Further praise for Kitchen Table
Su:

'Leadi
and ┠
provo
outco
Table
future
emoti
for ch

Sarkis:
compι
see in
of im,
improvι

'Even if there were whizzb........ ....; it
wouldn't be enough. People ....t be t..e solution, ..ot re..p.ent's o.
handed-down ideas. Like the community pro.esses described within,
this book provides the ..thi.. and pragmatic ways to get there.'

Gordon Price,
Director, The City Program, Simon Fraser University, Vancouver

'Wendy Sarkissian and her authorial team have brought together their
extensive practical experience and wisdom in an immensely accessible
book with which everyone can engage. The authors suggest so many
good questions for us to ask and offer us a storehouse full of useful
ingredients for making our own "meals" or actions. Creatively written,
without jargon, the book includes references to some excellent texts
and websites for the "meat lovers". There is definitely a place for
everyone at this kitchen table.'

Jean Hillier,
Professor of Town Planning, Newcastle University, UK

'*Kitchen Table Sustainability* is that needed gust of fresh air in the
sustainability debate. It reminds us that unsustainability is ultimately
a socio-behavioural problem, that community engagement, social
cohesion and mut.... trust – ....ab of mut..al coercion

– will move us closer and faster to the goal of human–nature harmony than all the techno-fixes the world has to offer.'

William E. Rees,
Professor, School of Community and Regional Planning,
University of British Columbia, Vancouver

'Traditional sustainability prescribes treatment for a diseased people. Wendy Sarkissian and her co-authors remind us that making us feel bad about ourselves is unlikely to bring about meaningful change. This book is about how to create processes and places that make us feel good, engaging our natural desire to protect the things we love.'

Stephen Hynes,
known as the 'Communitarian Capitalist',
President, Hynes Developments, Vancouver

'This is a most inspiring, stimulating and truly important book! Sustainable development is about the many small decisions and steps taken by all people in everyday life. Sarkissian and her co-authors have really captured the essence of community engagement!'

Henrik Nolmark,
Managing Director, Urban Laboratory, Gothenburg, Sweden

'Active citizen engagement has long been recognized as the critical component in building sustaining communities. This book is essential for those who want to know what needs to be done and how to go about creating this necessary engagement.'

Penny Gurstein,
Professor and Director, School of Community and Regional
Planning / Centre for Human Settlements,
University of British Columbia

'The perfect recipe book for those committed to creating a sustainable future. The authors have combined their wisdom built on decades of experience to provide us with the essential ingredients to effectively engage communities in sustainability planning and work. How delicious!'

Karen Umemoto,
PhD, Professor, Department of Urban
and Regional Planning, University of Hawai'i at Manoa

'As our Centre's focus is increasingly on community mobilization as an essential component of sustainable development, we are delighted to add *Kitchen Table Sustainability* to our teaching and research resources.'

Mark Roseland,
PhD, Director, Centre for Sustainable Community Development,
Simon Fraser University

'A very significant, highly accessible, community-based approach to the challenges facing all of us who wish to live a more sustainable lifestyle. Exemplary success stories and pragmatic guidance will inspire readers to sit at their own metaphorical kitchen tables and plan for more sustainable futures.'

Clare Cooper Marcus,
Professor Emerita, Departments of Architecture and Landscape
Architecture, University of California, Berkeley

'The face-to-face inter-generational sharing of knowledge and mutual support, which the authors describe so eloquently, reminds us that nourishment not only comes from food, community-building relationships and the self-renewing capacity of natural systems, but is a metaphor for understanding the differences between participating in the other non-monetized aspects of the cultural commons, and participating in the environmentally and community destructive consumer-dependent lifestyle. Essential reading for anyone who thinks in terms of technological solutions or has lost sight of the potential of what is shared in common as a source of wisdom.'

C. A. Bowers,
PhD, Emeritus Professor, Portland State University and author
of *Education, Cultural Myths, and the Ecological Crisis:*
Toward Deep Changes

'A great summary of common-sense and practical ways we can all help heal and save our planet.'

Thom Hartmann,
New York Times best-selling author of 19 books, including
***The Last Hours of Ancient Sunlight: The Fate of the World* and**
What We Can Do before It's Too Late

'What makes this book about engagement with sustainability so unusual and so impressive is its core understanding of these issues as profoundly ethical and value-based. This is a book rich in practical insights and advice, useful process and engagement tips and strategies, successful stories told and cases presented, but made all the more compelling because the underlying ethical assumptions and necessary moral guideposts for engagement are not pushed aside, but rather are brought to fore, made the foundation of community engagement – indeed the very legs of the kitchen table.'

Timothy Beatley,
Teresa Heinz Professor of Sustainable Communities,
Department of Urban and Environmental Planning,
University of Virginia

'Here, at last, is a book which transcends present anxieties, outdated myths and the paralysis resulting from a constant diet of bad news, scaremongering, half-truths and finger pointing. Instead, we are offered eminently practical yet nourishing recipes for re-engaging with our innate desire for better futures and a more holistic sense of community. Stories told within these pages offer hope and inspiration, together with proof, if needed, that we are capable of redesigning the underlying frameworks of our civilization in ways that do not deplete the quality of our lives.'

Richard David Hames,
PhD, Distinguished Professor & Director, Asian Foresight
Institute, Dhurakij Pundit University, Thailand

'An excellent resource with great "recipes" for those who hunger to make lasting, positive change in their community.'

Andrés R. Edwards,
author of *The Sustainability Revolution:*
Portrait of a Paradigm Shift

'This book is a fine example of practical kitchen table innovation for everyone committed to the future – involved in communities, leading community or community engagement initiatives.'

Anne Pattillo,
Vice President, International Association
for Public Participation (IAP2)

'Wendy Sarkissian and her team draw on their wealth of experience to offer practical strategies for working with communities and building a future based on care for each other and the planet. But this book is also a heartfelt reminder that this future is already here, if only we can take the time to create the spaces for listening to the wisdom that is all around us.'

Jenny Cameron,
Associate Professor, Centre for Urban and Regional Studies,
University of Newcastle, Australia

'The powerful stories and clear recipes in *Kitchen Table Sustainability* remind those of us in the development community of the need for the basic ingredients of thoughtful community engagement processes and a heartfelt response to community views to achieve the sustainable outcomes we all seek.'

Darren Cooper,
National Councillor, Urban Development Institute of Australia

Kitchen Table Sustainability

To the Living Earth, and all those who seek to
nourish and protect her,
including many dedicated and courageous activists
and innovators, who – often voluntarily and behind
the scenes – nurture community engagement
with sustainability.

Kitchen Table Sustainability

Practical Recipes for Community Engagement with Sustainability

Wendy Sarkissian with Nancy Hofer,
Yollana Shore, Steph Vajda and Cathy Wilkinson

publishing for a sustainable future

London • Sterling, VA

First published by Earthscan in the UK and USA in 2009

ISBN: 978-1-84407-614-7

Typeset by Safehouse Creative
Printed and bound in the UK by CPI Antony Rowe, Chippenham
Cover design by Susanne Harris
Illustrations by Steph Vajda

For a full list of publications please contact:

Earthscan
Dunstan House
14a St Cross St
London, EC1N 8XA, UK
Tel: +44 (0)20 7841 1930
Fax: +44 (0)20 7242 1474
Email: earthinfo@earthscan.co.uk
Web: **www.earthscan.co.uk**

22883 Quicksilver Drive, Sterling, VA 20166-2012, USA

Earthscan publishes in association with the International Institute for
Environment and Development

A catalogue record for this book is available from the British Library

Library of Congress Cataloging-in-Publication Data

Sarkissian, Wendy.
  Kitchen table sustainability : practical recipes for community engagement
with sustainability / by Wendy Sarkissian ; with Nancy Hofer ... [et al.].

      p. cm.
  Includes bibliographical references and index.
  ISBN 978-1-84407-614-7 (pbk.)
  1. Community development. 2. Sustainable development–Citizen
participation. 3. Economic development–Citizen participation. 4.
Regional planning. I. Title.

  HN49.C6S27 2008
  307.1'4–dc22
                    2008034694

The paper used for this book is FSC-certified.
FSC (the Forest Stewardship Council) is an
international network to promote responsible
management of the world's forests.

FSC
Mixed Sources
Product group from well-managed
forests and other controlled sources
Cert no. SGS-COC-2953
www.fsc.org
© 1996 Forest Stewardship Council

Contents

List of Figures and Tables

Figures

Tables

Acknowledgements

All five authors would like to acknowledge:

Karl Langheinrich, Shelagh Lindsey, Noel Wilson and Andrew Curthoys for editing assistance and reviewing; our publishers, Earthscan, including Rob West, Olivia Woodward, Alison Kuznets and Camille Bramall; and Nick Wates, Sam La Rocca and James Whelan, Jenny Cameron, Charlotte Humphries, Sarah Gall, Ann Forsyth, Leonie Sandercock, Darren Cooper, Trisch Muller, Mike Allen, Rebecca Cotton, Graeme Dunstan, Liz Coupe and Mary Maher for their ongoing belief, support and contributions; Kelvin Walsh, Yollana Shore, Wendy Sarkissian and Steph Vajda for photographs; Gordon Davidson for calligraphy; Andrea Cook and Steph Vajda for illustrations; Alan Arthur, President, Aeon, Minneapolis, for generously providing the developer pro forma for the Minnesota Block Exercise.

Wendy Sarkissian would like to acknowledge:

My four brilliant and generous co-authors and communities everywhere who have taught me about engagement. And: Karl for love, keeping the home fire burning, research, proofreading, reference checking, a sociological perspective, great cooking and a wild mind; Shelagh Lindsey for sharp editing, disciplined sociology and loving support; the editorial staff at Earthscan, including Rob West, Olivia Woodward, Alison Kuznets and Camille Bramall; Angel Kosch for pain-free photography; Keith Gillies for generous graphic support; Vivienne Simon for sparkling insights and keeping my feet to the fire; Peter Newman for a green heart, hopefulness and a generous Foreword; Leonie Sandercock for 34 years of loving support, great conversations and poetic and inspirational writing; Graeme Dunstan for wizardry, interviews and a wild heart; Ann Forsyth for a keen eye and a sharp mind, warm hospitality, the blessing of a long, rich friendship and for co-inventing the remarkable Minnesota Block Exercise; Jennie Moore and Cornelia Sussman for meticulous critiques and generous editing; Noel Wilson for a long friendship, thoughtful editing and a radical mind; John Forester for hospitality, inspiration and personally demonstrating the skills of deep listening; Nadia Carvalho for friendship and sweetly caring for me; Courtney Campbell for kind, skilful administrative and moral support.

And thanks to the following friends and colleagues who supported us in innumerable ways: Courtney Campbell, Andrew Curthoys, Des Connor, Brendan Hurley, Jeca Glor-Bell, Les Turner, Wendy Truer, Andrea Cook, Kelvin Walsh, Andrea Young, Peter Muller, Lynn McNeilly, Kevin McMillan, Jacqui Bridson, Anne Gorman, Sophia van Ruth, Chérie Hoyle, Urban Ecology Australia, Glenn Bailey, Jason Prior, Clare Cooper Marcus, Maged Senbel, Lis Miller, Penny Gurstein, Strider (this *is* a book about ecology), Tristia and the living Earth.

Nancy Hofer would like to acknowledge:

My dear friend Christopher Stephenson for all those wonderful conversations about all these things and more on our trips to visit our families in Kelowna; my very patient boyfriend Dylan Gothard for listening; my brother, Blake Hofer, who sees the world through a different lens and is always supportive; my mom, Renee Justinen, and Harold Justinen, for being interested in these ideas and wanting to make a difference; my two best friends Mona Zacharias and Megan Yamakawa for being great and cherished friends; Bill Rees for articulating so clearly the challenges we face; and Wendy, my professor, mentor, colleague and friend – thank you so much for this opportunity to be involved in this great work. You have positively influenced my ethic of caring for human communities and all living things.

Yollana Shore would like to acknowledge:

My husband, Will, for offering wholehearted belief and support in my work, as well as unconditional love and practical support; my daughter Erin for being a joyful contrast to the computer screen and inspiration to continue to engage with sustainability; my sister Fleur for unsolicited cups of tea and treats during long writing stints. I am grateful to my father, Noel, for his clear-thinking intellectual support; my mother, Leonie, for her loving and generous practical support; Brandon Bays who has taught me much about how writing – and living – can emerge from stillness; Mark Silver from *Heart of Business*, whose heart-centred approach to business and marketing will undoubtedly become evident in the publicizing of this book; the Climate Change Bootcamp which, together with this book, marked my return to a more active engagement with sustainability; to our author team – Wendy, Steph, Nancy and Cathy – for sharing the journey with me; and all those friends and strangers who have engaged in kitchen table conversations with me since I started contributing to this book.

I would also like to thank my neighbours, who provide me with a rich and nourishing experience of community; and the wider communities of West End and Northern Rivers, NSW, to which I belong.

Steph Vajda would like to acknowledge:

The Aboriginal and Torres Strait Islander Traditional Owners of Brisbane, where I live, and of Australia, whose sovereignty has never been ceded and who deserve respect and justice for 220 years of atrocities; Wendy and Yollana for constant support, love, openness and for the way in which we have been able to share our experiences and perspectives of life; Nancy and Cathy, our long-distance co-authors for their support and dedication. This book is for my Nana, who passed three years ago but will always be a symbol of strength and deep love, for my Mum for her wisdom, love and vulnerabilities and for sharing them so openly with me always and helping me to see and understand mine and for my Father for his constant support, love and keen interest. Respect and love to you Erin, for being exactly you and for enduring the days and nights filled with my work and then writing for months on end.

Thanks to those who have taught me the significance of what sustainability really is: Uncle Kevin Buzzacott, for your profound wisdom, mysticism and dedication to your people and land; Paul Dawson, for your lifelong friendship and your deep understanding of life and our place in it; Sam La Rocca, for your strategically minded, quick-thinking, straight-to-the-point, tireless approach to activism, friendships and life; Tim Collins for your fearless nature and deeper insights; John, Bec, Barry, Odin and Brad, Stradbroke Island activists who introduced me to a new world of activism; Brendon Radford for our initial forays into self-publishing and sustainability; Belle Budden for our times of Brisbane campaigning and desert learning; and more recently, Jade Lillie, for your support and belief and for so openly sharing the way you see the world.

Thanks also to all those educators, organizers, activists and change agents whose tireless dedication and boundless wisdom continue to motivate and inspire me. And thanks to my friends, including Jason, Thames, Mark, Abbie, Dave and Angel, who are still close after 18 months of my writing and often neglecting them. Lastly, thanks to the process of writing this book, which has made clearer the need for our own personal sustainability to permeate our global actions.

Cathy Wilkinson would like to acknowledge:

Wendy, Yollana, Steph and Nancy for welcoming me so warmly into this project; Luleå Tekniska Universitet for their flexibility in recognizing my contribution to this book as part of my doctoral studies; Libby Porter for her deep friendship always and mentoring on this project; Neil Houghton for introducing me to Bill Isaacs' work; Luleå for reconnecting me with Nature, providing the time and space to get involved in a project like this and enabling my children to experience a childhood without fences and close to Nature; and, my family – Matt, Calvin, Maya – as well as those far across the seas – for their love.

Foreword

Peter Newman
Professor of Sustainability
Curtin University

I collect stories of hope about sustainability. They are about cities that have taken down freeways and restored rivers like Seoul in Korea or Aarhus in Denmark; about building an eco-village in a central city like Christie Walk in Adelaide or in a degraded farmland area like Ithaca Eco-village; about a mining company like Argyle Diamonds deciding to leave a legacy for Indigenous people that goes well beyond the mine life...

One key characteristic of the stories I collected is that they all involved a community design process. They were all based on community values and were facilitated by a community process.

Is this a coincidence? No. Would they have happened anyway? No.

Community-based initiatives are essential for sustainability. They are not just helpful, they are essential. Sustainability is about tapping innovation for a future in our settlements that is much more resource-constrained, far lower in ecological footprint, yet resulting in much better places in which to live and work and play – all at the same time. So why don't we just call in the experts and get on with it?

That is the problem. There are no experts in the simultaneous achievement of these sustainability goals. Too many experts and professionals are trained to do the opposite: to create settlements that use more resources, have a bigger footprint and, in the days of expensive oil, are not much fun to live in.

Time and time again, communities demonstrate that they understand sustainability; they can see what they want and often they have good ideas about how it can be done in an integrated way. Sustainability comes from community values – it doesn't come from the professions or business or from government strategies that are big on rhetoric but small on implementation. It only comes when the glue of community values makes it clear that this is what they want. Then the community, professions, government and business have a chance to come up with solutions as a team.

The World Business Council for Sustainable Development calls this 'playing jazz'. They know that business alone or government alone does not work on sustainability issues. Only when community is engaged does the music begin to be played. Then you can get all kinds of renditions, with many different soloists playing their parts, but the total effect of them playing together is when the magic starts. Jazz is not easy but the synergies and partnerships that are created are providing the creativity we need.

Politicians are responding to communities and are looking for new and creative solutions to deep problems that have no easy solutions. They want to see how communities can reduce greenhouse gas emissions by 50 per cent before 2050, how we can begin to ecologically regenerate cities and their bioregions, how we can rediscover a local sense of place in a globalized economy.

The solutions to these issues will only begin to be found if community design processes are at their heart – starting from the kitchen table and moving out into the neighbourhood, the city, the planet. . .

Wendy Sarkissian, Steph Vajda, Nancy Hofer, Yollana Shore and Cathy Wilkinson have provided the tools for doing this. They are not a set of techniques that can be applied slavishly like an air traffic controller or engineer would do as they assess problems. They are a set of tools that communities can begin to apply if they seem to fit the kind of issues they face and the kinds of people they are. They are like a book of recipes open on the kitchen table, there to inspire and guide communities hungry for greater sustainability.

Wendy has been doing this for a long time. She was a pioneer in Australia, applying the rich insights of social science to the technical issues of development and planning. Thirty years ago, this was not often seen as being needed; the professions had all the answers in their manuals. If each set of manuals was applied then the result was surely going to be better. Why bother with the soft messy stuff when you could apply the numbers in the manuals? For a while, Wendy and others in community planning were tempted to compete with the manuals by producing a set of social manuals with all the numbers to compete with the engineers. Then something happened...

The ecological crisis appeared from over the horizon and showed that if we kept on doing what the manuals said then we would destroy the planet. Our cities and regions were eating into the natural capital upon which they depended, even causing the atmosphere to overheat. Wendy had a bit of a crisis like many in the professions. But as in most of Wendy's life, she chose to resolve this in a way that few others have. She went bush. She moved into an ecovillage community and built herself a house. She communed with nature and with her fellow villagers and soon found that the only solutions out there were to engage more deeply, to find solutions that communities could begin to apply that the professions could not even begin to see.

She came back to the city, wrote it all down in a PhD and took off to see if it would work. It did. She and her colleagues now have many stories of communities doing it for themselves, of different solutions found in ways that no one would have predicted, of real jazz being created.

Kitchen Table Sustainability is a book to be savoured. It should be used for experimentation and then taken as the basis for communities to achieve real outcomes. The process will generate hope and – like a good meal or a good piece of jazz – will help communities to face whatever else life will throw at them. I hope to hear some of the great stories that no doubt will be generated from *Kitchen Table Sustainability.*

Perhaps the World Ends Here

The world begins at a kitchen table. No matter what, we must eat to live.

The gifts of earth are brought and prepared, set on the table. So it has been since creation, and it will go on.

We chase chickens or dogs away from it. Babies teethe at the corners. They scrape their knees under it.

It is here that children are given instructions on what it means to be human. We make men at it, we make women.

At this table we gossip, recall enemies and the ghosts of lovers.

Our dreams drink coffee with us as they put their arms around our children. They laugh with us at our poor falling-down selves and as we put ourselves back together once again at the table.

This table has been a house in the rain, an umbrella in the sun.

Wars have begun and ended at this table. It is a place to hide in the shadow of terror. A place to celebrate the terrible victory.

We have given birth on this table, and have prepared our parents for burial here.

At this table we sing with joy, with sorrow. We pray of suffering and remorse. We give thanks.

Perhaps the world will end at the kitchen table, while we are laughing and crying, eating of the last sweet bite.

Harjo, Joy (1994) 'Perhaps the World Ends Here', in *The Woman Who Fell from the Sky*, W. W. Norton and Company, Inc., New York, p68

Preface

It's April 2008 Wendy, Steph and Yollana are sitting around the table on Wendy and Karl's porch, as the sunset plays long shadows through the frame of their partly completed home in a small Permaculture ecovillage in northern New South Wales. Wendy has just returned from two months in Vancouver working with Nancy, with a side trip to the Arctic Circle, where she touched base with Cathy in Luleå, in Swedish Lappland.

As Yollana passes Erin, her baby daughter, to her husband and he takes the child inside to settle into sleep, a troubled frown creases across the young mother's face.

'Worried about your babe?' inquires Steph.

Yollana sighs. 'Truthfully, sometimes this sustainability stuff gets me down.'

With a sympathetic frown, Steph leans over and pats her shoulder, as Wendy places a teapot and cups on the table.

'I just wonder what kind of future she will have,' Yollana continues, 'I mean, it's all very well to encourage communities to engage with sustainability. But will people listen? Will it be enough? Can we really change anything?'

'I know what you mean,' Steph offers. 'Your feelings about Erin are really natural, hey. I think that's how many people feel about this stuff, if they let themselves. It makes us all feel vulnerable.

'I was just reading in the paper today about how climate change impacts could be worse in Australia than almost any other developed country and how we are going to need greenhouse gas emission reductions of 70 to 90 per cent from all developed countries to avert that. I think people are listening now because we have to.'

'It's funny, though,' Wendy says, warming her hands around her cup, 'Here we are writing a book about sustainability ... and the truth is, we're just as bewildered as anyone. We're puzzling about how we can help make the difference that will mean a future for all of us who live on this precious Earth...'

She trails off for a moment to observe a wallaby bounding lazily past the unfinished house, its joey peering out from the pouch. Turning back to her friends, she smiles and continues, 'We may not have technical solutions, but together with Nancy and Cathy, I do feel we have a lot to offer.'

'Sure,' her husband Karl chimes in, 'Like all your collective knowledge of the professional and academic literature... And all those workshops!'

'Yes,' sighs Wendy, 'Didn't we say somewhere that we have a rich tapestry of stories from our experiences?'

'Yeah,' Steph agrees, warming to the topic, 'and we do all have a deep and heartfelt care for the Earth and its life and...' He nods toward the room where the baby now sleeps, 'for future generations.'

'You know what I think?' says Steph, leaning forward, 'I reckon it's our values that got us here. And it's values – a huge cultural shift – that will make the difference. Values got us here and values will get us out.'

Yollana shrugs, 'You mean like caring for each other...?'

'Yes,' exclaims Wendy, as Steph nods, 'and caring for Nature!'

'One more thing,' Karl chuckles as he clears the table, 'Do you really need a kitchen table to have these discussions?'

'Well,' replied Steph, raising his eyes from the newspaper, 'You know I just got back from Sri Lanka. There's some major poverty there and not everyone has a kitchen table but they're still having great conversations.'

'And,' whispers Wendy, gently closing the door to the shed where she has been checking on Erin, 'We don't even have a kitchen, let alone a kitchen table!'

List of Acronyms and Abbreviations

CaLD	culturally and linguistically diverse
CAS	Community Assistance Scheme
CCD	Community Cultural Development
CES	Community Education for Sustainability
CHI	Corridor Housing Initiative
CPTED	Crime Prevention through Environmental Design
CRP	Community Renewal Program
CSA	Community Supported Agriculture
CVHAT	Castle Vale Housing Action Trust
EFA	Ecological Footprint Analysis
ERAG	Eagleby Residents Action Group
IAP2	International Association for Public Participation
LEED™	Leadership in Energy and Environmental Design
LISC	Local Initiatives Support Corporation
LSF	Learning for a Sustainable Future
NGO	non-governmental organization
NLP	neurolinguistic programming
NVDA	non-violent direct action
PAC	Plaza Advisory Crew
PLAN	Planned Lifetime Advocacy Network
PSAP	Personal Sustainability Action Plan
SEPA-Q	Supportive Environments for Physical Activity in Queensland (project)
SIA	Stillness in Action
TCA	The Change Agency
UEA	Urban Ecology Australia

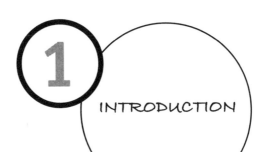

1

INTRODUCTION

We have such a brief opportunity to pass on to our children our love for the Earth, and to tell our stories. These are the moments when the world is made whole. In my children's memories, the adventures we've had together will always exist.

Richard Louv, 2006, p320

Everybody is a story. When I was a child, people sat around kitchen tables and told their stories. Sitting around the table telling stories is not just a way of passing time. It is the way the wisdom gets passed along. The stuff that helps us to live a life worth remembering. Despite the awesome powers of technology many of us still do not live very well. We may need to listen to each other's stories once again.

Rachel Naomi Remen, Kitchen Table Wisdom[1]

Introduction

When Wendy visited Minneapolis in early November 2006, she attended the launch of worldchanging.com, a solutions-based online magazine that works from a simple premise: that the tools, models and ideas for building a better future lie all around us. The editors explain their credo this way:

> *That plenty of people are working on tools for change, but the fields in which they work remain unconnected. That the motive, means and opportunity for profound positive change are already present. That another world is not just possible, it's here. We only need to put the pieces together.*[2]

This was a life-changing experience for Wendy. In the Minneapolis audience were hundreds of local people from all walks of life and from small, local organizations, who spoke up – one by one – after the formal presentations, explaining what they individually or their organizations were doing, affirming their commitment to both sustainability and to taking action. To putting the pieces together.

Wendy bought *Worldchanging* (the book) that day and read it on the long flight back to Australia. What a story it told! She described it to the rest of us as 'a Whole Earth Catalogue for the New Millennium'. *Worldchanging* presents us all with an invitation to be part of creating a better future, declaring:

1   *We need better tools, models and ideas for changing
    the world. Luckily, more are being created every day.*

2   *The more people know about these tools, models and
    ideas, the better their own ideas will get, and the more
    ideas will become available.*

3   *Anyone can join the conversation, and the more people
    do join, the better it gets.*

4   *The better the conversation gets, and the more people
    use the tools, the more exciting the adventure becomes,
    and the more likely its success.*[3]

We couldn't agree more. And we consider ourselves privileged to
be a part of this adventure. Privileged to be contributing to this
conversation together with a global community of dedicated and
courageous people – like the people at Worldchanging. And you.

This book is one volume in the 'Community Planning' suite of
books published by Earthscan in 2008 and 2009. The first book is
*The Community Planning Event Manual: How to use Collaborative
Planning and Urban Design Events to Improve your Environment*
(Wates, 2008). Other books authored by Wendy Sarkissian and
colleagues include *Creative Approaches to Community Planning:
Nurturing Inclusion with Insight and Method* (2009b) and
*SpeakOut!: The Step-by-Step Guide to SpeakOuts and Community
Workshops* (2009a). Nick Wates's second book is the second
edition of *The Community Planning Handbook: How People Can
Shape their Cities, Town and Villages in any Part of the World*. All
five books are backed up by *Communityplanning.net, the*
Community Planning website, an online version of *The Community
Planning Handbook* with current information and listings.

In this book, we seek to expand community engagement beyond
the realm of manuals for practitioners so that *anyone* can be confident that there's a place for them to influence community decisions
about sustainability. The challenges that all life on Earth now faces

are unique; they have never been faced on such a global scale. We have never been in the position where humans, and humans alone, can determine the future of all species. *Everyone* has skills, experience and expertise to offer on the journey toward sustainability. Now is the time to share them.

Our experience and research have convinced us that collaborative processes are the key to achieving sustainable transformations, particularly in today's increasingly complex world. We need people with specific and relevant skills to facilitate these collaborative processes in ways that acknowledge both nonhuman Nature and the voices of our diverse communities. Today, in so many ways, change and uncertainty are the dominant constants. Navigating more sustainable pathways within this context is challenging, requiring collaborative processes, experimentation and learning – among communities, government and industry. The eminent systems ecologist Buzz Holling advised Cathy at a recent international resilience conference in Stockholm that we must first establish an impossible vision, then take the first possible step, learn from that experience and then take the next step, together.[4]

Community engagement with sustainability is transformed by people like Maisie and Steph's mum, whom you'll meet in this book. People like us. We are community members first and practitioners second. And as professionals with experience in community engagement, we are eager to share what we know. Ultimately, community engagement with sustainability is transformed by people like *you*.

Everyone has skills, experience and expertise to offer on the journey toward sustainability. Now is the time to share them

Ultimately, community engagement with sustainability is transformed by people like *you*

What this book is about

This book explores the relationship between community engagement and sustainability. We aim to empower individuals to come together in community, to envisage, shape strategies, make decisions and take action for a more sustainable world. Sustainability is not only an important focus of community engagement; it is also *essential* for the transition to local and global sustainability. Communities are the heart and hands of the sustainability movement. Engagement helps communities articulate, develop and achieve their goals. However, we cannot design or specify one set of sustainability goals for every community. Ongoing processes of deliberation, questioning, refinement, agreement-making, experimentation, review and adjustment must underpin how each community defines its *own* quest for local and global sustainability.

Communities are the heart and hands of the sustainability movement

In *Kitchen Table Sustainability,* we do not focus much on ecological sustainability in a technical sense. Many other books do that.[5] While we have conducted research for this book, basically, it comes from the heart. Further, we do not offer comprehensive, step-by-step solutions to sustainability challenges. We are not sure that they exist. Instead, we offer a values-based approach for helping individuals and communities to engage with the wide range of issues that sustainability presents and to develop localized solutions.

Who this book is for

Kitchen Table Sustainability is for people who want to play an active role in developing sustainable communities

Kitchen Table Sustainability is for people who want to play an active role in developing sustainable communities. It's for social innovators and 'cultural creatives', communities and community groups seeking to organize around environmental and sustainability issues.[6] It's also for people in government – at all levels – ready to embrace an approach that embodies facilitation and empowerment. It's for educators and people everywhere who believe we need to share and communicate knowledge to uncover, develop and implement sustainable solutions. It's for professionals, sustainability consultants, environmental practitioners and natural resource managers who need to understand sustainability within a more holistic context. And it's for people in government, business and industry who want to engage with communities and their stakeholders about sustainability issues.

As planners, we hope that this book will be of particular interest to practitioners and clients in the land professions: planners, engineers, landscape architects, architects, urban designers and developers. It will also appeal to anyone organizing community engagement processes – from government to non-government organizations to facilitators, community development workers – and those working in Community Cultural Development (CCD). Finally, our book is for activists, environmentalists, social justice advocates and people in non-governmental organizations (NGOs).

Why kitchen tables?

Months after *Kitchen Table Sustainability* had been accepted for publication, Wendy was browsing in her favourite bookshop in Vancouver when she was drawn to a book. It was *Kitchen Table Wisdom* by Rachel Naomi Remen.[7] Wendy was delighted to find that the two books have more in common than their titles. While Remen's work focuses on individual healing from life-threatening diseases, our book is about reconciling our relationships with nonhuman Nature and with each other to support sustainability. Through the metaphor of the kitchen table, we build on Remen's work to expand this process of healing and reconciliation beyond the territory of experts with technical knowledge. We seek to put the power into the hands of individuals and communities who will exercise their common sense. We want to encourage conversations about sustainability at tables everywhere – in classrooms, workshops and meetings, offices and community centres. We take the metaphor of the kitchen table to mean *all* tables, *everywhere*.

For us, the kitchen table represents the place where we have casual but important conversations, we share meals and where people, even in a busy world, frequently come together. The hearth is the heart of the local, the family and the familiar – a place where many feel comfortable to speak openly about their real perspectives, ideas and concerns.

We seek to put the power into the hands of individuals and communities who will exercise their common sense

The hearth is the heart of the local, the family and the familiar – a place where many feel comfortable to speak openly about their real perspectives, ideas and concerns

We are aware that not everyone has happy memories of their kitchen tables, and many don't even have a kitchen table, or even a kitchen. In 2005, approximately three-quarters of the urban population of the world's least developed nations lived in slums.[8] More people in the developed world live alone so traditional notions of family mealtime and kitchen tables are challenged, In Melbourne, for example, 90 per cent of the growth in new households between 1996 and 2030 will be in single-person households.[9] The kitchen 'table' assumes many diverse forms in many different environments. Yet the 'hearth' that it represents is universal. Remen exclaims, 'I have glimpsed the true size of the kitchen table at which we sit and that we all have our places at it'.[10] Even people struggling to meet their basic needs have an important place at this table. Their stories are testament to the suffering that unsustainable practices have created, and inspiration for us to support transitions to a more sustainable world.[11]

'I have glimpsed the true size of the kitchen table at which we sit and that we all have our places at it'

As the beautiful poem by Joy Harjo explains, the kitchen table is a powerful place where we form our beliefs. It's the place where we all – from executives to activists to children – meet with those with whom we are close, often on a daily basis. It's a place we come back to, again and again, no matter what has passed before, to give and receive sustenance. It's also where people can begin to articulate and practise their visions for sustainability and explore their practical implementations. As our visions crystallize, we can have more intimate conversations with trusted friends and family and develop our own ideas and solutions. In terms of global and local sustainability, it is very important to create spaces where social innovators can be linked – to converse, share ideas, projects and support in the transition to sustainability.[12] We want this book to contribute to those relationships – to stimulate informed and productive conversations at these kitchen tables.

At the kitchen table, people do not use big words or complex terminology to tell their stories or voice their fears. Instead, we can speak from our hearts, using information, intuition and common sense. In the face of crisis, people often turn to 'experts' for solutions. While we are eager to include experts in our kitchen table conversations about sustainability, we also want to widen our conversations and reach beyond the aloof 'mask of knowing' that expertise sometimes brings. Everyday language has a wisdom that we must respect. Having real and relevant discussions can build family and household cohesion, community involvement and intergenerational understanding. It is the key to building a sustainable society where people understand the importance of working with – rather than against – Nature. Having real discussions about real issues and feelings is the secret to building a cohesive community that thinks globally and acts locally.

Everyday language has a wisdom that we must respect

The power of stories

To bring about a paradigm shift in the culture that will change assumptions and attitudes, a critical number of us have to tell stories of our personal revelations and transformations. (Jean Shinoda Bolen)[13]

You will find *Kitchen Table Sustainability* brimming with stories. In our own kitchen table conversations in Canada, Australia and Sweden, we have found that people relate more to stories than to data, 'evidence' or directives about what to do. Stories are powerful. They help us make sense of our lives and allow us to make meaning of past experiences. Stories encourage people to find and share their own stories. Spoken aloud, each story becomes a catalyst for others to tell their stories. When stories are shared, each person gains a new perspective. They glimpse their shared experience within the shared experience of the community. Telling stories around the kitchen table, we can go beyond the 'one-story' view of reality to embrace the multiplicity of stories that must interweave to create a sustainable world.

Stories are powerful. They help us make sense of our lives

Like individuals, communities live in and act out their stories. Future actions and responses are largely determined by stories we enact in community. As prominent American author and feminist Alice Walker once remarked, 'Stories differ from advice in that, once you get them, they become a fabric of your whole soul. That is why they heal you.'[14] Yet while some stories have healing qualities, others perpetuate sickness and disease. This is true on a personal level, but also on a global level. An example of a 'sick' story includes that of *Terra Nullius*, the 'empty land' that enabled the systematic and violent destruction of indigenous cultures in Australia, over two centuries.[15]

Another sick story is that of *cornucopia*. The cornucopia, or 'horn of plenty', is a symbol of food and abundance dating back to Greece in the 5th century BC. In environmental theory, it represents the story that the Earth has an infinite abundance of non-renewable resources for humans to use and exploit for our own pleasure.[16] This story is a far cry from the true recognition that the Earth has finite resources and that we are here to protect and nurture them. Yet the metaphors embedded within stories like this have had a powerful influence on our collective values and ultimately our behaviour.

As we discuss in the following chapter, environmental and educational philosophers Chet Bowers and David Orr claim that a complete 'reworking of our master metaphorical templates' is called for if we are to find a way of living that doesn't take more from the Earth than we can give back.[17] Thus a major task of this book is to help create and reaffirm sustainable stories that can guide us into the future and replace the outdated and unsustainable stories that have directed our lives in the past. In this book we want to share stories of a 'thousand tiny empowerments'[18] by willing agents of sustainable change – people like you – acting 'as if the world could be saved'.[19]

Organization of this book

We are interested in the critical relationships among three important things in this book: sustainability, communities and community engagement. We see sustainability as the overall goal, communities as the means to achieving that goal and community engagement as the ongoing, underlying process that enables the journey to continue. Thus, in Chapters 2 and 3, we discuss these components in this order.

At its core, *Kitchen Table Sustainability* is our approach to community engagement with sustainability, referred to as ***EATING***. Eating is nourishing, nurturing and sustaining. It transforms the bounty of our Earth into energy we can use. It is one of the most basic human activities and is often done together (at the kitchen table). We introduce the ***EATING*** approach in more depth in Chapter 4.

> Eating is nourishing, nurturing and sustaining. It transforms the bounty of our Earth into energy we can use

The ***EATING*** approach consists of six components – food groups if you like – **E**ducation, **A**ction, **T**rust, **I**nclusion, **N**ourishment and **G**overnance. With respect to community engagement with sustainability, we view each of these as a necessary part of a well balanced diet. All components must be included – or the diet (the engagement process) – will be deficient and we will not be sustained. The six elements of ***EATING*** are introduced in the subsequent chapters as follows:

Chapter 5: Education asks what information and knowledge do we need to impart and share for community engagement with sustainability? It seeks guidance from adult and environmental education and presents our new model, Community Education for Sustainability (CES). We also describe a community-based, participatory approach to growing local knowledgeability about sustainability and community building.

Chapter 6: Action explores two key questions: 'How can the frustration of inaction be overcome in community engagement processes?' and 'What actions are required to achieve transformative change for sustainability?' The chapter discuss how to achieve systemic change to established regimes, with a particular focus on the role of activism. We identify ways in which the activist in each of us can be harnessed to work beyond the traditional 'us' and 'them' categorization of actors involved in community engagement processes.

Chapter 7: Trust examines the persistent problem of trust in community engagement: what happens when trust is broken and how trust can be nourished in hard times with difficult problems to address. We identify principles and approaches to tackle trust and help communities form trusting relationships about sustainability issues.

Chapter 8: Inclusion highlights the diversity of our communities and the need for 'listening across difference', emphasizing the valuable roles that children and young people can play as engaged citizens and not 'citizens-in-the-making'. Our approach to inclusion is about everyone sitting at the table – all tables – speaking and being heard.

Our approach to inclusion is about everyone sitting at the table – all tables – speaking and being heard

Chapter 9: Nourishment provides some solace for the worried community member and embattled sustainability practitioner by drawing attention to some ancient and basic principles, including that we cannot nourish the Earth and our communities if we cannot nourish ourselves. We explore ways to nourish – and be nourished by – self, community and Nature. With this support, we can effectively engage with community and sustainability.

Chapter 10: Governance argues that very specific governance approaches should underpin community engagement with sustainability – notably participatory governance and transformative management. We include stories and several detailed case studies to illustrate fundamental principles. And we describe common-sense tools and practices for good governance consistent with these principles.

Case studies and examples in the book are drawn from our own experience and that of our friends and colleagues around the world – particularly in Australia, Sweden and Canada. They are diverse in content and scale – from personal stories told around the kitchen table, to town centre redevelopments, engagement with children and young people, community renewal, local activism and creative visualization.

In our final chapter, **Conclusions**, we identify challenges and opportunities for everyone: governments (local, state, provincial and federal); developers and the private sector; consultants in the land professions; community engagement practitioners; social, environmental and community activists; NGOs; artists and community development practitioners; teachers and academics; children and young people and their parents; and citizens. Finally, we lay down 'The Mother of all Challenges': to *create caring communities*.

Finally, we lay down 'The Mother of all Challenges': to *create caring communities*

The book concludes with a comprehensive list of References.

What changes can we expect by implementing the *EATING* model?

Our recipes should help nurture more effective partnership approaches among government, industry and community, including community activists. And finally, we look forward to experiencing a revitalized role for government as sustainability *facilitator*, helping local people and community organizations with visioning, strategizing, resources, partnerships, infrastructure, action and, ultimately, genuine engagement.

2

THE
SUSTAINABILITY
STORY

Perhaps the most difficult and yet essential aspect of this work is to change our stories.

Richard Louv, 2006, p320

... the sustainable life is inseparably intertwined with full participation in social life, democratic decision-making, self-esteem for both women and men, a relaxed approach to daily life, good food, and a stable population. The key seems to be that we humans can successfully survive on this planet only so long as our presence contributes to and meshes with the life of the Earth.

Chellis Glendinning[1]

Introduction

In January 2008, while we were writing this book, Wendy and Karl were weathering dramatic rainstorms as unprecedented flooding inundated much of south-eastern Australia, including their community. It was the region's wettest summer in over 200 years since European settlement. Flooding occurred on a massive scale in 2007 and 2008. In a different bioregion, just two hours' drive away from Wendy, Steph and Yollana lived with Level 6 water restrictions as drought tightened its grasp on Brisbane. Residents were discouraged from showering for more than four minutes. At the same time, in Swedish Lappland, just south of the Arctic Circle, Cathy was experiencing the mildest winter in recorded history, with the thermometer hovering around zero instead of sub-20 to 30. This dramatic change played perilous havoc with the hibernation patterns of local animals. A few months earlier, in Vancouver, Nancy was picking her way through streets littered with fallen trees after a violent windstorm felled over 3000 huge conifer trees in the city's Stanley Park.

Scientific research has demonstrated conclusively that, as a global population, we are living unsustainably and are irrevocably changing natural systems. There are many indicators of this process: our diminishing energy supplies, mass extinctions and a subsequent narrowing of biodiversity, desertification, rising temperatures and sea levels, extreme storms, droughts and our inability to manage

'The key seems to be that we humans can successfully survive on this planet only so long as our presence contributes to and meshes with the life of the Earth'

Scientific research has demonstrated conclusively that, as a global population, we are living unsustainably and are irrevocably changing natural systems

toxic wastes. All are examples of how our current lifestyles jeopardize the quality of life for future generations of all species.

As we face an unprecedented global crisis, we must ask ourselves, how did we get here? How could we, the 'clever' species, let ourselves live so far beyond our means that our very survival is threatened? Why are we, with our highly developed languages, specialized communication skills and revolutionary means of communication, still at war – unable to negotiate between cultures and nations? These questions lead to deeper questions. As we consider our sobering predicament, described above, we must ask:

What are the unsustainable stories that have led us to this situation? What are the unsustainable stories that have led us to this situation? And which sustainable stories will carry us out?

Stories are the strong and resilient foundation for the conversations, recipes and ingredients presented in *Kitchen Table Sustainability*.[2]

To create a sustainable world requires nothing less than a paradigm shift, a complete change in worldview, a new story To create a sustainable world requires nothing less than a paradigm shift, a complete change in worldview, a new story. These changes, at the level of concept and meaning, are the foundation for real change at the level of action. We trust that this book will inspire individuals and communities to uncover the unsustainable stories that have driven them in the past and begin urgent conversations to create new sustainable stories to influence them in the future. In this book, we focus on providing inspiration, empowerment and practical tools for individuals and communities to begin these urgent conversations and to initiate community engagement processes for sustainability.

Why community engagement with sustainability?

As community engagement practitioners, we are unashamedly environmentalists. In our work, we seek to facilitate deep and lasting changes and empower communities, rather than assisting them to 'fit in' with existing social, economic or ecological frameworks. We believe strongly that the cultural and social dimensions of sustainability must be given more emphasis within sustainability discourse, which is partly the reason we have written this book. Our direct experience with 'sustainability practitioners' leads us to believe that many approach sustainability in a 'technical' way, without appreciating the important role of culture as a building block of community sustainability. Our views on sustainability are strongly influenced by social and cultural theorists, as well as our experiences in community engagement and non-violent direct action.

Nevertheless, we recognize that while our long-term view focuses on 'changing the master metaphorical templates' of our consumer-driven culture, the planetary crisis demands immediate, constructive action. To facilitate this we must ensure that cultural, environmental, social and economic development occurs within a strong framework of sustainability objectives, with clearly identified goals. Those goals, we believe, must emerge from community-based dialogue, as well as from 'experts' and planners. Our approaches to community engagement, therefore, aim to help communities address all aspects of sustainability and to avoid focusing on only one dimension. We are eager to help communities create solutions that benefit Nature, society, local cultures and the economy, now and well into the future. To achieve this, we must also find ways to strengthen communities and help them work more effectively.

Community development must be an outcome of community engagement with sustainability. It is a component that has often been ignored by sustainability theorists and that is one reason why we emphasize both action and governance in this book. When communities work together in culturally appropriate ways, with facilitation, capacity strengthening and resourcing, local people can find approaches to explore how economic, community, cultural and environmental outcomes can be achieved together and in a collaborative manner. Then the different dimensions of sustainability can

Our direct experience with 'sustainability practitioners' leads us to believe that many approach sustainability in a 'technical' way, without appreciating the important role of culture as a building block of community sustainability

Community development must be an outcome of community engagement with sustainability

be both inclusive and mutually supportive. This holistic thinking is at the core of our approaches to community engagement with sustainability and particularly relevant to our innovative Community Education for Sustainability (CES) model presented in Chapter 5, Education.

This book contains a strong emphasis on environmental ethics. For many of the pioneering community engagement approaches we use, we are indebted to environmental philosophy and, in particular, Deep Ecology. While some might argue that sustainability is not environmental ethics, we disagree. Perhaps a better term would be 'sustainability ethics'. Our direct experience is that communities are able – and eager – to explore the ethical underpinnings of sustainability decisions. Further, the holistic thinking that underpins environmental philosophy can inform and enrich community discourse. As community members develop new literacies and learn to think holistically – and ethically – they can help to ensure that what have been seen in the past as 'isolated silos' of thinking and professional activity (economy, society, culture and environment) can now be considered together. As the sustainability discourse moves more deeply into mainstream policy and change processes, we need to ensure that this movement does not bypass people in local communities and is not occurring in ways that are separate from their immediate concerns.

Our direct experience is that communities are able – and eager – to explore the ethical underpinnings of sustainability decisions

In the sorts of communities in which we work, people do not think in silos or disciplines. They think in stories. Life, in community, is made up of stories. And storytelling is the ultimate holistic medium. Cultural historian and 'Earth scholar' Thomas Berry aptly proclaimed: 'The deepest crises experienced by any society are those moments of change when the story becomes inadequate for meeting the survival demands of a present situation'.[3] In this chapter, we focus on changing the sustainability stories from outdated ones we have heard in past decades to new, community-based stories that are accurate, relevant, inclusive and empowering.

Bearing in mind our desire to ground our approach in current research and practice, we have taken a leaf from the book of our colleague, Peter Newman, whose elegant Sustainability Framework, based on *Hope for the Future: The Western Australian State Sustainability Strategy* (Newman and Rowe, 2003) gained international acclaim. In this Strategy, we find strong support for our approaches, particularly in two of the Strategy's principles: Accountability, transparency and engagement; and Hope, vision, symbolic and iterative change.

With respect to the first, the Strategy argues that:

- people should have access to information on sustainability issues
- institutions should have triple bottom line accountability on an annual basis
- regular sustainability audits of programs and policies should be conducted
- public engagement lies at the heart of all sustainability principles.

With respect to the second, the authors contend that:

> The 'magic' of sustainability ... does not occur unless part of the 'policy learning' process involves community engagement. Therefore, deliberative democracy processes have become totally enmeshed in what sustainability means for cities and regions... Politics will always be part of planning in cities, but the processes of community engagement will enable much of the learning that needs to be done as the basis for any public debate. Sustainability can only be a legitimate approach to the city if it is encompassing the values of its citizens about their long term visions for the city.[4]

Sustainability can only be a legitimate approach to the city if it is encompassing the values of its citizens about their long term visions for the city

We acknowledge the long-standing, dedicated and groundbreaking work of sustainability theorists and practitioners, like Australian Peter Newman and Canadian Bill Rees and many others, who have brought the global predicament and sustainability discourse to the attention of communities. That alone is a huge triumph. Our contribution, through this book, is hopefully to empower the voices of communities in processes of framing sustainability discourse, as well as in implementing decisions that support sustainability outcomes.

How wide and how deep does sustainability go?

Sustainability academic Bill Rees constantly reminds us that there is no such thing as becoming more or less sustainable. Achieving sustainability is like being pregnant: you either are, or you aren't. In essence, the concept of sustainability is straightforward – protect and look after the Earth so that future generations of all species can enjoy it without it being diminished. In the original model of sustainability, popularized by the Brundtland Commission in *Our Common Future*,[5] and adapted by Peter Newman for the *Western Australian State Sustainability Strategy*,[6] sustainability occurs at the centre of the diagram, where the spheres of society, economy and the environment coalesce (see Figure 2.1). This model illustrates how sustainability requires our economic, social and ecological systems to be working together, in harmony, mutually benefiting each other in the present and indefinitely.

Achieving sustainability is like being pregnant: you either are, or you aren't

However, we must recognize a basic fact: all three components are not equal. This is because there is only one biophysical reality, which is the basis upon which all life depends. Many theorists, such as Bill Rees, now assess the validity of sustainability writing according to the extent to which the authors acknowledge biophysical realities and the Earth's carrying capacity. Thus, while there is merit in representing sustainability by the three interlocking circles, there are also limitations associated with this representation.

In another model of sustainability, originally conceived by Emeritus Professor and President of the Australian Conservation Foundation Ian Lowe, the circles are nested, rather than interlinked (see Figure 2.2). We have adapted his original model to build upon the work of authors such as Jon Hawkes by including the element of culture[6].

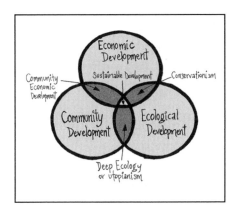

Figure 2.1 The interlinking circles model of sustainability
Source: Newman and Kenworthy (1999), p4
Figure 2.2 The concentric circles model of sustainability
Source: Lowe (1994)

Figure 2.2 reflects the reality that economic systems are embedded within social systems, societies are embedded within culture and all three are completely dependent upon the environment or Nature, which encompasses them.

New ideas about sustainability

When we find ourselves losing our way in despair, we can turn to the great thinkers in sustainability policy and environmental education, whose work we discuss at length in Chapter 5, Education. David Orr argues that our role should be to frame questions to create the possibility that they might someday be resolved. This framing involves:

Our role should be to frame questions to create the possibility that they might someday be resolved

- integrating social, cultural and economic needs within ecological constraints
- acknowledging that we are all part of Nature and that all learning, education, interactions, governance and decision making must be based on our relationships with Nature
- acknowledging that the sustainability debate is based on our cultural perspectives. The way we do or don't relate to sustainability emerges from our values and this is the place to create change that is ongoing and which will ultimately bring into effect true sustainability.[8]

Orr reminds us that a sustainable society meets basic needs and ensures individual and community safety. It fosters democratic process and promotes civic participation and engagement for all. These sorts of societies identify and resolve systemic barriers to social inclusion, and acknowledge collective responsibility for children and young people (and they are given their own voice, which is actively included and respected). Further, these communities give a high priority to skill development and education, foster well-being, value heritage, art and culture and ensure that physical design increases opportunities for a healthy lifestyle, play and social interaction.[9]

Philosophically, we support principles of Deep Ecology and deep economy.[10] Our approach also aligns with principles of biocentrism or ecocentrism. To us, sustainability involves a dynamic interplay of qualities, some easy to grasp and others very challenging. Our integrated sustainability model must be sufficiently robust and resilient to help us manage our impacts and allow us to tread lightly and live efficiently, while developing supportive and renewable practices. Living sustainably means we must lessen our ecological footprint and live within our means and the Earth's carrying capacity.

Living sustainably means we must lessen our ecological footprint and live within our means and the Earth's carrying capacity

We briefly highlight some key aspects of cultural, social and economic sustainability below.

Cultural sustainability

> ... community wellbeing is built on a shared sense of purpose; values inform action; a healthy society depends, first and foremost, on open, lively and influential cultural activity amongst the communities within it; sustainability can only be achieved when it becomes an enthusiastically embraced part of our culture.
>
> Jon Hawkes[11]

Culture is the essential and often ignored ingredient in the creation of sustainable societies.[12] Our values, dreams and beliefs about the world and the actions we take reflect our culture. Values are transmitted as we translate our beliefs and actions into cultural artefacts and creations. Yet when decision makers define culture as an 'artistic matter', they often obscure its wider value. Culture is the context in which we can articulate and manifest social meanings and guide public action. We need this broader understanding to make sustainability a reality in our communities.[13]

Culture is the context in which we can articulate and manifest social meanings and guide public action

Culture is not about creating communities of sameness where everyone believes the same things or holds the same vision. It is about people sharing value-based ideals that inform their participation in their geographical communities and communities of interest. New ways of conceptualizing and redefining culture will help us to create sustainability. How we craft our recipes for cultural success and the ingredients we use to achieve cultural integrity are topics of wide international debate. 'This debate is about values; it is a cultural debate,' claims Jon Hawkes[14]. If we neglect our cultural needs, we ignore an essential ingredient of sustainability.

Social sustainability

Sustainable communities theorist Maureen Hart argues that an ecologically sustainable community is also inherently a socially sustainable community:

> *Sustainability is related to the quality of life in a community*
> *– whether the economic, social and environmental systems*
> *that make up the community are providing a healthy,*
> *productive, meaningful life for all community residents,*
> *present and future.*[15]

Indicators of unsustainability include social breakdown, cultural disconnection, few incentives for people to participate and lack of awareness and understanding of what constitutes unsustainable practice

Sustainable communities acknowledge that there are limits to the natural, social and built systems upon which we depend. Many communities – not the least of which are in our home countries of Australia, Canada and Sweden – are both socially and economically unsustainable. Indicators of unsustainability include social breakdown, cultural disconnection, few incentives for people to participate and lack of awareness and understanding of what constitutes unsustainable practice. These factors lead to and reinforce inaction and inability to press for action. By contrast, communities actively working to implement social sustainability reflect new structural systems, including connectivity, networking and incentives for people to participate and act.

A socially sustainable community shares benefits and responsibilities across generations and into the future, ensuring opportunities that include everyone in decision-making processes. Social sustainability must also be consistent with cultural sustainability. This requires balancing respect for tradition and innovation, self-reliance and self-confidence. Social sustainability relies upon locally relevant and positive practices, including intergenerational approaches to community networking, accountability, social capital management, retention, enhancement and growth. (We discuss social capital below and in greater depth in Chapter 7, Trust.) Such initiatives represent important steps towards socially sustainable communities and should involve groups comprising people from diverse backgrounds.

Economic sustainability

Ecological Footprint Analysis (EFA) modelling predicts that we would need several additional Earth-like planets to raise the present world population to North American levels of consumption.[16] Clearly our current economic system is not sustainable. Economic sustainability requires, first, that we recognize and adopt the story that the economy is fundamentally dependent on the finite resources of Nature. To manifest this recognition within our economies requires substantial changes to current economic systems.

Economic sustainability requires, first, that we recognize and adopt the story that the economy is fundamentally dependent on the finite resources of Nature

The Post-Autistic Economics movement articulates how neoclassical (mainstream) economics is but one of many approaches to economics which has, in the words of Nobel-prize-winning economist Joseph Stiglitz, suffered 'a triumph of ideology over science',[17] where a single view of economics has been promoted at the expense of dialogue and enquiry about alternative economic theories. This shortcoming has become increasingly problematic as the world has evolved beyond 19th century society from which neoclassical economics emerged: consumer societies, corporate globalization, economic-induced environmental disasters and the accelerating gap between rich and poor.[18]

Many alternative models now challenge mainstream neoclassical economics. Sustainable economics and ecological economics are based on an accurate understanding of our relationships with and dependency on the biosphere.[19] Participatory economics aims to create circumstances that involve all those affected by economic transactions, including the broader community and Nature.[20]

Valuing different types of capital

There are (at least) four types of capital essential to sustainability: natural capital, cultural and human capital, social capital and economic and human-made capital

Clearly, we need to rewrite all aspects of our stories about the meaning and accumulation of wealth. One helpful way is through reviewing and renewing our definitions of capital. Traditionally, capital referred to a good of some kind used to produce further assets. This understanding of capital is reflected in our cultural obsession with the accumulation of financial wealth, trumping care for people, cultures and Nature. This has been another unsustainable story. We embrace a more sustainable story when we recognize that there are (at least) four types of capital essential to sustainability: natural capital,[21] cultural and human capital,[22] social capital[23] and economic and human-made capital. According to cultural economist David Throsby, we should regard each form of capital as an inheritance from the ancient or recent past, where natural capital is 'a gift of Nature' and cultural capital is the fruit of human creativity.[24] Again, natural capital (or Nature) is the basis or 'precondition' for all other types of capital; therefore we should accord it the highest priority.[25]

As with economic wealth, sustainable 'wealth' involves living off the natural interest, not the natural capital which generates it

As with economic wealth, sustainable 'wealth' involves living off the natural interest, not the natural capital which generates it. Approaching retirement age, Wendy has been asking herself whether she should cash in her pension plan and put the money into the construction of her ecological home. That would be using up the capital and not living on the interest. It's a risky thing to consider. Wendy's dilemma is the global dilemma in a nutshell. The difference is that Wendy can probably create further capital. The Earth's natural capital is finite.

Airing old, unsustainable stories: finding new sustainable stories

As we have seen, many approaches to sustainability require us, firstly, to shift our thinking and then to change our world. Unsustainability means living beyond our means. Our unsustainable actions are perpetuated by values embedded in the stories we tell ourselves about how the world works. Unsustainable stories thrive in darkness and ignorance – in conditions where sustainable stories are not being told.

A major culprit is our acceptance of economic growth and material well-being, which – in our global story – has erroneously surpassed our need to live sustainably on this Earth. Environmental educators Chet Bowers and David Orr claim that we need nothing less than a complete 'reworking of our master metaphorical templates' to regain the balance we have lost.[26] We need long-term solutions, involving changes both in consciousness and the language we use to describe all aspects of our lives.

We see these 'master metaphorical templates' as collective world-views, or paradigms, shaped by the confluence in patterns among billions of 'stories'. These stories reside in the minds and hearts of millions of people, living with diverse beliefs and values, life experiences, education, resources and immediate challenges. Far from being a linear process, changing our master metaphorical templates involves the awakenings, realizations and inner changes of many individuals to change many, many stories... All the outdated stories, in fact.

In this chapter, we discuss some unsustainable stories that are already 'in transition'. We believe that through kitchen table conversations, in communities around the world, we can work together to do the important work of creating a sustainable world, one story at a time.

> **Our unsustainable actions are perpetuated by values embedded in the stories we tell ourselves about how the world works**

> **Through kitchen table conversations, in communities around the world, we can work together to do the important work of creating a sustainable world, one story at a time**

Alarming realities

Internationally, we see many frightening examples of communities using up their natural and social capital, living off the principal rather than the interest. Many of our great fisheries have been seriously depleted. Rainforests are being logged at an ever increasing and unsustainable rate, primarily to support the global resource trade.[27] As a result, local temperatures and precipitation rates change, animals lose their habitats and precious soils are lost to erosion.[28] The list of related environmental and social damage is endless. In the United States, particularly in water-thirsty California, aquifers of clean water have been emptied without hope of recharging. Socially, we are witnessing a widening gap between wealthy and poor, and crime and drug use are tearing apart the fabric of our communities.

The size and complexity of these environmental problems, coupled with the frailty of our current remediation approaches, can be profoundly distressing. In 2006, Steph compiled some basic research about the likely implications of climate change and unsustainable growth in regional Queensland for participants in a community event. When Wendy presented a list of moderate predictions, compiled from the most basic and conservative Internet and journal resources, the council's project manager burst into tears. She had not integrated news about sustainability into a vision for her community's future. Yet her young son, aged 11, told her he already knew everything that was in the report. Like many, she feared the outcome of our unsustainable ways of living but did not know what to do. When Wendy suggested that she had been 'in denial', she quickly agreed.

A constant stream of media reports confronts us about the impacts of our unsustainable behaviour: ice melts, bleached coral reefs, species extinction, automobile dependence, logging, drought, flooding and bushfires. Nihilistic responses to the ever present 'alarming realities'[29] manifest in many ways: boredom, paralysis, addiction and fragmentation.[30] Processes are urgently needed to re-engage people – in community.

Bringing the discussion back to the table means making it accessible. Kitchen table conversations are grounded in the local and the real. They involve listening and sharing with family and friends, with community, and with people who care because they have a stake. At the kitchen table, no one is a remote stranger or an objective voice of false authority. We are all simply people with opinions, values, hopes and fears working to secure a sustainable future for the Earth we share in common.

At the kitchen table, we are all simply people with opinions, values, hopes and fears working to secure a sustainable future for the Earth we share in common

Dialoguing with experts

Scientific, technical and professional experts have much to offer community engagement with sustainability. However, their knowledge is not always properly understood by community members without the same scientific, technical or academic training (nor, sometimes, by the experts themselves). Expert knowledge is often presented or received as an ultimate 'truth'. This popular perception ignores an important truth: the scientific method – which contextualizes the basis of much formal expertise – never claimed to reveal 'the truth'. Rather, it attempts to approach the truth by continuously refining theories to better approximate observable objects, patterns and events.

On the one hand, we believe that communities need to take expert knowledge more seriously. The alarming ecological realities outlined above make this point clear. And while there are many unknowns regarding the implications of climate change, for example, we cannot deny that it is occurring, that it threatens life on Earth and that we need to take immediate and drastic action to address it. We need to listen to the experts and get on with creating a sustainable world.

On the other hand, some people with expertise can give the impression that their opinion is beyond debate. It is not. 'Experts' may tend to constrain debate to what is known (by them) and exclude opinions not based on research (such as emotional and intuitive understandings, for example).[31] They often undervalue local knowledge, preferring opinions that don't challenge the status quo. Some cling to their status-based 'power' and fail to recognize the power of facilitating the education and empowerment of others. We acknowledge that specialized or technical knowledge is important in achieving sustainability. We need scientists, technicians and people who know things that others may not. However, what needs to change is the 'trump value' of this knowledge over other forms. We need to frame community discussions about sustainability – and many other issues, for that matter – in ways that avoid denial and allow for debate.

How we navigate to sustainability

Once recognized and embraced, new stories that support sustainability can be translated into practical models and frameworks – 'recipes', if you like. And we can implement them in a sustainable society. We briefly discuss below some models that can be developed within cultural, social and economic systems to support ecological systems and broader sustainability.

From compartmentalization to interdependence, interconnectedness and embeddedness

This separation from Nature is the fundamental source of our abuse towards Nature and each other

Since the Enlightenment, in so-called 'educated' societies, we have been trained to categorize, classify and compartmentalize. This compartmentalization of Nature, in relation to our economic, political and social systems, mirrors our compartmentalization of society in general.[32] We see ourselves as 'skin-encapsulated egos', separate from the living world.[33] Environmentalist and therapist Chellis Glendinning argues that this separation from Nature is the fundamental source of our abuse towards Nature and each other.[34] We cannot continue rationalizing Nature according to our economic and non-renewable resource needs. It is simply not sustainable.

In reality, our bodies and our communities are completely reliant upon Nature. Cathy became acutely aware of this story when, in January 2006, she moved from Melbourne to Luleå, in northern Sweden. As a new immigrant with two young children, no local language skills and daily temperatures as low as –25 degrees Celsius, she found it challenging, to say the least. Yet it was also invigorating. Cathy discovered that she needed a deep engagement with the locals and with Nature to learn to read the climate, to respect the limitations it imposed and to keep the children safe.

Forced to be out in Nature every day with no car and an energetic two-year-old, Cathy discovered unaccustomed blessings in the astonishing beauty and fragile interdependence of Nature. With her children, she learned to listen for the first magical sound of dripping water after six months of snow and ice. They learned where the wild raspberries were hiding. They witnessed the devastating consequences of a hibernation cut short by erratic winter temperatures... As her literacy expanded, Cathy experienced at first hand some of the damaging environmental consequences of unsustainable urban lifestyles in cities across the world that remain highly car-dependent, land-hungry and Nature-blind.

From linear progression to a complex web of interactions

Cathy was reminded that we are part of a complex system, a system that we cannot control. We need both humility and knowledge to operate within such a system. Until the 4th century BC, most people believed that the Earth was flat. That sort of thinking persists today, with many accepting the convenient stories we are told by the media and others. Despite all our knowledge about how extraordinary and unpredictable Nature can be, many people still believe that complex systems like globally connected societies,

We are part of a complex system, a system that we cannot control. We need both humility and knowledge to operate within such a system

economies and ecological systems demonstrate relatively simple, and linear, causal relationships. They don't. A growing body of science based in complexity theory[35] and resilience theory[36] demonstrates the falsity of assumptions of stable, predictable and linear behaviour for socio-ecological systems. We need to carefully examine this research because it shatters the illusion that solutions based on partial sustainability considerations will deliver transformative change. We cannot tinker at the edges and expect beneficial results.

Sustainability requires a holistic, integrated approach that addresses issues from root causes to outcomes

A piecemeal approach is ineffective with complex natural systems and with social, cultural and economic systems, let alone the interactions among them. Sustainability requires a holistic, integrated approach that addresses issues from root causes to outcomes. Real change means not merely a change in a technology but a fundamental change in the human values that drive it. We need to experience and relate with Nature in new (some would say, old) ways. We must also embrace cultural and social sustainability, and develop more sustainable models for our economy.

Many government and industry policy responses still treat sustainability as an entirely environmental matter, not recognizing the intrinsic connections among our natural, social, cultural and economic systems. Approaches that focus solely on technological or economic responses, such as developing wind or solar power or taxing carbon emissions, are a product of what Glendinning calls 'techno-addiction': 'a way of being, a way of seeing the world, a way of asking certain questions and not others, a way of feeling certain emotions and not others, a way of experiencing that is linear, mechanistic, exclusionary, and distorted'.[37]

We now understand that linear-based understandings of complex socio-ecological systems are no longer valid

We now understand that linear-based understandings of complex socio-ecological systems are no longer valid. We must experiment with new adaptive management approaches to transform our economic, social, cultural and environmental systems at the systemic, strategic and tactical levels. A new sustainability paradigm must respect the role of local cultures in framing, implementing and evaluating change. We dream of a sustainable community and lifestyle that allows us to live at as high a standard as possible (within levels that do not impair the Earth's capacity to support future generations), while minimizing our impacts. Many obstacles impair the transformation of these impossible visions into possibilities.

Communication: The discursive key

The primary means by which we can transform our unsustainable stories into sustainable ones is communication. By questioning the assumptions that underlie them, we help change our unsustainable stories, one story at a time, until whole communities begin to embrace a new story and, eventually, the whole new world. In this way, we believe that communication is a discursive key to achieving sustainability outcomes, as The Tragedy of the Commons (told below) story illustrates. As we see later in this book, as we tell various stories about the Eagleby community in Queensland, Australia, telling a new story is a powerful way to build sustainable communities.

> By questioning the assumptions that underlie them, we help change our unsustainable stories, one story at a time

The discursive key is an important concept to explore here, as we return to it in Chapter 8, Inclusion. A discursive key 'turns' the discussion from one conception to another. It can shift the 'storyline' of policy debate from one account to another and perform 'the critical transformative work which allows an issue to be re-framed'.[38]

This is a small but powerful example of how a different story can lead to reworking our master metaphorical templates. In hindsight, of course, and in the context of this book, it seems obvious. (To us, at least.) Of course, communication is the discursive key to sustainability outcomes. Of course, the Earth isn't flat!

The Tragedy of the Commons revisited

Most finite natural resources on our Earth are managed as common property. Because their use by some can disadvantage others, governments or institutions normally control access to them.[39] This situation is supported by the classic economic model developed by ecologist Garrett Hardin in 1968. Hardin's model, known as The Tragedy of the Commons, predicted inevitable and unsustainable overharvesting within common resources in the absence of private or central government ownership.[40] Yet Hardin's model assumed that resource users would always seek to maximize private returns to the ultimate detriment of the natural resource. By questioning Hardin's original assumptions, including, critically, the absence of communication among the actors,[41] Elinor Ostrom and her colleagues turned this classic model on its head.[42] Recreating the resource dilemma in an experimental laboratory, they showed that the model's original predictions are correct only when participants interact anonymously and cannot communicate.[43] When participants were allowed to communicate, trust and reciprocity were achieved, which provided for better and more sustainable resource management.

When participants were allowed to communicate, trust and reciprocity were achieved, which provided for better and more sustainable resource management heart and hands of the sustainability movement

Conclusion

In this chapter, we have avoided repeating research about sustainability and the planetary crisis reported in numerous recent publications. Wise mentors advised us to 'take that as read'. Rather, we have explored the realms of stories and storytelling, arguing that we need a completely new story – in fact, many new stories – to guide us in creating a sustainable world. Deeper and more expanded, inclusive stories. Stories that resonate with our deepest dreams and are consistent with our cultural values. We need these new stories to guide us both in personal and community engagement with sustainability and the challenges these processes present.

These sustainability stories can be understood and integrated through effective conversations spreading throughout our local communities and our broader communities of interest. A great place to start is with open conversations around our kitchen tables. These conversations can then expand to encompass community engagement processes.

Our next chapter explores in greater detail concepts of community and community engagement and how they relate to sustainability. We examine meanings of community and community engagement to prepare for our discussions about how community engagement can help us build communities committed to achieving sustainability objectives.

3 COMMUNITY ENGAGEMENT: A PATHWAY TO SUSTAINABILITY

Sustainability always involves the whole community. This is the profound lesson we learn from nature.

Fritjof Capra, 2005, p24

If we face an unprecedented planetary crisis, we also find ourselves in a moment of innovation unlike any that has come before. We find ourselves in a moment when all over the world, millions of people are working to invent, use, and share worldchanging tools, models, and ideas. We live in an era when the number of people working to make the world better is exploding. Humanity's fate rests on the outcome of the race between problem solvers and the problems themselves. The world is getting better – we just have to make sure it gets better faster than it gets worse.

Alex Steffen (ed)
Worldchanging: A User's Guide for the 21st Century[1]

At roughly the same time Wendy was thumbing through *Kitchen Table Wisdom* in Vancouver, Steph was at his mum's place in Brisbane, sharing a meal…

A kitchen table conversation

It was that time of the evening, after dinner, just relaxing. I was over at Mum's place for dinner and, with her husband John, we were hanging about and talking.

It had been a really sustainability-focused week. The Stern report had been released and the subsequent media and scientific frenzy was in full swing. Stern had described the largely economic impact of moderate climate change and suggested that switching to renewable low-emission energies could have enormous economic benefits. Despite the focus on economic measures of sustainability, Stern had presented a comprehensive study incorporating his assessment of the economic and societal costs of moderate climate change impacts. He stated bluntly that politicians had to act both radically and quickly. It was on all the news, well, all the news I was consuming, anyway.

So, when I looked up and saw Mum washing the dishes one at a time, with the hot water flowing freely, I thought it important to say something. At the time here in

Continued

> **The sight of that tap billowing water while Mum turned to talk with John and me started me thinking about local, household sustainability, the bigger picture and how we are all involved**

Brisbane, we were on level 4 and soon to be level 5 (now level 6) water restrictions. The sight of that tap billowing water while Mum turned to talk with John and I started me thinking about local, household sustainability, the bigger picture and how we are all involved. The conversation that followed moved me even further to think about the kinds of conversations we all needed to have around kitchen tables, just like the one where we were sitting:

'You know that we're on restricted water, hey? The dams are really low...' I trailed off, kind of uncertain how best to approach this.

'Yeah', she snapped back, turning around, hands dripping, looking straight at me, water flowing in the background. There was an air of 'so what?' in her voice and she was suddenly looking pretty upset.

'Well, I thought, maybe, it would be less wasteful to fill the sink up instead of...' Trailing off again, I thought it best to leave the conversation there.

It wasn't that Mum was unable to understand what I was saying. She's a progressive thinker in many ways. No, it was more that I was challenging her understanding of the relationship between humans and Nature and this informed her core values. By questioning the way she used water, I was reminding her about the need to limit our use of natural resources, which was linked to new lifestyles, sacrifices and opportunities: enormous changes for us all to understand and embody. Our inability to talk about it in any meaningful way, at her kitchen table, represented just how disconnected many of us are from the reality of what sustainability might look like.

Introduction

Steph's story above about his conversation with his Mum illustrates just how difficult communication can be – even if it is around the kitchen table with those we know and love. And even if it's about sustainability issues that seem pretty straightforward. Yet as we learned at the end of Chapter 2 and as many of us know

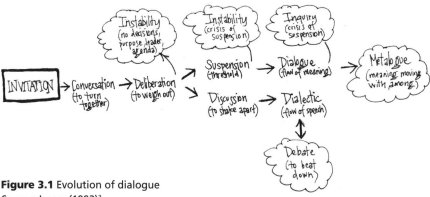

Figure 3.1 Evolution of dialogue
Source: Isaacs (1993)[3]

instinctively, communication is critical to achieving sustainability outcomes. Effective communication can mean the difference between competition and cooperation, between natural resource devastation and sustainable management.

Communication is critical to achieving sustainability outcomes

A *continuum of communication* ranges from 'conversation' to 'dialogue' (see Figure 3.1 above).[2] When we engage in communication at the 'dialogue' end of the spectrum, we can transcend different ways of understanding and different value systems. This is the type of communication Steph and his mum needed to achieve a sustainability outcome around their kitchen table. They needed a dialogue.

This book makes a commitment to community engagement processes to achieve sustainability outcomes because, if conducted well, they provide forums for communities to communicate. Sometimes, fortunately, they provide opportunities for communities to have a dialogue and through that process to be empowered and achieve transformative change that challenges our 'master metaphorical templates'.

As the global emergency deepens, we need the best possible approaches to community engagement to achieve sustainability outcomes. Thus, we need to understand what a community is – and what it could be. We also need to understand

As the global emergency deepens, we need the best possible approaches to community engagement to achieve sustainability outcomes

community engagement and how to design inclusive and appropriate approaches for different community contexts. To this end, this chapter examines concepts of community, community engagement and sustainability.

What is community?

The word *community* derives from the Latin *communis*, meaning 'common, public, shared by all or many'. It also means the changes or exchanges that link. Community is the practical expression of our commonly owned goods, including the infrastructure in our streets, the services we depend on, our communications and exchanges **A community** and the ways we actively build the world around us. A community **is any group** is any group that shares a location, interests or practices, defined by **that shares** patterns of interaction among individuals, perceptions of common- **a location,** ality or common interest and/or geography. **interests or practices**

Nancy, Yollana, Wendy, Steph and Cathy are all – or have been – members of the planning community. Nancy, at the time of writing, was a member of a student community and Wendy, her supervisor, a member of that academic community. Wendy is a member of a small rural community, an international feminist community and a community of eco-philosophers interested in eco-spiritual approaches. Wendy, Steph, Cathy and Yollana are members of an Australian community; Wendy and Nancy are members of a Canadian community. Cathy is part of a Swedish community. Nancy and Yollana belong to Generation Y, Steph and Cathy to Generation X and Wendy is a Baby Boomer. All are members of a wider global community. Cathy and Yollana are parents; Cathy, Wendy and Yollana are married.

So what does this mean for community engagement processes? It means that while we are members of more than specific geographical communities, our geographical locations are important. This book does not deal exclusively with place-based community engagement processes. However, as communities engage with the challenges of the planetary emergency, many of those will need to be confronted in a specific locality. So, while we may be members of many communities, as the authors of this book are, we must also engage with local, geographically specific issues. Engagement specialist Desmond Connor offered Wendy a brief working definition of community that has stood the test of time: 'people, living in a place, who develop a sense of identity and a common culture, and who create interdependence in a social system'.

So, while we may be members of many communities, we must also engage with local, geographically specific issues

Exploding the myth of the common community goal and embracing communities of difference

In Western democracies, we often view community as a positive term to describe well-functioning collections of people. But that is not always the case. Iris Marion Young in *Justice and the Politics of Difference* (1990) explained that the meaning of community has become so distorted by people's reactions to their present situations or sense of belonging (or not) that it has become idealized. People's perceptions of community relate to how they would prefer to feel. Young rejects what she calls 'the assimilationist model' and affirms a positive sense of group difference. We need to broaden our sense of community to include our *interactions*, as well as what we create and build.

There is now broad acceptance that communities are complex, diverse and tangled places. An easily identified single view rarely emerges about any given issue. When those in power try to define a community based on notions of unity and sameness, they often exclude or alienate those people or 'elements' who do not 'fit' this perceived balance. They are then called the 'other'. If we are not vigilant, we can relegate certain elements or ideals to the 'outside' of a so-called homogeneous community. Iris Marion Young argued that, 'there is no universally shared concept of community'.[4] One study that asked, 'What is a community?' found that for most

Communities are complex, diverse and tangled places. An easily identified single view rarely emerges about any given issue

people it is a small 'home area', much smaller than a local authority. This definition of community excludes those members whose views differ from the dominant view. This process of exclusion legitimizes the majority view as an expression of the democratic process.

Wendy and her husband Karl had a fascinating experience of transformation into the 'other' when they lived in a flat in Brisbane, within walking distance from Steph's and Yollana's homes and the office the three of them shared. Owner-occupiers for several years, they sold their flat and for a year were renters, as the new purchaser did not want to move in right away. Having listened to the racist comments of Body Corporate (Strata Corporation) members about 'those dirty Samoan renters using the pool', they were now classified as 'others' – the vilified renters. Yet they were the same residents, in the same household, living the same lives and maintaining the same housing standards.

The changing nature of communities

To complicate matters, our communities are changing – and rapidly

The stories of our place-based communities are becoming more complex. And our community engagement practices must be alert to the ever changing nature of communities

To complicate matters, our communities are changing – and rapidly. Wendy finds the Vancouver where she grew up and where Nancy now lives almost unrecognizable in terms of its cultural and ethnic mix. When Wendy, Steph and Yollana worked in Bonnyrigg, a western Sydney housing estate, in 2005, they had to translate all community engagement material into eight local languages and employ bilingual community educators to deliver community capacity-strengthening sessions to local residents. Half of the residents spoke no English or little English at home. In the Swedish Lappland city of Luleå, population 70,000, Cathy spent a year studying Swedish at the Adult Education Centre in a class with students from no less than 25 different countries – from Nepal to Nigeria to Azerbaijan. Most immigrants intended to stay in Sweden but many were waiting for civil war in their own countries to calm so they could return. The stories of our place-based communities are becoming more complex. And our community engagement practices must be alert to the ever changing nature of communities.

What is community engagement?

Sustainability always involves the whole community.
This is the profound lesson we learn from nature.

Fritjof Capra[5]

There is no widespread consensus about the meaning or purpose of community engagement, despite a huge professional and academic literature and hundreds of manuals, checklists and models for practitioners.[6] Engagement is generally believed to be 'real' when participants can determine the outcome and therefore 'bogus' when the outcome is determined elsewhere.[7] The term *community participation*, rather than *consultation*, indicates *an active role for the community*, leading to significant control over decisions. North Americans almost exclusively use the term *citizen participation*, rather than *community consultation* or *engagement*, although *engagement* is definitely gaining popularity. Community engagement is sometimes contrasted with 'citizen action', seen as at the opposite end of a continuum, defined as an activity *'initiated and controlled by citizens for purposes that they determine'*.[8] The term *consultation* generally means *sharing of information but not necessarily of power*.

There are two key rationales for community engagement:

1 *It is ethical:* In a democratic society, those whose livelihoods, environments and lives are at stake should be consulted and involved in the decisions that affect them directly.
2 *It is pragmatic:* Support for programmes and policies often depends on people's willingness to assist the process. It is also often *necessary* because 'If planners will not involve the citizens, citizens will involve themselves'.[9]

This book has relevance for all types of community engagement

In a democratic society, those whose livelihoods, environments and lives are at stake should be consulted and involved in the decisions that affect them

with sustainability at a variety of scales. It's particularly designed for community members who are trying to build their own literacy and understanding of how global pressures can affect local communities (for example, rising fuel prices and automobile dependence, food security, planning for higher density housing, transit-oriented development). Our approach to community engagement in any location has always assumed that there is no single entity that we could call 'the community'. Views such as ours are now widely shared.

Our approach to community engagement in any location has always assumed that there is no single entity that we could call 'the community'

Community engagement processes are often weakened by an exclusive focus on identified stakeholders, with the assumption that these people share a common community goal. Proponents (particularly developers) often prefer to deal exclusively with identified 'stakeholders' (the principal of the local school, the manager of the childcare centre, the head of the volunteer fire brigade, the youth worker, the childcare centre manager...). But we know that these people rarely reflect all views or even share a common community goal. How, for example, can a youth worker speak on behalf of youth? He or she can speak confidently on behalf of youth workers. But not for youth.

How, for example, can a youth worker speak on behalf of youth? He or she can speak confidently on behalf of youth workers. But not for youth

Typically, when social planners like Wendy, Yollana and Steph design community engagement processes to help communities build sustainability, we accept a consultancy, do some background reading or talk to some people and show up in an unfamiliar place, asking, 'Who lives here and what's going on here?' At the outset, we are searching for a definition of what the local community is and why local people need to strengthen it. Only if there is opportunity for everyone to be involved can we collectively explore ways for cooperation and coordination.

Community engagement with sustainability

There are many reasons why community engagement is central to achieving sustainability. First are ethical and practical reasons: in a democratic society, those whose livelihoods, environments and lives are at stake should be engaged and involved in decisions that directly affect them. Community-initiated projects and processes empower people to take action in local community development. Canadian planning academic and practitioner Peter Boothroyd recently reminded Nancy, his student, 'To participate is to be human.'

Second, community engagement provides opportunities for developing a holistic sense of sustainability, where people make decisions using local wisdom, values, information and knowledge. Third, community engagement contributes to the efficiency of a project or programme. Targeting local needs and preferences always saves time and money. Fourth, by addressing local social and cultural needs, community engagement processes can help develop micro-scale policy approaches that fit the community and its particular resources, skill sets and preferred approaches. And finally, community engagement helps to build local accountability.[10]

Existing tools for community engagement

A variety of community engagement tools can be used to determine the appropriate types and levels of engagement for different contexts and the benefits and weaknesses of different methods.

The Public Participation Spectrum

One model that is widely used is the *Public Participation Spectrum* developed by the International Association for Public Participation (IAP2).[11] The Spectrum is seen as a development of Sherry Arnstein's *Ladder of Citizen Participation*, first published in 1969.[12] The Spectrum's stages are: *Inform, Consult, Involve, Collaborate* and *Empower*. Each stage has an objective, a *Promise to the Public* and *Example Tasks*.

One of the Spectrum's benefits is its powerful *Promise to the Public* that is appropriate to the 'level of community impact' of the public participation process. For example, the 'promise' at the 'inform' level is simply 'we will keep you informed', whereas at the 'empower' level it is 'we will implement what you decide'. We discuss the importance of clarifying participants' contributions further in Chapter 6, Action.

The Wheel of Participation

Another tool is the Wheel of Participation (or empowerment), developed by the Shire of South Lanarkshire, Glasgow (see Figure 3.2 below). We prefer the Wheel to the Spectrum because it does not suggest (as ladders, continua and spectra might) that moving up or along the ladder is necessarily the preferred approach.

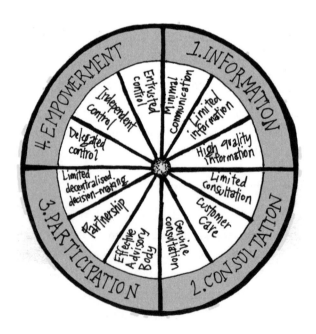

Figure 3.2 The Wheel of Participation
Source: South Lanarkshire Council, www.step.gb.com/consultation/index. htm#The%20Wheel%20of%20Participation

50

A feature of this model is that each quadrant identifies appropriate responses and approaches. An example of how the Wheel could work was delivered to Wendy's letterbox in Brisbane in 2002. The Lord Mayor explained that the Council had purchased new 'split trucks'; the letter contained a drawing that illustrated two separate compartments: one for general waste and one for recyclables, designed to avoid contamination. (See Figure 3.3.)

As an environmentally conscious resident, Wendy felt the letter met her information needs – an example of good-quality information (Quadrant 1). If, however, it had foreshadowed changes to the City's waste management policies, Wendy would have been on the telephone or email immediately. In this case, as the Wheel rightly suggests, the requirement was only for high-quality information. In this case, information sufficed.

How the split truck works

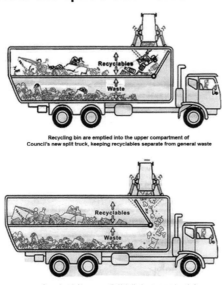

Recycling bin are emptied into the upper compartment of
Council's new split truck, keeping recyclables separate from general waste

General waste bins are emptied into the lower compartment of
Council's new split truck, keeping general waste separate from recyclables

Figure 3.3 For information only: The split truck
Source: Brisbane City Council (2002)

The coproduction model

Coproduction implies a shared responsibility between the community and public officials

Wendy visited Belgium in 2007 and found that there and throughout much of Europe, practitioners and planners are increasingly using the term 'coproduction' to describe the sorts of community engagement processes we advocate in this book. It's an attractive term because it implies a shared responsibility between the community and public officials in planning and producing services and managing development processes. The term also implies the intention to continue involvement to the implementation stage.[14]

The aim is to work together constructively through the inevitable tensions and conflicts, negotiating outcomes with recognized sharing of power and responsibility. The discussion has been going on in Europe for 25 years, with scholars Susskind and Elliott commenting in 1983 that coproduction 'epitomises the power sharing that residents in some cities are seeking'. There will be no one stable way, but a changing, evolving pattern, where appropriate roles can be agreed between citizens and public officials for a current position.[15]

Coproduction is characterized by direct involvement of non-elected interest group representatives in the operation of government. It involves decision making through face-to-face negotiation between decision makers and those who claim a major stake in particular decisions. The model acknowledges the inevitable tensions among local government, community members and business groups. A key complement of the coproduction model is that community members have a say in *how resources are expended*. This greatly expands their 'advisory' role.[16] From our perspective, achieving sustainability depends on deep engagement processes like coproduction. We would like to see more coproduction in the English-speaking world.

The current state of community engagement

All of us share the view that not enough people – including some of our clients – recognize the importance or value of community engagement. Further, those responsible for community engagement processes are generally not aware that methods already exist or adopt new buzzwords (e.g. *capacity building, community cultural development, placemaking, community partnerships and strengthening communities*) with inadequate appreciation of their deeper potential.

Previous publications by Wendy and others summarized eight underpinnings of community engagement arising from theory and practice, listed below.

> **Those responsible for community engagement processes often adopt new buzzwords with inadequate appreciation of their deeper potential**

Eight underpinnings of community engagement[17]

1　People know more than they realize.
2　People cannot participate satisfactorily unless they can understand the language being used.
3　People often fear giving opinions, especially in their home locality.
4　People's involvement improves the quality of local government.
5　Synergy is more likely to occur when people collaborate.
6　Specific skills are required.
7　Relevant professionals should be involved from the start.
8　There is community value in sharing participatory experiences.

These underpinnings are a useful starting point for anyone embarking on the design of a community engagement process. Even though principles and protocols may be in place, however, political will is often lacking. Wendy frequently speaks at conferences about cases from her consulting practice. She's spoken with practitioners in many countries who tell a similar tale: people are aiming too low. Apparently terrified of 'raising expectations without being able to deliver', they collapse under the barrages of risk-management advisers and often are reluctant to gather a group of residents together unless they have 'all the answers' or at least 'a viable plan'. A senior manager with a prominent development firm proudly told Wendy in 2003 that they had 'never held a public meeting'. They would not allow their 'enemies' to congregate together in case they might 'gang up against them'.

Apparently terrified of 'raising expectations without being able to deliver', they collapse under the barrages of risk-management advisers

In terms of the state of community engagement practices, across the board, methods are poorly implemented. Attention to detail is critical – from layout of workshop spaces, to what organizers wear, to how participants' responses are recorded. It all matters. There are too many examples of poor practice, even where processes started out innovatively – as the Open House Vancouver example below attests. We provide many practical suggestions in this book that can help raise the bar.

This book is for people eager to create sustainable futures by using engagement processes that reach into the fabric of communities and touch people deeply

This book is for people eager to create sustainable futures by using engagement processes that reach into the fabric of communities and touch people deeply. We emphasize depth in this book because of the demonstrated failure of shallow engagement processes. In this context, we challenge readers to choose methods appropriate to the anticipated level of public involvement and impact. If the impact is likely to be high, we recommend experimenting with a collaborative or empowerment approach, as shown in the IAP2 Spectrum. But it is important to do this with the support of experienced community engagement practitioners.

Why community engagement processes for sustainability can fail

Community engagement processes for sustainability fail for many reasons, some of which are touched on below. In practice, we do not find that the components of our *EATING* model are being used or even discussed. We need a richer discourse.

Inadequate involvement of community at the strategic decision-making level

Formal statutory processes exclude many community members from decisions with great impact on their lives and all life on Earth. Within communities, we find little community discussion about the potential of community engagement strategies to shape sustainable futures.

Use of process to ratify existing decisions and actions

At a local level, in many countries, governments and development managers use community engagement processes almost exclusively for ratifying plans for urban development, managing open space, developing transport options and environmental management.

Mismatch of techniques and needs

Many developers and government authorities are painting with a very limited paint box, with few 'colours' – and little variety – in the techniques and methods they select.

Inadequate resourcing

Processes rarely demonstrate continuity or consistent resourcing for true engagement, capacity building and development (rather than project-based approaches).

Inadequate succession planning/capacity building

When the 'engagement champion' leaves the agency or firm, the whole culture of community engagement he or she fostered can collapse virtually overnight. We have seen that happen recently in a major high-profile Australian project.

Within communities, we find little community discussion about the potential of community engagement strategies to shape sustainable futures

Lack of integration

Lack of integration of engagement approaches within and between departments, projects and communication processes, followed by a limited understanding of the dimensions of sustainability, contributes to shallow engagement processes and inadequate outcomes.

Fear of challenging the status quo

Among other barriers is a popular view that commitment to building genuine sustainability will decrease economic viability.

Inadequate connection with communities

Many bureaucrats and senior people in planning, development agencies and consulting firms have little connection with the communities with which they work

Many bureaucrats and senior people in planning, development agencies and consulting firms have little connection with the communities with which they work. They may not understand them sociologically or culturally or be able to empathize with their problems and needs. This is particularly the case with professionals working in low-income communities. Wendy recalls a terrible experience, blessedly fading from her memory after 20 years, in which a senior architect insisted on wearing a striped double-breasted suit and a bow tie to a public workshop in a low-income community slated for redevelopment.

As chair of the workshop, she begged him to reconsider. He presented his redevelopment plan to about 200 angry residents. Of course, this decision backfired and a loud male voice was heard yelling (in characteristic Australian style) from the back of the room: 'Who's that pompous pri*k in the bow tie?' It took Wendy's team weeks of hard work to compensate for this error in judgement. And the community never trusted that architect. Ever.

Lack of respect for local knowledge

In the same workshop, Wendy encountered the problem of the 'experts' not respecting local knowledge. The consultant engineers assured local residents that there would be no flooding problems on the site. 'It will never flood here', the engineer announced, flourishing his one-in-a-hundred-year-flood plan. Wendy noticed an elderly woman (who lived across the street from the workshop venue) shaking her head and mumbling. When Wendy nodded to her, she rose and countered in a shaky but clear voice:

> *What a load of old rubbish. Where do you so-called experts get your ideas? There was a big flood here only a few years ago and I was rescued from my basement by the fire department. In my nightie. Don't tell* **me** *it doesn't flood here. I was up to my waist in it when they finally got to me! No flooding problem? Ha!*[18]

The engineers checked their statistics and, sure enough, they found the potential for significant flooding. Severe flooding in that neighbourhood had been recorded as far back as 1881.

The 'expert' problem

We have already discussed the role of experts in Chapter 2, Sustainability. Here we reiterate our point. Community engagement processes need to draw on the knowledge, skills and resources of 'experts'. Yet people with expertise must continue to acknowledge the limitations of their knowledge and respect the local knowledges of diverse communities. We must recognize that different individuals draw upon different intelligences (see our discussion on multiple intelligences in Chapter 5, Education). We must not allow 'intellectual' intelligence to take precedence over local knowledge. An old spiritual adage reminds us that 'the mind is a wonderful servant but a lousy master'. Similarly, experts are the 'mind' of our communities. We believe that expertise should be employed to serve the community's own visions themselves, not to control them.

We believe that expertise should be employed to serve the community's own visions themselves, not to control them

A tale of two approaches to community engagement

This book contains many stories of terrible and inspirational examples of community engagement processes. Below are two recent stories told in some detail, as we will return to the principles that they demonstrate, either by good or bad example.

A tale of decline in quality of community engagement: From CityPlan to Open Houses, Vancouver

An example of how effective processes can be diminished appears to be the City of Vancouver, which is very diverse ethnically and linguistically. In earlier books in the *Community Participation in Practice* suite, Wendy and her co-authors praised Vancouver's innovative CityPlan process, conducted over four years, costing $Can 1.5 million, plus $Can 1.5 million for internal staff.[19] Initiated in late 1992, the visionary process was heralded as a 'Cadillac approach' to community engagement. While some saw it as a bit top–down and elitist, the future-oriented process aimed to inform citizens, allow for a high level of community engagement from a broad cross-section and put the ideas of citizens first.

> While some saw it as a bit top–down and elitist, the future-oriented process aimed to inform citizens, allow for a high level of community engagement from a broad cross-section and put the ideas of citizens first

The original CityPlan process was organized on two levels – local 'City Circles' with a neighbourhood focus, and then forums, fairs and travelling shows to provide a city-wide focus beyond identified stakeholders. Representing work in progress was written material in five languages and material specifically designed for people with visual impairments. The programme for youth included classroom circles and workshops on 'Kids in City Hall' and 'Build Your City'. A senior planner and manager, now retired, oversaw all CityPlan work and reviewed it regularly.

Fifteen years later, in Vancouver in late 2007, a controversial sustainability project was launched using a community engagement model technique called the 'open house'.[20] This process has had a chequered career in the USA, Canada and Australia, as proponents have pared away the essential qualities of the original model and reduced it to little more than a drop-in session, perhaps with some informal discussion.

Nancy and Wendy attended one such open house in Vancouver in December 2007. The proposed project was an innovative 'neighborhood energy utility' in the inner city.[21] It will be an interpretive facility to showcase innovative use of sustainable technology and is expected to achieve Leadership in Energy and Environmental Design (LEED™) Gold or Platinum certification. Given the contentious nature of the proposal (using sewage waste to heat the facility's water), our assessment was that the open house failed on all reasonable engagement criteria. A planner colleague attended in the role of an imaginary, well-educated Afghani woman and reported that she (hypothetically) had to leave after three minutes because none of her needs was met.

There was no explanatory information in 'plain words' and nothing to explain to a neophyte what was expected at an open house (as though everyone would automatically know what an open house was). The presentation by the expert engineer after the drop-in period was in incomprehensible technical language, over the heads of three of us (all with environmental science degrees). The engineer gestured at complex plans and diagrams, not visible to anyone seated farther back than the third row.

None of the interpretive information was translated into any local languages. No arrangements were made to accommodate children or young people. The Council staff, consultants and experts wore no identifying nametags. Interpretive material was presented in complex, dense panels with large slabs of text accompanied by complicated diagrams. During the discussion session, no indication was given of who (if anyone) was taking notes and no offer was made to provide a summary to participants. Subsequent inquiries to

The Council staff, consultants and experts wore no identifying nametags. Interpretive material was presented in complex, dense panels with large slabs of text accompanied by complicated diagrams

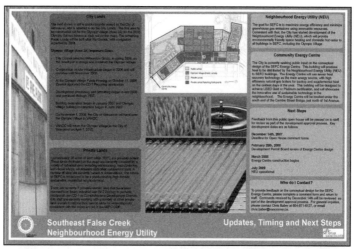

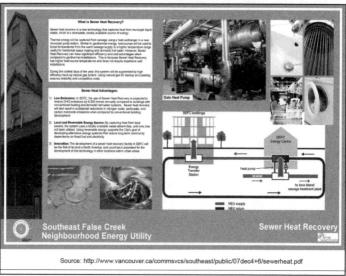

Source: http://www.vancouver.ca/commsvcs/southeast/public/07dec4+6/sewerheat.pdf

Figure 3.4 Display panels, Open House, Vancouver, December 2007

the Council revealed that, 'the open house comments are not public documents'. Nevertheless, we were told, 'generally the public was supportive of the initiatives and direction of the project'.

This example is particularly distressing because of the high profile of the City of Vancouver in international circles with regard to sustainability, community engagement and urban design.

The photographs of some display panels in Figure 3.4 convey, to some extent, a weakness of the process.

A tale of excellence: The Corridor Housing Initiative, Minneapolis

In November 2006, Wendy experienced a marvellous example of kitchen table sustainability in a workshop featuring the 'Minnesota Block Exercise'. The workshop was hosted by the Minneapolis Center for Neighborhoods[22] and conducted as part of the Corridor Housing Initiative (CHI). The CHI community engagement process took a whole year to develop and was initially imagined by Gretchen Nicholls, then Executive Director of the Center for Neighborhoods (now continuing with Twin Cities LISC (Local Initiatives Support Corporation)), who, remarkably, had no formal design training. One of the designers of the process is Wendy's long-time friend and colleague, Professor Ann Forsyth, whom we meet again as a younger woman in Chapter 9, Nourishment.

Ann Forsyth tells us that in the CHI such workshops were tailored to each neighbourhood by a steering committee of local residents, city staff and the CHI technical team. Importantly, the process involves three separate workshops for the same participants. The 'block workshop' is typically preceded by a detailed briefing session for local people, focusing on opportunities and challenges in the neighbourhood, with presentations about issues and brainstorming sessions to identify local priorities regarding neighbourhood character, density, identity, livable communities, transit-oriented development, neighbourhood fit and open space, for example. The block workshop is then typically followed by a third session with local developers and business people conveying their senses of local circumstances. Then there are working sessions with the public or the steering group, focusing on refining the vision and developing guidelines that can be given to developers.

Importantly, the process involves three separate workshops for the same participants. The 'block workshop' is typically preceded by a detailed briefing session for local people

Wendy observed the second workshop, where the Block Exercise was conducted. It was opened by the Mayor and attended by the developer, facilitators, staff and a handful of participants reflecting the socio-demographic mix of the neighbourhood: blue-collar workers, artists, immigrant businesspeople and professionals. While there are relatively few participants at any one block exercise, wider public participation occurred in the broader planning process and then when specific developments were proposed. The exercise gives developers opportunity to work on improving the design (having meetings about *how* the development could be done, not *if* the development could be done). **It aims to show community leaders that** (including those who had led the charge against higher density and affordable housing) that **much needed high-density housing could be attractive and well designed and was not just a result of greedy developers making huge profits**. Workshop results are summarized and distributed through highly active neighbourhood associations and advertised in local newsletters.

A key tool in the exercise is the developer's 'development pro forma': a dynamic spreadsheet designed to help participants understand the financial feasibility of various development scenarios. It contains assumptions about unit and site character, parking, developers' fees, construction costs and potential subsidies (for example, for low-income housing). It was displayed on the wall and provided as part of participant handouts.

The photographs in Figures 3.4 to 3.9 show the workshop Wendy attended in November 2006.

Each table was provided with a detailed, high-quality orthophoto map: an aerial photo adjusted to the curvature of the Earth, with labelled streets, a north point and a scale. About a square metre in size, these bold maps gave a sense of place nearly impossible to reproduce on a line map. Also on each table were coloured housing blocks, sized to the map scale. Several different sizes represented

Figure 3.5 Developer with Pro Forma on the wall, Minnesota Block Exercise, Minneapolis

Figure 3.6 The Development Pro Forma, Minnesota Block Exercise, Minneapolis

different-sized dwellings and the three different housing types (houses, rowhouses (terraced houses) and apartments) were printed on different coloured paper glued onto the blocks.

Wendy describes the process she observed this way:

Without much ado, participants began selecting house blocks and moving them around on the site

> My table had three participants, a facilitator and a sketcher. Other staff circulated between tables and helped out as necessary. Because they had already attended a briefing workshop, without much ado, participants began selecting house blocks and moving them around on the site, clearly marked on the map. The group was small (two men and one woman) and it was easy for everyone to have a say. When the participants were happy with their design solution and had finished 'building', the facilitator asked the group to decide on the architectural style of the building. She then called for a photographer, who took three Polaroid photographs of the construction and gave them to the sketcher.

The facilitator then completed a *Scenario Record Sheet* she had been filling in and took it over to the developer, who began typing the figures into his pro forma on his computer. Then the group knocked down the blocks with a child-like flourish and began building again.

The sketcher (a qualified architect) began drawing up a perspective rendition of the first design using the three Polaroid photographs and the notes she had taken during the first building session. But this was no rough notional sketch. She worked from a carefully pre-prepared perspective outline based on a panoramic photograph of the site prepared before the workshop.

By the time the sketcher had finished, the small group was part-way through their second attempt at designing the housing for the site. They applauded the sketcher's drawing of their first attempt,

Figure 3.7 Participants working together, Minnesota Block Exercise, Minneapolis

declaring it to be 'just what they imagined'. Then the developer came over with his pro forma. 'You've lost me four million dollars this time', he smiled. The group members looked crestfallen. 'But', he said, 'I can tell you how to fix it. I know you think it's best not to have too much subsidized housing but it's those subsidies that can help developers like me make a profit. So I suggest that you change the dwelling mix and also get rid of some of that commercial on the ground floor. It's not all that helpful, really.'

Then the developer came over with his pro forma. 'You've lost me four million dollars this time', he smiled

The second attempt was also a losing effort in financial terms, but this time the developer, having crunched the new numbers, found that it was only $1 million short of breaking even. 'I can see how to fix it', he smiled at the relieved team members. 'I could make this one work. Congratulations'.

Buoyed by their success and thrilled by the appearance of the building in a new sketch, the group had another try and this time succeeded in designing a viable development by getting the mix of dwelling sizes, types and tenures, parking, green space and

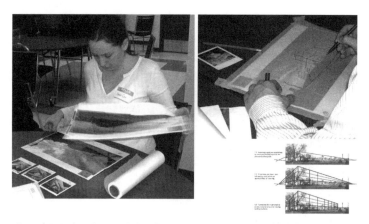

Figure 3.8 Sketcher and sketch, Minnesota Block Exercise, Minneapolis

Figure 3.9 Developer explaining the Pro Forma results, Minnesota Block Exercise, Minneapolis

I was impressed that the process looked interesting and fun. People clearly loved the process and there was lots of buzz and enthusiasm

commercial and residential uses in balance. I was impressed that the process looked interesting and fun. People clearly loved the process and there was lots of buzz and enthusiasm.

What Wendy witnessed is a breakthrough in community educa-tion for sustainability. The CHI takes participatory design work-shops to a new and sophisticated level by acknowledging that local people need to understand what is going on. The multi-award-winning community capacity-strengthening and engagement process focuses on transit corridors and town centres.[23] It aims to create viable development projects that include affordable housing options along corridors to meet city goals and neighbourhood inter-ests and brings together neighbourhood people, a technical team and city staff to develop a strategy for attracting well-designed, higher density and affordable housing to transit corridors and town centres.

It aims to encourage high-density and affordable housing (or housing intensification) and is supported by a wide range of user-friendly educational materials, templates, spreadsheets, photos, fact sheets, posters, kits, websites, design briefs, maps, handouts, PowerPoints, a video and advisory material for facilitators and community members.[24] The final outputs are development guide-lines or principles handouts developed by a steering committee, aimed at helping developers understand local opportunities and values and neighbourhoods to be better prepared to negotiate with developers.[25]

The Block Exercise is 'a hands-on opportunity for community members to explore different development options and find out whether their development ideas are financially viable'.[26] The process 'helps people understand the financial issues and tradeoffs a developer will be working with when considering options for a specific site'. Wendy observed one group of local people from one community working together on a real site available for redevelop-ment, engaging with the site, design, transit-oriented development issues, affordability and costs issues to generate responses that were viable in planning, design and financial terms. In the process of coming to grips with all the site-specific realities and challenges,

The Block Exercise is 'a hands-on opportunity for community members to explore different development options and find out whether their development ideas are financially viable

people overcame their fear of higher density (and particularly high-*rise* housing) and came to understand that density is a more complicated matter than they originally imagined.

In subsequent conversations with Ann Forsyth, Wendy learned that the CHI operates on multiple levels. The long process, which has many steps and must be overseen by a steering committee, is a model of community engagement for sustainability and the most exciting and promising example of this work we have seen. It allows local people to break through the 'intractable problems' of redevelopment and public resistance. People with very different values and of different political persuasions can participate effectively. In every case, people report that they had more fun than they had imagined and they imagined different things from what they thought would 'work' on site.

This exercise builds trust, as profits were discussed openly

This exercise builds trust, as profits were discussed openly. The developer was upfront in building a 10 per cent fee into the pro forma to pay for the work of finding land, getting permits, managing construction and so forth. Participants discovered that even 10 per cent was difficult to attain. While breaking even was the main point of the exercise, there was a sense of fun and 'competitiveness', as each group sought to make the development more profitable. Ann very perceptively pointed out that, 'The problem with community acceptance of high-density and affordable housing is not generally with design. It's community resistance.' Therefore an educational process like this one can 'show people how their values *can* be achieved. They need to see options.'

When Wendy later asked Ann about the 'green' credentials of the process, she replied that, 'The basic "green" idea is higher density–transit orientation which is where big energy savings are to be had. Even with the super energy regulations in Minneapolis, single-family homes use a lot of heating. It saves land, water and so forth. Further, major funders of affordable housing – like the

Enterprise Foundation nationally, the local McKnight Foundation and the main funder of CHI (the Family Housing Fund) – have "gone green". This means that those receiving funding from them would be required to build green buildings.'[27] It was also encouraging that some partners are interested in green building and have incorporated this work into their guidelines.[28] Further, the Metropolitan Design Center has prepared advisory materials on sustainable landscaping and incorporated that in the information materials available to communities.[29]

What's so special about this process?

This process is special because it has been so well researched and resourced. It can be used on a range of sites without great investment in preliminary work. All the material, templates and communities education materials are freely available. Careful attention to detail means that participants can concentrate on 'designing' the housing and not worry about irrelevant technical or process issues. The process developed from a grassroots initiative (through the Center for Neighborhoods) has had wide professional support and support from municipal government. It offers important roles to professionals and 'experts' in ways that serve the community interest, rather than imposing professional or expert views. The developer is a fully fledged member of the team, working with real dollars on a real site with real development opportunities. Further, as there are priorities in both metropolitan and city government to increase housing density and land prices in Minneapolis are increasing, thus encouraging redevelopment, several of the projects Wendy discussed with Ann are now proceeding. Clearly, as communities' priorities continue to emphasize livability and green space, good design can make a significant difference. Helping communities understand density and design is a significant contribution.

Clearly, as communities' priorities continue to emphasize livability and green space, good design can make a significant difference.

Helping communities understand density and design is a significant contribution

In terms of community engagement with sustainability, the CHI process builds understanding, strengthens community capacity, is grounded in the reality of a local context, addresses social and economic justice issues though an emphasis on housing affordability, encourages and rewards creativity, allows for expressiveness and expansiveness and has the potential to contribute to new relationships with the natural world. We believe that this innovative model deserves further investigation and piloting in other contexts. When Wendy recalls passionately negative responses to many failed medium-density housing initiatives of state governments in Australia over several decades, she wishes they'd had processes and models like the CHI and the Minnesota Block Exercise in those days. And today.

Conclusions

In this chapter we explored the community and community engagement dimensions of sustainability and raised a number of questions about our effectiveness in involving communities in decision making if current approaches continue. We need new, updated and inclusive conceptions of community *and* vastly improved and updated approaches to community engagement. If we do not make these changes, community engagement will continue to exclude ordinary people from decisions about sustainability. The roles of experts will be strengthened without the countervailing force of public opinion and public judgement.

We need new, updated and inclusive conceptions of community *and* vastly improved and updated approaches to community engagement

Examining the potential of community engagement approaches, we need to remind ourselves that *sustainability* must be our goal, our primary focus. In this and the previous chapter, we outlined many reasons why we are not achieving sustainability. In our view, this is because the majority of people – at least in the cultures we know and have studied – do not really understand sustainability or what is at stake. They cannot relate to what is happening or cannot see what is in it for them. And many decision makers and experts either do not understand the concept themselves or are manipulating its interpretation to promote particular interests or beliefs. To

The majority of people do not really understand sustainability or what is at stake

achieve sustainability through community engagement, we need a three-part approach: *sustainability* is the goal, *community* is the means and *community engagement* is the strategy.

We bring to this book our open hearts, open minds and decades of shared experience in planning and social planning, activism and research. And we are sharply aware of the limits of what we can discuss and the outcomes we advocate. Developing sustainable communities offers people connections to others who live locally or who do similar things and perhaps who do or do not share similar values. It can foster cultural awareness and sharing across difference and help people develop local solutions and networks and creates opportunities for knowledge and skill-sharing that generic systems cannot offer. However, all of this requires an expansion of our limited, homogeneous models of community, our limited community engagement processes, our limited professional visions as planners and a reconceptualization of the 'expert' view. It involves, as we shall see in Chapter 9, Nurturing, more heart-centred and direct approaches to listening to the wisdom of communities.

All of this requires an expansion of our limited, homogeneous models of community, our limited community engagement processes

In the next chapter, we introduce the components of our proposed approach – the *EATING* model for community engagement to achieve sustainability.

4

THE *EATING* APPROACH TO COMMUNITY ENGAGEMENT WITH SUSTAINABILITY

This movement's key contribution is the rejection of one big idea in order to offer in its place thousands of practical and useful ones. Instead of isms it offers process, concerns, and compassion.

Paul Hawken, 2007, p18

Introduction

In the first three chapters of this book we addressed the need for transformative change to challenge our unsustainable 'master metaphorical templates'. Sustainability cannot be achieved without these changes. But it is no easy task. The central argument of this book is that community engagement processes can help. They can bring together diverse communities in inclusive ways to generate solutions to intractable sustainability problems. However, the ways in which these community engagement processes for sustainability are carried out have absolute bearing on the outcome. The 'devil' or the 'divine' dwells in the details.

The remaining chapters of this book provide common sense guidance for community engagement with sustainability processes based on our *EATING* approach.

The *EATING* approach to community engagement for sustainability

At the core of *Kitchen Table Sustainability* is the *EATING* approach. *EATING* is an acronym for the six components we believe are critical for community engagement for sustainability: *Education, Action Trust, Inclusion, Nourishment* and *Governance*. These are the basic food groups, if you like, that must be on the table when designing community engagement processes for sustainability. Each of the six *EATING* components is necessary for a well balanced diet. All six must be included or the diet (the engagement process) will be deficient and we will not achieve optimum functioning. As addressed in Chapter 9, *EATING* is also about nourishment, nurturing and sustaining: the most basic human activity, often done together. It's about meeting basic survival needs.

Each of the six EATING components is necessary for a well balanced diet

In the same way that eating is literally one of our basic human needs, the *EATING* approach put forward in this book is a basic need that must be met in community engagement processes for sustainability. And if we were to extrapolate a hierarchy of societal needs in this time of crisis, we would argue that community engagement for sustainability is foundational, as food, personal safety and shelter are in Abraham Maslow's famous hierarchy.[1]

Community engagement for sustainability is foundational, as food, personal safety and shelter are

Throughout the next six chapters, we employ the *EATING* metaphor to ground our discussions and remind ourselves that we are talking about something as basic as eating here: something that sustains life. When we speak about setting the table and preparing the meal, we mean that it's important to take care in opening up a discursive space and preparing for discussions in the family or the wider community. Preparing the meal is about the actions we take to implement local and global sustainability. Cleaning up after the meal could mean engaging in critical reflection and evaluation. It could also mean cleaning up our environment. We could continue: washing the dishes could be part of the governance mechanisms necessary to enable community engagement processes to continue. And then there's feeding the chickens and putting out the compost. We'll leave that to your imagination.

Finally, we celebrate the transformative quality of *EATING*: it converts the energy from the Sun and the Earth into energy that animals like us can use. Experience has taught us that community engagement processes, designed and managed collaboratively with the community, can have transformative qualities. A dear friend, Liz Coupe, an Australian community activist struggling with terminal cancer, told Wendy and Karl in 2005 that the personal empowerment fostered by an open and collaborative engagement process in her community had given her 'something to live for'. Our *EATING* model is for Liz and others like her.

An open and collaborative engagement process in her community had given her 'something to live for'

The six components are described briefly below.

Education: Chapter 5

Chapter 5 explores the foundational fields of adult education and environmental education, asking the question, 'What information and knowledge do we need to impart and share in community engagement processes with sustainability?' We present our new model, *Community Education for Sustainability* (CES), which incorporates leading-practice approaches to environmental education, recognizing that community participants will have a variety of learning styles and multiple intelligences. We describe processes that underpin a community-based, participatory approach to growing local knowledgeability about sustainability and community building.

Action: Chapter 6

Chapter 6 explores two key questions: 'How can the frustration of inaction be overcome in community engagement processes?' and 'What actions are required to achieve transformative change for sustainability?' We discuss the broad range of actions and actors required to achieve systemic change to established regimes, with a particular focus on the role of activism. Through illustrative case studies and a summary of recent research on social innovation and transformative management, we identify ways in which the activist in each of us can be harnessed to work beyond the traditional 'us' and 'them' categorization of actors involved in community engagement processes.

'How can the frustration of inaction be overcome in community engagement processes?'

Trust: Chapter 7

This chapter explores the ever-present problem of trust in community engagement: what happens when trust is broken and how trust can be nourished in hard times with difficult problems to address. It highlights community engagement principles and approaches that tackle issues of trust in sophisticated ways, helping communities to form trusting relationships with each other about sustainability issues across the divides of difference.

helping communities to form trusting relationships with each other about sustainability issues across the divides of difference

Inclusion: Chapter 8

This chapter highlights the diversity of our communities and the need for 'listening across difference'. Taking the position that children and young people are citizens, it argues that an engaged citizenry must not exclude any social, cultural or age group and promotes the inclusion of everyone's knowledge as valid and valuable. Inclusion is about ensuring that everyone sitting at the table can speak and be heard.

An engaged citizenry must not exclude any social, cultural or age group and promotes the inclusion of everyone's knowledge

Nourishment: Chapter 9

This chapter provides some solace for the worried community member and embattled sustainability practitioner by drawing attention to some ancient and fundamental principles, including that we cannot nourish the Earth and our communities if we cannot nourish ourselves. It explores heartfelt and practical ways to nourish – and be nourished by – self, community and Nature so that we can engage with community and sustainability, using our energy in balanced, consistent and sustainable ways.

We cannot nourish the Earth and our communities if we cannot nourish ourselves

Governance: Chapter 10

This chapter deals with the housekeeping. We argue that specific governance approaches should underpin community engagement with sustainability – notably participatory governance and transformative management. We include stories and several detailed case studies to illustrative key principles. We describe common-sense tools and practices for good governance that are consistent with these principles.

What changes can we expect by implementing the *EATING* model?

It would be exciting to have a conversation after you have read the following six chapters to see how your views about community engagement with sustainability might have changed. We invite you to visit our website (www.kitchentablesustainability.com) to continue the conversation with us. We are confident that using the recipes and ingredients presented below will enable much greater decentralization of decision making and encourage integrated approaches within organizations (with all departments communicating effectively). It should signal an end to closed processes and enable wider sharing of information and strengthening of community capacity and knowledgeability. As an outcome, we should see more integrated policies that reflect the social, cultural, economic and environmental dimensions of sustainability, rather than those that focus solely on technical or scientific aspects.

Our recipes should help nurture more effective partnership approaches among government, industry and community. And finally, we look forward to seeing a revived role for government as sustainability *facilitator*, helping local people and community organizations with visioning, strategizing, resources, partnerships, infrastructure, action and, ultimately, genuine engagement.

When the recipes and ingredients are combined in balanced and creative ways, with a true chef's flair, we should delight in greater use of sophisticated 'deep' models like the Corridor Housing Initiative and the complementary Minnesota Block Exercise described above in Chapter 3. And fewer 'shallow' models.

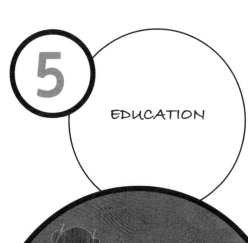

5

EDUCATION

We must educate for love of place, and then we must gather and disseminate the knowledge required to preserve the places we love ...

Nell Noddings, 2003, p131

Information is not knowledge, knowledge is not
understanding and understanding is not wise action.

Janet Moore[1]

'Information is
not knowledge,
knowledge
is not
understanding
and
understanding
is not wise
action'

Wendy's story: Maisie and the constructed wetland

During the dinner break in the public workshop, I was discussing the design of a proposed artificial wetland with Maisie, who lived in a house overlooking the park. The wetland had been designed to deal with severe ecological problems caused by the rubbish buried in the park near Maisie's house. We were standing by the table with the cardboard model of the proposed constructed wetland. She appeared agitated and not satisfied with my reassurances that the proposed wetland was only four metres deep. Proud of the cardboard model prepared for exactly this situation, I lifted out the wetland piece and held it up to demonstrate the great distance between the top of the wetland and the entrance to her house.

'It'll come up to my front door, Wendy. I am sure of that!' Maisie was trembling, tears in her eyes. She looked down.

'No, Maisie. No. That's just not the case,' I exclaimed. I gestured at the model. 'The wetland is only going to be four metres deep. It's a long way from your front door. Trust me, Maisie. The engineers have done all their calculations and you can see your house clearly on this cardboard model. There's no way the wetland's going to come anywhere near your front door. The wetland is only four metres deep!'

Maisie looked up. She looked embarrassed. She turned around to see if anyone was listening. We were in a corner of the lunchroom and other people were chatting animatedly. She bowed her head again and inquired in a soft voice, 'Wendy, how big is a metre?'

'Oh, Maisie', I whispered back. 'It's a yard – that's all. Just one yard!'

'Oh, Wendy', she cried, tears brimming over. She raised

Continued

her hands to her head. 'Why didn't you say that in the first place? It's only four yards deep? I had no idea what you were talking about! Only four yards!'

She gestured to the high ceiling of the heritage building.

'Only that high? Why didn't you say that before, Wendy? Only four yards? Oh my God! Now that I understand, I'm sure it'll be fine.'[2]

Introduction

This chapter is for Maisie. It's about community education to achieve sustainability. It is also about the *relationships* between community education and community engagement. The central message of this chapter is that education can be a leverage point in the transition to a sustainable future, *but only if* it allows us to present accurate information about the challenges we face, to search for the root causes of those challenges, to integrate that deeper knowing with community knowledge and to promote 'wise action' to transform those challenges into sustainable opportunities.

In this chapter, we explore how and why we need education for successful community engagement for sustainability. We accept the definition of education as an 'open-ended process that helps people to make sense of an increasingly complex world'.[3] We strongly believe that everyone involved in decision making has something to gain from community education. People participate most effectively in the sustainability debate when they are given opportunities – through community education and engagement – to identify their individual and collective values and build and share their knowledge, skills and expertise to realise these values.

A key to community education is using existing community processes to promote an attitude of learning. If community engagement can be consciously infused with learning opportunities, we can help a community do three things:

Education can be a leverage point in the transition to a sustainable future, *but only if* it allows us to present accurate information about the challenges we face, to search for the root causes of those challenges, to integrate that deeper knowing with community knowledge and to promote 'wise action' to transform those challenges into sustainable opportunities

1   Assess the knowledge and skills it collectively has to offer in making a decision.

2   Recognize the need for outside assistance and expertise.

3   Take charge of the outcomes to ensure successful implementation, evaluation and adjustment of community goals.

So how can communities participate in collecting, creating and understanding the relevant knowledge they need? And how can they transform this knowledge into sustainable decision making?

Transformational learning

To achieve the transition to a sustainable society, education must be *transformative*, not simply *informational*. Change expert Don Wolfe identifies two kinds of learning: informational learning and transformational learning – or *head learning* and *heart learning*. Informational learning, he claims, predominates in our educational system. By contrast, transformational learning empowers people to discover answers for themselves: 'It's a slower process, but much more profound. That's why it's transformational.'[4] Transformational learning is akin to reflective learning, whose two components are 'finding the unstated assumptions' and 'reframing in a more non-judgmental and compassionate form'. Reflective learning strives to transcend the separation between head and heart.

To achieve the transition to a sustainable society, education must be *transformative*, not simply *informational*

A learning society

A *society of learners* comprises individuals committed to educating themselves to better their chances of participating in the system. Everybody is pursuing their own goals as best they can, hoping that they will be better off. In contrast, a *learning society* is a collective whole that embodies an ethos (or commitment) of learning from its collective actions, research and policy directives. In a *learning society* the emphasis of education is on *adaptive capacity* rather

In a *learning society* the emphasis of education is on *adaptive capacity* rather than learning how to do the same things better

than learning how to do the same things better.[5] This approach emphasizes ownership (of the problems) and change, as opposed to conformity to the status quo. To foster a learning society is to recognize that for us to develop, evolve and live sustainably, we must be willing to evaluate our decisions, learn from our mistakes and pass on knowledge gained from our successes. This is the type of learning we focus on in this book.

Later in this chapter, we present our new learning model, *Community Education for Sustainability* (CES). But first we explore what we can learn from existing education models.

Learning from existing education models

There's no point in developing new education models for community engagement for sustainability if we do not respect the important work already undertaken in related fields.

The fields of environmental and conservation education teach us about the environment, Nature and sustainability. From adult education, we glean tools for understanding our world, so we can 'make appropriate decisions about how to live in it, relate to ourselves, to others and our environment, and how to act accordingly and responsibly'.[6]

Learning from environmental education

In its broadest sense, contemporary environmental education has the following three aims:

1   Heal the distortions in human expectations caused by the hubris of anthropocentric thinking (in plain language, think love of Earth, not power over it).
2   Rekindle an ethos of citizenship and responsibility rather than of individualism and rights.
3   Educate broadly, perceive systems and patterns and live as whole persons.[7]

Environmental education teaches us that the process of learning is facilitated by approaches that increase awareness, compassion, energy for action, a sense of cohesion with like-minded people and hopefulness. In Table 5.1, we outline specific approaches that hinder or help – approaches that can also be applied to community engagement for sustainability.

Table 5.1 Approaches to environmental education that facilitate trust[8]

Environmental education is hindered by approaches that ...	Environmental education is facilitated by approaches that ...
Do not build and maintain trust	Promote openness and respect to build and maintain trust
Make people appear foolish or incompetent	Are tailored to different backgrounds and levels of preparedness
Stress behaviour people consider unfeasible, impractical, inconvenient or without personal benefit	Build and strengthen people's capacity to respond rather than their obligation to respond
Emphasize disconnection between current behaviour and environmental values	Incorporate reflective activities to restore people's embedded beliefs and values so they can transform them into action
Lack support for feelings of anxiety, loss, despair, insecurity and vulnerability. Induce information overload	Permit flexibility. Give permission to make and learn from mistakes. Acknowledge emotional and spiritual connections, and foster a sense of wonder and curiosity
Focus exclusively on global problems	Encourage local leadership roles

What works and what does not work?

There is wide agreement in both adult education and environmental education about what works and what doesn't work. We have applied that learning to community education for sustainability in Table 5.2.

Table 5.2 What works? Principles from environmental and adult education[9]

Component	Environmental education: What works?	Adult education: What works?
Foundational assumptions	A lifelong learning ethos	Accept life skills as prior learning
		Build on earlier activities and prior learning experiences
Degree of involvement	Active, rather than passive, participation	Encourage active learner participation
Reflexivity	Allowing people to see that their learning can have an impact and be effective	Allow learners to assess their own skills and develop strategies that work for them
Power distribution	Opportunities to replace an external with an internal locus of control	Collaborative modes of teaching and learning. Co-planned and shared teaching processes and activities

Problem framing	Critical thinking opportunities	Promote question-asking *and* question-answering, problem-finding and problem-solving, and allow for uncertainty, inconsistency and diversity
	Competence building: knowing *how* and not simply *why* to do something	
Learning style	Creative learning approaches	Cater for visual, auditory and kinaesthetic learning styles
		Problem- and experience-centred learning, using comparison, analogies and examples
		Multidimensional communication
Feeling outcome	Enjoyable experiences	Enhance sense of self-esteem and pleasure
		A conducive learning environment: a non-threatening atmosphere that supports experimentation and recognizes different learning styles
Assessment methodology	Continual feedback	Feedback and evaluation

Four lessons from existing education models

From these existing education and learning models, we can distil four important lessons for community education for sustainability:

1 Incorporating education about sustainability into a community engagement process is not a simple task.
2 There is no single right way to educate people about sustainability.

There is no single right way to educate people about sustainability

3   We need new approaches to framing engagement exercises.

4   We must regularly update our education models.

Lesson 1: Incorporating education about sustainability into a community engagement process is not a simple task

As we began our journey to develop a learning model, we grappled with questions like these:

- What does it mean to 'educate' a community about sustainability?
- What are our expectations about who is to be educated?
- Whose knowledge is being emphasized?
- How is it being used to frame issues?
- What roles can the 'expert' scientist, politician, planner or engineer play?
- Who else might have something to teach?
- Do we have targeted approaches for people from culturally and linguistically diverse backgrounds?
- Do we have ways to work effectively in communities with low levels of formal literacy?
- Can we work effectively with people who are not skilled in using electronic technology?
- How do we reach hard-to-reach people?
- How do we include children and young people in ways that empower them and honour their learning styles and needs?

These questions help communities make their values, assumptions and expectations explicit, which supports clarity, trust and collaboration and ultimately helps build consensus. These are the macro framing questions that we *must* ask at the very beginning of any community engagement process for sustainability.

Lesson 2: There is no single right way to educate people about sustainability

Given the complex, interrelated and contextual nature of the challenges we face today, we cannot expect one single approach to education to be effective. If one community member wants to focus on energy security, while another champions food reliance and yet another wants more educational campaigns to promote sustainable behaviour, we need to encourage *all* these approaches. As Wendy's husband Karl, a talented Gypsy cook, exclaims, 'the more variety in the ingredients the better for a tasty stew'.

Learning about ecology and the social environment can (but doesn't have to) grow from deeply experiencing a place the land, the water, plants and animals. Wendy recalls a powerful team meeting on

Learning about ecology and the social environment can grow from deeply experiencing a place

Figure 5.1 Site visit, Williamstown Rifle Range, Melbourne, 1989
Photograph: Kelvin Walsh

Wendy remembers those 'slow' moments in a busy consultant's life when informal discussion led to learning about others' perspectives and an appreciation for the land and its life

a greenfield suburban site in Melbourne, where members of an interdisciplinary consultant team spent a day walking the site and talking informally about their feelings about it. Now when Wendy visits Roxburgh Park, population 25,000, she remembers those 'slow' moments in a busy consultant's life when informal discussion led to learning about others' perspectives and an appreciation for the land and its life. On another Melbourne project which had been stopped by community action, a facilitated site walk with hundreds of local people before a participatory design workshop helped bridge differing views and clear up misunderstandings.[10]

Lesson 3: We need new approaches to framing engagement exercises

When we frame the purpose of an engagement exercise as learning, sharing and community renewal, rather than focusing exclusively on outcomes, we open a space for collective and community learning.[11] Shifting our emphasis from *outcomes* to *learning* can alleviate pressure for participants. Opening a 'discursive space' – where everyone is a learner – creates places for deeper listening and reflection.

Collective exercises, in which ideas are shared, cross-pollinated and grown into new ideas, *consistently* result in more ideas (and *more creative* ideas) than the sum of the individual ideas before the sharing

Collective exercises, in which ideas are shared, cross-pollinated and grown into new ideas, *consistently* result in more ideas (and *more creative* ideas) than the sum of the individual ideas before the sharing. The result is always more than the sum of the parts. And the act of brainstorming itself encourages people to be intellectually cooperative and mutually reflective.[12] Learning and transformation in community engagement also require patient and sustained commitment *for the long term*. Educators know that small steps are important. In this context, any work that decreases the spiral of 'unsustainability' is empowering, whereas it's often disempowering to focus only on the larger end goal.

Lesson 4: We must regularly update our education models

We found that most of the existing environmental education models we reviewed were too limited for our purposes. Early approaches focused on information dissemination, viewing Nature as something separate from humans, to be managed with proper scientific knowledge and appropriate technical approaches. This approach does not accurately represent biophysical and social realities. More progressive models recognize that it is not *the environment* that needs managing, but rather humans and our behaviour. This realization has profound implications for how we approach sustainability.

It is not *the environment* that needs managing, but rather humans and our behaviour

Fritjof Capra suggests that what is necessary is education for *perceptual shifts,* which include shifting:

- from the parts to the whole
- from objects to relationship
- from objective knowledge to contextual knowledge
- from quantity to quality
- from structure to process: systems develop and evolve
- from contents to patterns.[13]

One thing is clear from our research: we cannot rest on our laurels. As we cannot yet know which methods and tools will be successful for transforming worldviews and promoting widespread cultural change, we need to experiment with alternative learning models. While we experiment with environmental education within a community engagement context, educational researchers are discovering new territories and finding out what works and what doesn't. We must continually refer to this research.

Our Learning Model: Community Education for Sustainability (CES)

Our learning model, *Community Education for Sustainability* (CES), emerges from a comprehensive review of learning models, environmental and adult education literature, current research into sustainability issues and our understanding of how community members need to be engaged in sustainability debates, based on our professional experience. Our six-part CES learning model comprises the following ingredients:

- **Ingredient 1:** Understanding
- **Ingredient 2:** Community capacity strengthening
- **Ingredient 3:** Grounded in reality
- **Ingredient 4:** New relationships with Nature
- **Ingredient 5:** Justice
- **Ingredient 6:** Creativity and spirituality

We describe each of these ingredients in more detail below.

Ingredient 1: Understanding

Foster broad understanding of all dimensions of sustainability based on science, experience, ethics, values and the intersection of diverse beliefs.

We do not aim solely to educate people to operate within the existing paradigm but rather to build the skills of an enlightened citizenry so that people can engage with and question that paradigm in effective ways This ingredient reflects and extends successful environmental education models, as a major weakness of some models is their reluctance to challenge the established paradigms that drive our lives. The transformational education we advocate requires a complete rethinking of our 'master metaphorical templates' (as discussed in Chapter 2). We do not aim solely to educate people to operate within the existing paradigm but rather to build the skills of an enlightened citizenry so that people can engage with and question that paradigm in effective ways. This ingredient also highlights the need for processes to support community understanding of the complexity of sustainability challenges by opening up community discussions of ethics, human responsibilities to Nature and the multidisciplinary and holistic nature of the sustainability crisis. We must assess community knowledge levels so we can target capacity-strengthening activities appropriately. It is a difficult balance. In

Maisie's community, for example, attempts to rewrite complex engineering material about the proposed wetland backfired badly, not only with Maisie, but with local residents trained in engineering. They told Wendy they did not trust the local council and were suspicious that the information oversimplified and 'dumbed down' engineering facts to hide the truth.

Ingredient 2: Strengthening community capacity

Build stronger, more connected and skilful communities that foster learning and learning environments.

This ingredient is about how to strengthen community capacity, skills and social capital. It requires us to focus on strengthening community ecoliteracy and scientific and technical capacity. We must offer opportunities to build both *hard* and *soft* skills, as well as opportunities for collaborative learning and decision making. In this work, education must have long-term benefits, support mentoring and intergenerational learning opportunities, be relevant to local contexts, foster learning and learning environments and offer significant skill-building opportunities for citizenship.

Strengthening capacity is not as easy as it seems. Returning to the story of Maisie, Wendy's cardboard model, designed specifically to help local people engage with the proposed constructed wetland, failed dismally in strengthening Maisie's capacity. Further, earlier presentations by technical experts and engineers in the workshop sessions were clearly lost on Maisie, who imagined a metre to be perhaps a storey of a house – three metres or more. Maisie needed more than informational capacity. Of the three types of capacity in communities: informational, participatory and integrative, we have found that we rarely achieve more than the 'informational' stage.[14]

In working with activists and community leaders, we find that people frequently change roles, shoulder new or fewer responsibilities and form new allegiances and groups

In working with activists and community leaders, we find that people frequently change roles, shoulder new or fewer responsibilities and form new allegiances and groups. We need to be flexible and responsive in designing community education within community engagement processes. Equally as important as lifelong learning is the concept of education for the life of the *community*. We must recruit and train new members, strengthen their capacity and help them with the 'business' and protocols of community engagement. In Nimbin, Wendy's village community, the Climate Action Group has seen people drop out, partly to deal with the impacts of months of harsh weather during the region's wettest year since European settlement. Newcomers need to be brought up to speed and a new activist agenda is emerging.

Asset mapping

A valuable way to strengthen community capacity and discover what is happening in any community is through asset mapping and capacity inventories. We often use this approach, especially in SpeakOut community events and discuss this approach extensively in a forthcoming Earthscan book.[15] The process has transformative qualities. As the editor of *Worldchanging* explains, '...the real magic of the community asset map goes beyond making these capacities visible: the map generates *new* capacities by drawing people out of a mindset of dependency on outside resource, and into a creative process of mapping their own paths to the future'.[16]

The next century may bring an Age of Amateurs, when citizen exploration yields much of our greatest learning as a society

Citizen science

...into the twenty-first century – indeed, we may be bound to leap beyond professionalism. As education levels keep rising, more of us have leisure time and access to vast amounts of publicly available knowledge. The next century may bring an Age of Amateurs, when citizen exploration yields much of our greatest learning as a society.

A. Steffen, *Worldchanging*[17]

Citizen science is a participatory process that involves the public, government and industry directly in public-interest research to bridge the gaps between science and the community and between scientific research and policy, decision making and planning. We can learn a great deal from local environment groups for our community engagement processes. Hands-on, practical processes that build and strengthen skills can encourage participants to learn more and take action toward sustainability goals.

Promoting collaboration via mentoring and intergenerational learning

An important characteristic of a well-functioning community is the members' effectiveness in working together to achieve sustainability objectives. Often, community engagement processes raise people's understanding and consciousness, encourage participation and build literacy, but lack ongoing processes to help people strengthen interpersonal or organizational skills. One of the characteristics of a sustainable society is that current members seek to preserve life, resources and opportunities for members of *all* species into the future. This is the principle of intergenerational equity. Intergenerational *learning* – sustainable transfer of knowledge and learning – means developing forums and support to help participants address intergenerational conflicts or misunderstandings and work toward bridging divides.

An important characteristic of a well-functioning community is the members' effectiveness in working together to achieve sustainability objectives

Intergenerational learning also means valuing *all* forms of education, not simply formal education and training. In our processes, we can highlight different ways of knowing and learning. We can foreground the role of elders as mentors. Further, we can ask, what can we learn from and through children and young people? In the workshop Maisie attended, a group of high school students presented their plan for repairing the park's ecological systems to an audience of adults. It became clear as they spoke that their work was of a higher quality than that of most of the adult participants.

Intergenerational learning also means valuing *all* forms of education, not simply formal education and training

Embarrassed, some adults mocked them. That should not have happened. We need processes designed to help adults, children and young people to engage in intercultural mentoring, based on common support and understanding.

The powerful model of the Corridor Housing Initiative (CHI) in Minneapolis and the method of the Minnesota Block Exercise (discussed in Chapter 3) are highly sophisticated examples of collaborative community learning processes. Both landmark processes can be used to confront common barriers to community education for sustainability in an engagement context. It's useful to summarize some of their features here:

- Early briefing sessions strengthen community capacity and help participants learn and express their views in a supportive setting.
- It's a hands-on process.
- It is relaxed, fun and engaging.
- It does not rely on participants' abilities to read plans or interpret drawings.
- It can accommodate different design styles and tastes.
- It provides realistic representations, using accurate sketches to represent the proposed development.[18]
- Participants learn by doing and are never made to feel 'stupid' or look incompetent.
- With good facilitation, this can be a highly inclusive process.
- The process could easily be modified for use by young people or children.
- It accommodates different learning styles and intelligences.
- Rapid feedback and opportunities to have 'another go' allow participants to see easily the results of their labours and opportunities for improvements.

Ingredient 3: Grounding in social and biophysical realities

Focus on practical outcomes that increase people's empowerment and participation by being grounded in physical and social realities.

This ingredient requires us to be grounded in the biophysical realities and limits of the living Earth, as well as grounded in credible and reliable information and data. Our work should lead to individual and group understanding and empowerment. In engagement, we should aim to provide practical learning experiences, offer valid assessment and evaluation opportunities and allow for rearrangement of planning and development priorities consistent with ecological limits. Research about how knowledge is transformed into action consistently emphasizes the importance of hands-on, practical and grounded activities. In a forthcoming book, *Creative Approaches to Community Planning* (2009a), we describe this approach as 'embodied engagement'.[19]

The collective social memory of past social and ecological changes is an educational resource grounded in social and biophysical realities that must be passed on to future generations. Stephan Barthel, a systems ecologist with the Stockholm Resilience Centre, drawing on a detailed study of allotment gardening in Stockholm, argues that 'society needs to draw on, and actively reproduce such memories to navigate evolutionary processes into more sustainable outcomes'.[20] The people working in the community garden allotments had detailed experiential knowledge of the local ecosystem. Yet various formal community engagement processes that affected them failed to recognize this knowledge.

The collective social memory of past social and ecological changes is an educational resource grounded in social and biophysical realities that must be passed on to future generations

Before any educational or engagement process begins, facilitators, leaders and advocates need a solid understanding of the community and its ecological context. We need to understand both the knowledge our group already has and the general group characteristics and morale. We can get to know participants through a range of methods, including focus groups, surveys, interviews, public meetings and workshops. If we ignore this stage, our educational efforts may not be well received; at worst, we can create fragile relationships, destroy trust and endanger future engagement prospects. We discuss the delicate matter of trust in Chapter 7.

Ingredient 4: New relationships with Nature

Develop opportunities for new relationships with Nature and actions to support Nature.

It is important to speak openly and explicitly about environmental ethics and our responsibilities to nonhuman life We believe that it is important to speak openly and explicitly about environmental ethics and our responsibilities to nonhuman life. This means we must focus on direct experiences with Nature and the emotions they invoke. It helps if we uncover our deeper, spiritual connections with Nature, sharing the energy of the Earth and its life and discover, or rediscover, our mutual dependencies. In this way we become aware of the previously hidden environmental effects of our everyday living.

Direct experience of Nature

We have to know a place in order to make it better, because a given urban-planning tool never works for every city, and because the more we know and love a place, the more we want to participate in determining its evolution.

A Steffen, *Worldchanging*[21]

This ingredient deepens our conversations by exploring the ways we can strengthen our connections with Nature. Ecologist and biologist Edward O. Wilson explains our fundamental attraction to and *need* for Nature as *biophilia* or love of life. We can say it is in our DNA. Given that, for much of our development, the human species lived closely with Nature, it would be surprising if it were not![22] By fostering this relationship with nonhuman or greater-than-human others, we come to respect, learn from and value Nature. Stephen Jay Gould's famous quotation captures this sentiment: 'We cannot win this battle to save species and nature without forging an emotional bond between ourselves and nature as well – for we will not fight to save what we do not love.'[23] Everyone knows at a visceral level that frequent interaction with other living things is good for the heart, mind and soul. If we are to nurture the hearts, minds and souls of our communities in engagement processes, we need to design community engagement processes that acknowledge and celebrate this precious interaction.

Thus, in community processes, we need to incorporate regular opportunities for direct contact with Nature to sustain the connection. It goes without saying that this work requires skilled facilitation. Michael J. Cohen, who calls his work 'sensory environmental education', developed 97 hands-on Nature-connecting activities. To be part of a life system, any entity, humans included, must communicate with that system. Otherwise the entity may, to its cost, stray from it.[24] Direct experiences of Nature reduce our estrangement; its pain and adverse effects and can induce critical thinking, allowing feelings of love and understanding to be expressed and validated. Importantly for planners, this process also 'gives natural areas added value as renewers of our biological and spiritual integrity'.[25]

American Robert Greenway, formerly a planner, began conducting wilderness trips in 1969 for a wide range of participants, from university students and faculty to senior executives, and reported on post-experience evaluations with 1400 participants.[26] He describes 'a lifetime spent in the high tension between nature and culture' and reminds us that we are 'awash in nature, for the most part unaware of it', and that the issue is 'how much we leave culture behind'. Greenway reports the following remarkable statistics: 90 per cent of participants said they felt 'an increased sense of aliveness'. Astonishingly, 90 per cent had been able to break an addiction; 80 per cent found the return to 'the everyday' really positive,

Direct experiences of Nature reduce our estrangement; its pain and adverse effects and can induce critical thinking, allowing feelings of love and understanding to be expressed and validated

while 53 per cent experienced depression shortly after their return. And, for 77 per cent of participants, the course resulted in 'a major life change' on return.[27]

Learning societies: Lessons from the Heart Group

When Wendy's office was in Melbourne in 1990, she and a group of colleagues met fortnightly in what they called the *Heart Group*. Founded on the principles of *Heart Politics* espoused by Fran Peavey, this self-managed learning society sought to help members (about ten in all) explore ways of learning to be heart-centred in their everyday work in planning, design and development.[28] The group consisted of activists, planners, artists, community develop-ment workers, landscape designers, a developer and one much-loved accountant. The group met for only nine months but through support and mutual learning strengthened friendships and profes-sional relationships. Several of its members work together to this day. As a member of the Heart Group, Wendy experienced the three main characteristics of a learning society: many forms of knowledge are valued; it is inherently democratic; and we can pass on knowledge through learning webs, rather than unilaterally. Today, with our understanding that the future of life on Earth is at stake, learning societies have great potential in helping us develop approaches for community engagement with sustainability.

Blending knowledges: Native wisdom

In community education for sustainability, we need to understand two broad categories of knowledge: the rigorous and systematic generation of theoretical constructs that apply everywhere (known as scientific principles) and knowledge that stems from an expe-rience of place, known as 'native wisdom'.[29] Landscape architect and ecologist Randy Hester defines native wisdom as knowledge 'grounded in observation, sensing, and an awareness of kinship with the surrounding world'. Hester is confident that this knowl-edge is 'embedded in each person who strives every day for higher meaning in relationship to place'.[30]

This aspect of education celebrates the 'local' and asks us which knowledges we value. Do we know more about faraway lands than the lands in our own communities? Did we learn about Nature from books or *in* Nature? Environmental educators like Michael Cohen and Robert Greenway use simple processes to help people understand their place in their bioregion and their local ecology. Deborah Churchman in *American Forests* recommends recreating with children 'all the dopey, fun things you did as a kid':

> Take them down to the creek to skip rocks – and then show
> them what was hiding under those rocks. Take a walk after
> the rain and count worms... Turn on the porch light and
> watch the insects gather... Go to a field ... and watch the
> bees diving into the flowers.[31]

Do we know more about faraway lands than the lands in our own communities? Did we learn about Nature from books or *in* Nature?

To protect both adults and children from 'nature-deficit disorder', environmental author and commentator Richard Louv recommends: 'Find a ravine, woods or a windbreak row of trees, a swamp, a pond, a vacant and overgrown lot – and go there, regularly'.[32] It is important to make time to 'soak in a place' and be able to return 'to ponder the visible substrate of our own personality'. Then, 'knowledge of a place – where you are and where you come from – is intertwined with knowledge of who you are'.[33] Community engagement processes that bring together people from a wide variety of backgrounds to experience and discuss a common place can create rich opportunities to blend these knowledges and nurture a learning society.

Find a ravine, woods or a windbreak row of trees, a swamp, a pond, a vacant and overgrown lot – and go there, regularly

Ingredient 5: Justice

Protect and enhance social, environmental and economic justice for all peoples, beings and life forms.

There is now wide acknowledgement, reinforced by the disastrous social and economic impacts of Hurricane Katrina, that the impacts of environmental change and especially climate change, are not felt equally by all people. Research suggests that those who are most adversely affected by impacts of climate destabilization (extreme weather events, heat waves, sea level rise, warming ocean temperatures, flood and drought) are least responsible for the emissions that cause climate change.[34] Many predict increased risks and economic instability as a result of climate change. Local, regional, national and international mitigation and adaptation strategies and plans are needed.

Research suggests that those who are most adversely affected by impacts of climate destabilization are least responsible for the emissions that cause climate change

What we are talking about here is environmental justice: the fair treatment and meaningful involvement of all people regardless of race, colour, national origin or income with respect to the development, implementation and enforcement of environmental laws, regulations and policies.[35] As one example, communities need to be aware of the impacts of these changes to protect human health. In northern Australia, for example, increases in dengue fever and malaria are predicted, as predator species are lost. Most experts agree that local relevant policy development, based on public support and emphasizing community resilience, is the most promising direction. Poor and vulnerable communities, expected to shoulder the largest burdens, need help to understand and address these complex issues. Inter-jurisdictional collaboration will be required, as will intensive community engagement. While members of some communities will become 'climate refugees', others will need to receive those refugees into their communities. Wendy and Steph's experience in explaining this prospect to local government managers has not been very successful. Everyone is going to need to learn about climate – and the natural world. Rural communities are likely to be particularly vulnerable to the effects of climate change. The fairness of policies to address climate change will need to be discussed thoroughly by those – and other – communities in public forums.

Ingredient 6: Creativity and spirituality

Employ visionary and creative approaches to community education that enable communities to imagine and communicate their own visions of a sustainable future.

This ingredient challenges us to employ creative and visionary approaches, using storytelling and creative visualization to envisage and create possible futures. We can select approaches that are culturally appropriate and grounded in local cultures and encourage the use of indigenous approaches to storytelling and placemaking. Importantly, we should acknowledge a variety of learning styles and multiple intelligences in selecting approaches. This ingredient supports a variety of new ways of engaging with communities and educating communities about innovative approaches to complex problems, as well as visions of a sustainable future. It draws heavily on research in the wisdom traditions, spirituality, environmental psychology and philosophy, as well as art and community cultural development.

Select approaches that are culturally appropriate and grounded in local cultures and encourage the use of indigenous approaches to storytelling and placemaking

Creativity

We have had great success using creative visualization approaches (discussed below in Chapter 9) as a means of practising cooperation and collective learning. We've also had great results with role-playing. Turning an issue into a performance, a piece of art, a story, dance or song, has a way of making that issue special and directly relevant. 'Making special' can be an important step to making something worthy of our care. We can also use the arts to measure change over time and use mapping exercises and drawings to depict land-use change.[36] With appropriate modifications, these approaches can be used with all ages, genders and cultures.

Spirituality

All five of us have experienced despair, immobilization and even apathy as we have learned more about the state of the Earth. We have been strengthened by spiritual practices which have helped us to access what poet and philosopher Mark Nepo calls our 'unencumbered spot, free of expectation and regret, free of ambition and embarrassment, free of fear and worry, an umbilical spot of grace'.[37]

There is no *right* way to get in touch with that unencumbered spot. So we encourage people to explore for themselves and embrace the practices that bring them to that place. Our explorations have been influenced by a variety of wisdom and spiritual traditions, including Christianity, Buddhism, Sufism, Indigenous spiritualities, Deep Ecology, New Age practices and poetry. In these and other traditions, we find common threads of 'just being', meditation and contemplation, inner listening, visioning and enfolding our personal will within a greater purpose. For each of us, Nature has been our great solace and inspiration. When we approach Nature with a sense of wonder and humility, we find ourselves enfolded in a process greater than ourselves – in the sights and sounds of ocean waves rolling in, entranced by the trickle from a melting icicle, startled by the beauty of the night sky, standing strong against the trunk of a massive, ancient forest tree. We experience our hearts opening and our minds becoming quiet. We fall in love and find it is as environmental educator Meryl Sundove suggests: 'Pick any species. Go into depth about its life. Find out all about it and you'll fall in love with it.'[38]

When we approach Nature with a sense of wonder and humility, we find ourselves enfolded in a process greater than ourselves

What skills do communities need to embrace our education model?

Hard skills

What Wendy witnessed was a focus on hard skills, such as information and practical 'development' projects, and a neglect of the need for soft skills, such as community networking, authentic involvement in governance and decision making and

Hard and soft skills in an eco-community

In the early 1990s, Wendy lived in an intentional community near Darwin on 320 acres of fire- and cyclone-damaged
land. There, 26 residents (in eight households) had carved
out an eco-community in rough and hot conditions. The
adults' 'hard' skills were enviable: they selflessly engaged
in clearing firebreaks, bridge-building, road-building,
house-building, drilling bores and constructing windmills.
Their ethic was strongly fostered by their commitment to
ecological literacy and community education; their deep
involvement and engrossment in the natural world (their
piece of bush); hard work; a commitment to learning how
to work better; the experience (though not the expectation or requirement) of reciprocity; idealism; and frequent
discussion about ethical and moral issues and what consti-
tuted a right relationship with the land. These residents
engaged with environmental ethics as 'everyday fare'.
Learning how to be in relationship with Nature was almost
all there was. They modelled for their children an ethic of
caring for Nature. And the children learned well from their
elders.

What the children did not learn about, however, was governance. The community had no 'succession strategy' and
despite the fact that several local children were teenag-
ers, they played no role in the community meetings while
Wendy lived there. Wendy saw this as a significant over-
sight, given the high levels of ecological literacy among
the dozen or so resident children. She experiences the
same phenomena in her present community.

In Wendy's view, the adult community members' 'soft'
skills were somewhat deficient. One weakness was the lack
of an explicit fostering of connection between community
residents. Some critical interpersonal relationship aspects
appeared to be ignored. Community meetings were often
acrimonious and unproductive. Wendy's observation was
that feelings were not allowed to be expressed in productive ways and were seen as a sign of weakness. Members
ran sometimes from meetings in tears. Wendy's assessment, after a year's study as a participant observer, was

Continued

that community members had learned to care for the land, vegetation and nonhuman inhabitants and to manage it with great attention and love. They had highly developed *hard* land-management skills. With regard to the *soft* skills of caring for each other, they still had work to do.[39]

strengthening community capacity. We have identified three characteristics or knowledge bases of all hard skills that need to be reflected in practice:

1   Enhance social and ecoliteracy by situating humans in the web of life.
2   Highlight the relevance of native wisdom, grounded and situational knowledge.
3   Manage information and knowledge so that it is useful and effective to the context.

When these knowledge bases are in place, it's easy to learn the more technical and practical skills of road-building, farming, gardening and so forth because the building blocks have been established.

Hard skill 1: Social and ecoliteracy

The Canadian organization, Learning for a Sustainable Future (LSF), summarizes 15 types of *knowledge* needed today by ecoliterate and responsible citizens.[40] Here are the first two:

1   Knowledge of the Earth as a finite system and its elements that constitute the planetary environment.
2   Knowledge of the resources of the Earth, especially soil, water, minerals etc., their distribution and role in supporting living organisms.

LSF also listed 14 attitudes and values we need to acquire to enhance these ecoliteracy skills:

Fourteen attitudes and values needed by ecoliterate and responsible citizens[41]

1 appreciate the resilience, fragility and beauty of Nature and the interdependence and equal importance of all life forms
2 appreciate the dependence of human life on the resources of a finite planet
3 appreciate the role of human ingenuity and individual creativity in finding appropriate and sustainable solutions
4 appreciate the power of humans to modify the environment
5 experience self-worth and rootedness in our own culture and community
6 respect other cultures and recognize the interdependence of the human community
7 maintain a global perspective and loyalty to the world community
8 recognize disparities and injustices and commit to human rights and peaceful conflict resolution
9 appreciate the challenges we face in defining processes needed for sustainability and implementing necessary changes
10 maintain a sense of balance in deciding among conflicting priorities
11 embrace a sustainable lifestyle and commit to participation in change
12 maintain a realistic appreciation of the urgency of challenges we face and complexities demanding long-term planning
13 foster a sense of hope and positive personal and social perspectives
14 appreciate the importance and worth of individual responsibility and action

Real ecological literacy is radicalizing in that it forces us to reckon with the roots of our ailments, not just their symptoms

Ecological literacy is not separatist but rather activist and unashamedly politicizing. As David Orr explains, 'Real ecological literacy is radicalizing in that it forces us to reckon with the roots of our ailments, not just their symptoms.'[42] An ecologically literate person

An ecologically literate person is engaged, informed and active, with local knowledge and a sense of place, keen to experience their kinship with life and seeking to assert and practise civic competence is engaged, informed and active, with local knowledge and a sense of place, keen to experience their kinship with life and seeking to assert and practise civic competence.

These people know not to treat the environment as a separate subject, but rather as the basis of other subjects. They also recognize their own and human limitations, both physical and epistemological (to do with how we know things). Physical limitations include concepts such as the finite nature of resources and carrying capacity of the Earth. Epistemological limitations include our inherent human limits to knowledge and understanding. When we offer community education for and about sustainability, we seek to encourage a perceptual shift from strictly *anthropocentric* (human-centred) perspectives to include *ecocentric* and *biocentric* (life-centred) perspectives. Community education for sustainability should provide opportunities for people to discuss this foundational knowledge as the basis for other forms of knowledge.

Hard skill 2: Native wisdom, grounded and situational knowledge

Native wisdom, described above, is 'grounded in observation, sensing, and an awareness of kinship with the surrounding world'.[43] It's about knowing about a place. Let's imagine we are conducting a community engagement process. We could ask the following questions to ground people in their local realities and strengthen their skills of observation and attitudes of awareness:

- What was this place before?
- Who keeps the sacred stories of this place?
- Who lived here and what did they do here?
- Which places are sacred and powerful?
- What was the original vegetation like?
- What grows well in these soils?
- What materials are locally available for building?
- Where does your water come from and where do your wastes go?

- How are the seasons and the climate changing?
- What do the old-timers say about this drought? These floods? The mosquitoes? The mice plague?
- How do I need to live differently in this bioregion now that I am aware that all these changes are occurring?

Hard skill 3: Information and knowledge management

Knowledge and literacy are not enough. We must also manage information. To help people understand the complexities of sustainability, we must provide information that is accessible and digestible, as well as accurate, current, credible and professional. This raises questions about how to frame information for community engagement. How much detail? How complex? How current? Which sources can we trust? Because some people have difficulty with the abstract nature of sustainability, a wise approach is to introduce practical tasks linked to the bigger picture. This helps people make long-term commitments.[44]

We must provide information that is accessible and digestible, as well as accurate, current, credible and professional

Some approaches to knowledge-building work especially well with community groups, like beginning with a logical and gradual introduction to sustainability concepts, rather than shocking people into a sense of concern.[45] Awareness-raising is the first step, as we cannot expect people to change their behaviour if they do not recognize that there is a problem with it. Communities can learn, grow and change very fast, as many people already have heightened and sophisticated awareness of the challenges we face. But simply *knowing* does not necessarily bring about action, and if they see nothing happening people may turn off and become cynical. We must avoid increasing cynicism. We need to allocate time for full discussions and discover what lies underneath the cynicism. Sometimes we have found that fear, even grief, are present.

Simply *knowing* does not necessarily bring about action, and if they see nothing happening people may turn off and become cynical

Soft skills and knowledge: Educating for civic life and democratic decision making

Soft skills have to do with how people relate to each other and usually involve interaction with other human beings. They are as important as hard skills.

Soft skill 1: Accessing multiple intelligences through a variety of learner models

Smart, clever or wise?

In Australia, the current fashion is for everything to be called *smart*: smart cars, smart transit tickets, smart housing, smart wiring and smart government. Queensland calls itself 'The Smart State'.[46] But there is more to life – and sustainability – than 'smart'. We need new definitions of intelligence to address our complex problems. For David Orr, 'education can be a dangerous thing', because of 'the modern fetish with smartness'.[47] Orr points out,

> *What we call intelligence and what we test for and reward is more akin to cleverness. Intelligence has to do with 'the long run' and is mostly integrative, whereas cleverness is mostly preoccupied with the short run and tends to fragment things.*[48]

Ecological intelligence

Australia's love affair with 'smart' reflects modern views of intelligence as 'smartness' that began, says Chet Bowers, with the individually centred view of intelligence. Bowers proposes instead *embodied intelligence* and an *ecological view of intelligence*, based on the long-term sustainability of the Earth's ecosystem as the primary criterion. These ways of thinking lead to *patterns* of thinking that relate to ecosystems: *interdependence, ecological cycles, energy flows, partnership, flexibility, diversity* and *coevolution.*[49] These are intelligences Indigenous people have traditionally developed to a high degree. To embrace embodied or ecological intelligence, we must place greater emphasis on transgenerational communication and develop new criteria for evaluating success.[50] Donella Meadows would say that this approach encourages us to 'pay attention to what is important, not just what is quantifiable'.[51] Our colleague, educator Noel Wilson (Yollana's father), reminds us that, 'Any quantification represents a reduction in meaning and in the depth of what is the object of meaning. In other words, quantification inevitably leads to a reduction in the quality of evaluation.'

Concluding a community engagement process, we would be obliged to ask: Have we placed the life of the ecosystem at the centre of our deliberations and decisions? Further, have we acted wisely on our knowledge?

Emotional and social intelligence

Skilful community engagement requires self-awareness, skilful handling of emotions, empathy and social skills. This means we need to demonstrate and cultivate *emotional intelligence*: to perceive emotions, reason with and about emotion, access and generate emotions to assist thought, understand emotions and emotional knowledge, reflectively regulate emotions to promote emotional and intellectual growth, and combine feeling with thinking and thinking with feeling.[52]

Particularly relevant for community education for sustainability is Daniel Goleman's concept of *social intelligence*, which expands the notion of multiple intelligences.[53] Social intelligence has two major components: social awareness and social facility. Like emotional intelligence, it necessitates a conscious effort. However, social awareness in itself does not guarantee fruitful interactions. Those require *social facility*, which builds on social awareness to allow smooth, effective interactions. Goleman's views of intelligence align with those of Bowers and Orr. He emphasizes nurturing relationship skills, especially empathy and altruism, claiming that empathy is

Concluding a community engagement process, we would be obliged to ask: Have we placed the life of the ecosystem at the centre of our deliberations and decisions?

Empathy is 'the root of caring'

'the root of caring'.[54] Thus, to educate community members about sustainability within community engagement processes, we must maximize all *our* intelligences and be alert to participants' multiple intelligences.

Multiple intelligences

Although Goleman's work on 'emotional intelligence' has caught the popular imagination, earlier work by Howard Gardner on a 'theory of multiple intelligences' initially proposed seven types of intelligences:

1   Linguistic intelligence (*word smart*)
2   Logical-mathematical intelligence (*number/reasoning smart*)
3   Spatial intelligence (*picture smart*)
4   Bodily-kinaesthetic intelligence (*body smart*)
5   Musical intelligence (*music smart*)
6   Interpersonal intelligence (*people smart*)
7   Intrapersonal intelligence (*self smart*).[55]

If we aim to educate community members about sustainability as part of community engagement processes, we need to be alert to their different learning styles and multiple intelligences Later Gardner added naturalist intelligence, spiritual intelligence, existential intelligence and moral intelligence.[56] The clear message from this research is that if we aim to educate community members about sustainability as part of community engagement processes, we need to be alert to their different learning styles and multiple intelligences. The 'one-size-fits-all' approach that has characterized limited capacity building and strengthening in community engagement processes will definitely not work for all participants. We must acknowledge diverse learning styles for the richness they bring to the learning situation. As planners, we need to be particularly wary. Wendy's earlier research revealed that the personality types of planners generally fall into a very 'narrow band', with few in the 'feeling' category.[57]

Soft skill 2: Communication

As we have noted in Chapter 3, communication is a two-way street and communication skills are valuable soft skills in community engagement. Helping people to talk and *listen* to one another is a primary ingredient. In many of our engagement exercises, people came together to state their views, but they were not willing to listen to others' positions. We draw the distinction here between hearing and listening, where the latter involves an *attentive* approach to attempting to *understand* what the other person is saying. Here, we draw from a core assumption of neurolinguistic programming (NLP) which contends that the meaning of any communication is determined in the response of the listener.[58]

We draw the distinction here between hearing and listening, where the latter involves an *attentive* approach to attempting to *understand* what the other person is saying

Listening

Kanji are the Chinese symbols used in a form of modern Japanese writing. The *kanji* for listening includes the four components you listen with: your ears; your eyes; your undivided attention; and your heart.

Figure 5.2 The Chinese character for listening
Calligraphy by Gordon Davidson

The *kanji* 'Ting', representing the verb 'to listen', explains the difference between simply hearing and truly listening. By integrating representations of our ears, eyes, heart and the selfless act of undivided attention, this character captures the essence of 'listening' (see Figure 5.2). In community engagement, when we listen in this way, we show respect for the other and open ourselves to understanding larger truths. Planning theorist and educator John Forester, also distinguishes between hearing and listening:

> We can hear words, but miss what is meant. We can hear what is intended, but miss what is important. We can hear what is important, but neglect the person speaking... We can make a difference by listening or failing to do so, and we can be held responsible as a result.[59]

True listening is an active process of hearing and reflecting In community engagement processes, we've found that true listening is an active process of hearing and reflecting. Listening also nurtures relationships. Critical listening contributes to the evaluation of a community recommendation or decision, as we identify, integrate and come to respect different worldviews and social practices. The artfulness of this soft skill is in deep listening, which can be challenging, particularly when negativity surfaces. But listening is always worth the challenge.

Finally, we need not confine our 'listening across difference' exclusively to humans. Thoreau sagely reminded us: 'All nature will fable if we will but let it speak.' In Chapter 8, Inclusion, we discuss the potential of listening to the voices of nonhuman Nature.

Soft skill 3: Critical and reflective thinking

We use the term *critical thinking* to describe analytical and systemic thinking, precaution and foresight, recognition of consequences, evaluation and assessment of outcomes and a commitment to learning. A critical learner knows how to frame appropriate questions to guide relevant study and research, develop hypotheses based on balanced information, critical analysis and careful synthesis and test them against new information and personal experience and beliefs. Critical thinkers apply definitions of fundamental concepts, such as *environment, community, development* and *technology*, to local, national and global experiences and can assess bias and evaluate different points of view.[60] A critical thinker also knows that easy solutions do not exist and is constantly evaluating situations to assess success even after a decision has been made. Critical thinking is important in many arenas, not only in civic life. We discuss it here because it is a fundamental ingredient of all good recipes for decision making.

In community engagement, *reflective thinking* is as important as critical thinking. If critical thinkers seek to solve problems, reflective thinkers allow their minds to wander, look back and make sense of situations. Reflective thinking involves thinking about thinking, understanding and caring about different perspectives and ethical reasoning. In Chapter 9, Nourishment, we describe a workshop Wendy and Yollana facilitated to heal broken relationships in a Sydney public housing estate. We observed that our creative and visionary approaches had the effect of nurturing reflective thinking. Then participants put on their critical thinking hats to decide how to implement their collective vision of a harmonious working relationship.

If critical thinkers seek to solve problems, reflective thinkers allow their minds to wander, look back and make sense of situations

Soft skill 4: Personal development

It's an old (yet pertinent) adage that we cannot save the Earth if we cannot save ourselves. The same applies to community engagement for sustainability. We cannot lead people where we are not willing to go. It takes personal skill and commitment to practise the soft skills described above. While educating for sustainability should not focus exclusively on individual success, we must respect each individual's unique needs, boundaries, barriers and potentials. We all know activists who have burned out through overwork and lack of self-care. To open ourselves to the soft skills we've advocated, we must be grounded in our own selves, a topic we discuss in Chapter 9, Nourishment.

As we integrate these hard and soft skills into the ways we educate and learn alongside communities, we are aware that the distinctions between them may begin to blur. People will recognize that, for example, it doesn't matter how well you understand solar technology if you can't explain it to a confused or sceptical neighbour.

Kitchen table conversation starters

Kitchen table conversation starters are questions you can ask your friends, your family, your neighbours, your local politicians and anyone else whom you find at – or can bring to – your kitchen table, including yourself! We call them 'starters' because we are aware that conversations about sustainability must be deep and broad to be effective. And each of these questions will likely raise many more questions. Yet the important thing is to begin. To be part of the conversation:

- Which topics related to sustainability and your local community are you unclear about?
- What information do you need to and how can you get it? Who within your community has the answers to your questions? Or do you need to look further afield?
- Which forces represent the status quo in your community? What learning would you require to confidently challenge the status quo, where it is unsustainable?
- What have you learned about sustainability from people who are older or younger than you?
- Which knowledge, concepts, skills and educational resources would you want to bequeath to your children and/or future generations?
- Which places in your neighbourhood support opportunities to learn in and from Nature? Are they protected or at risk? How can you enhance and maintain the learning opportunities that these places provide?

For more opportunities to continue the conversation about community education for sustainability, please visit www.kitchentablesustainability.com.

Final thoughts

Education is the first chapter in the *EATING* model. It sets the table for a feast: a rich smörgåsbord of theories, recipes and ingredients to come. Critically, it's followed by the Action chapter. Our community *education* processes in engagement for sustainability must yield *action* – action that leads to transformative change. In a planetary emergency, we must make sure that we're acting differently – doing more than merely talking about doing.

6

ACTION

As I kneel to put the seeds in careful as stitching, I am in love. You are the bed we all sleep on. You are the food we eat, the food we ate, the food we will become. We are walking trees rooted in you.

Marge Percy, 1983

Never doubt that a small group of thoughtful, committed citizens can change the world. Indeed, it's the only thing that ever has.

Margaret Mead[1]

The Great Bear Rainforest[2]

The Great Bear Rainforest encompasses 15 million acres, stretching between Bute Inlet (some 200 kilometres north of Vancouver, where Nancy lives) to below the Alaskan border on Canada's west coast. A temperate rainforest, it accounts for approximately 25 per cent of the coastal rainforest in the Province of British Columbia. While some areas have been heavily logged for many years, the Forest includes as many as 100 pristine valleys that have never been logged. It has a high biodiversity value and is treasured for the white bears that give the Rainforest its name.

The Forest is highly contested and subject to competing claims from environmental activists, logging companies, researchers and First Nations communities. Since the mid-1990s, the Forest has been the focus of significant non-violent activism and ongoing conflict among various interest groups. Yet in 2007, a breakthrough solution was achieved that resulted in a World Wildlife Fund Gift to the Earth Award.

This remarkable transformation resulted from a wide range of actions at different scales over many years. The first scale was at international and national levels. On the one hand, financial redistributions occurred as a result of the increasing sophistication of First Nations groups, who took legal action against national and international governments over treaty claims previously ignored. And they won. Large tracts of land, previously ceded to logging companies, were essentially 'taken back', reducing the supply of logging land. At same time, campaigns starting as early as 1992, led by Greenpeace and Friends of Clayoquot Sound, included high-profile expeditions to Europe to pressure consumers to stop buying timber from old-growth forests. The result of those campaigns was a

This remarkable transformation resulted from a wide range of actions at different scales over many years

Continued

At that table – as a result of exceedingly hard work and determination by many actors with deep, if not always reconcilable, motivations to stay at the table – generative relationships were formed and a fertile ground for innovation was created

dramatic decrease in demand from Europe. These two factors prompted a restructure of the forestry industry in British Columbia. Previously dominant players, recognizing their power was impeded in this new context, also saw threats to profitability. For the first time, they could see the benefits of coming to the table. At that table – as a result of exceedingly hard work and determination by many actors with deep, if not always reconcilable, motivations to stay at the table – generative relationships were formed and a fertile ground for innovation was created.

Working through the agreements created a demand for 'ancient forest-friendly' products. Then a conservation economy was born. Vast areas of land were subsequently protected (21 million acres under environmental management, 5 million acres protected outright). Social financing was established (First Nations forestry, community-based initiatives value-added for the logging industry, retraining of forestry workers) and new logging technologies were developed. This transformation in the flow of resources, priorities and relationships continues today.

Introduction

To achieve sustainability, we need transformative change – such as the systemic change eventually achieved in the Great Bear Rainforest. It's very clear that we must act differently from our accustomed ways. An authentic community engagement process can be an effective step towards transformative change. In itself, it can be a powerful action. Yet there should be plans for many actions to continue beyond it. And many actions must come before it. Often, as in the case of the Great Bear Rainforest, sustained activism *outside formal processes* is the catalyst for bringing people to the table for more formal engagement processes.

The focus of this book is on community engagement with sustainability. In discussing the role of action in this context, we emphasize *action to achieve transformative change,* as opposed to actions that maintain the status quo. No matter how large or complex the subject of community engagement processes, we believe that there is always potential for outcomes to challenge currently unsustainable beliefs and practices. However, we need innovative and improved approaches to action if we sincerely seek transformative change. When we make this commitment, we need to change how we go about community engagement processes.

This book focuses on action directed towards sustainable outcomes. Action focuses on what we do. Governance, by contrast, is 'the whole system of interrelated actors performing these activities'.[3] Governance is about systems of organizing relationships among actors and about actions and is ultimately about how we go about this work. Clearly, the two are closely related, even though they may be pulling in different directions. Chapter 10 addresses the issue of governance in more detail, including the critical issue of accountability for the implementation of agreed outcomes.

Governance is about systems of organizing relationships among actors and about actions and is ultimately about how we go about this work

In Chapter 9, we explain that positive and regular early experiences of Nature can be powerful predeterminants of people's capacity and willingness to engage in sustainable action.[4] The same principle applies to community engagement. Positive and regular early experiences of good community engagement are necessary if people are going to engage in future processes. Community engagement processes will become increasingly important as we work together to find solutions to sustainability problems. Those currently involved in designing and conducting community engagement processes must find ways to deliver on their promises. Participants will not continue in community engagement processes if they perpetually fail to deliver tangible actions or outcomes.

In this chapter we:

- unpack some sources of frustration with community engagement with sustainability processes caused by 'inaction'

- apply lessons from existing social change approaches to community engagement with sustainability
- provide six recipes for action to achieve transformative change through community engagement processes for sustainability.

Approaches to action

In strengthening community engagement with sustainability, it is important to recognize that every participant brings a different preference for being and different preferences for action. All of these approaches are important. Most transformational change occurs when diverse people work together toward the same goal using a range of different approaches. Thus, processes of engagement with sustainability must acknowledge personal styles, preferences for ways of being and the full spectrum of actions necessary to achieve transformative change. Here we present two ways of conceptualizing roles and approaches to activism.

Most transformational change occurs when diverse people work together toward the same goal using a range of different approaches

Four roles of activism (Bill Moyer)

Social change activist Bill Moyer believes that there are commonly four roles played by social change activists:

- *Citizen*: promotes positive, widely held values, e.g. democracy, freedom, justice and non-violence.
- *Reformer*: uses official channels and a variety of means such as lobbying, legal action and elections to make change.
- *Change Agent*: employs grassroots organizing approaches to educate and involve citizens based on strategic approaches to long-term movement-building and to creating alternatives and paradigm shifts.
- *Rebel*: employs protest and civil disobedience to put problems in the public spotlight.[5]

Each of these diverse roles calls for and gives priority to different types of action. To create transformative change, we need all these approaches. To create transformative solutions in the Great Bear Rainforest, people needed to take action in all these roles. Indeed, a coalescence of diverse activist roles was necessary to challenge and ultimately supersede the dominant paradigm of unsustainable resource extraction. *Rebels* engaged in sustained non-direct violence in the Forest, *reformers* lobbied politicians to amend laws, *change agents* educated consumers about 'ancient forest-friendly' products, in the process creating demand for an alternative industry. Many different actors, many different roles, all working for the same sustainability outcome: protection of the Great Bear Rainforest.

> Indeed, a coalescence of diverse activist roles was necessary to challenge and ultimately supersede the dominant paradigm of unsustainable resource extraction

Five 'ways of being' (SIA)

Another useful approach to understanding different approaches to action is the *Stillness in Action* (SIA) model developed by the Australian organization, Interhelp. It describes five 'ways of being' in the world:

- *Resisting*: holding actions, stopping the worst abuse.
- *Strengthening*: building resilience in communities, organizations and systems.
- *Creating*: finding alternatives, developing new ways of doing and being.
- *Renewing*: working to reform institutions, professions, social and economic systems.
- *Serving*: caring for others – humans and all beings.[6]

While each of these is a valuable role to play, we do not need to be deeply involved in all of them. In fact, as we caution in Chapter 9, Nourishment, that would probably not be personally sustainable. Most people function best when they can focus in the area that feels most comfortable to them, acknowledging that this may change over time. Yollana recently visited her godmother in

> Most people function best when they can focus in the area that feels most comfortable to them, acknowledging that this may change over time

Creating: A new EcoCity at Christie Walk, Adelaide

Because much damage has already been done to natural systems in this urban location, from the start everyone involved embraced a nurturing ethic that sought to reverse damage, rather than simply avoid further damage

Christie Walk is the first EcoCity development in downtown Adelaide (population one million plus), a practical prototype for inner city, ecologically responsible design. It was conceived and built through a genuinely community-driven development process, supported by Urban Ecology Australia (UEA),[7] with funding from residents and other ethical investment sources. Because much damage has already been done to natural systems in this urban location, from the start everyone involved embraced a nurturing ethic that sought to reverse damage, rather than simply avoid further damage.

Christie Walk excels in environmental performance in areas such as energy, water use and use of non-toxic materials. In dramatic contrast to drab new townhouse housing nearby, the EcoCity's 27 dwellings are a study in diversity and community: four straw-bale detached cottages, a terrace of four townhouses, an apartment block of six apartments and the final building of 13 apartments, laundry, kitchen, meeting room, toilets and the Centre for Urban Ecology. A community garden features food plants, a substantial roof garden has comfortable, paved sitting areas (using materials recycled from the site), and shade in this hot Mediterranean climate is provided by a few large trees. There is no through-traffic for cars. Christie Walk has two underground rainwater tanks, photovoltaics, and all dwellings have solar-powered hot water or a heat exchanger. The effluent from the sewage works provides underground watering for a healthy park.

The future residents acted as architect, planners, developers, landscapers, builders (for some buildings) and financiers, and sold all the dwellings before final construction. This was an enormous and sometimes arduous undertaking. However, because of the strong commitment by UEA to community education, many have learned about ecological development through the process and that knowledge is widely available to other communities. Today, many residents are still involved in ongoing community activities and hosting site tours for visitors.[8]

Adelaide, South Australia, whose efforts in developing the EcoCity where she now lives are a fine example of a *creating* approach to action.

The frustration of 'inaction'

Community engagement processes are often frustrating, with the root cause being real and/or perceived lack of follow-up action. Within democracies, some sort of community engagement processes should be the starting point for most sustainability initiatives. However, as citizen education activist, Lotte Scharfman, has famously declared, 'democracy is not a spectator sport'.[9] People who take part in community engagement processes want to see tangible changes demonstrating that they have been heard. And most of the time they want that action to be immediate and lasting.

People who take part in community engagement processes want to see tangible changes demonstrating that they have been heard

In 2003, Wendy, Steph and Yollana facilitated a series of public workshops for Redland Shire Council,[10] located on Moreton Bay to the east of Brisbane in subtropical coastal Queensland. They designed these workshops to maximize community contributions to the Local Area Plan for Cylinder Beach on North Stradbroke Island. The Island's residents expressed a strong wish to preserve and maintain local ecological qualities, principally by reducing vehicle traffic to the foreshore and beaches. Conflict ensued, as the Council was keen to enlarge the parking area and add a bus turn-around area to support economic development. While the engagement activities were effective in involving a large proportion of residents and others on the small island, the subsequent differences between Council's preferred options and the community's clearly articulated and recorded views created resentment and conflict. Local wishes were largely ignored. Outcomes like this can destroy people's confidence in community engagement and paralyse opportunities for future action. Such ongoing conflict inevitably diminishes the quality of actions that might result from engagement.[11]

Outcomes like this can destroy people's confidence in community engagement and paralyse opportunities for future action

We address governance issues, including the critical issue of accountability for implementing agreed actions in Chapter 10. In the next chapter, we discuss trust issues, including the importance of clarity about the scope of community engagement and how outcomes will inform follow-on actions. We will not repeat that material here. Instead, we focus on *how to identify the most effective actions to achieve transformative change through community engagement with sustainability.*

With so many diverse interests involved in community engagement processes, it is always difficult to achieve agreement on which actions should be prioritized. The range of participants in any one process can include government bureaucrats, community engagement consultants, technical consultants, citizens, activists, peak body representatives, politicians, journalists, academics... Each has different personal and professional values and priorities. It is no wonder, then, that action (or inaction) resulting from community engagement processes can often be a problem.

Activism: A response to 'inaction'

Nonviolence works by destroying the ability of those in power to use force without losing the essential support of those on whom their continued stay in power depends.

A Steffen, *Worldchanging*[12]

Some people managing or engaged in *formal* community engagement processes have difficulty understanding the necessity of other approaches. The following story provides some clues.

The Gully and the Woolworths Maleny story told later in this chapter are local examples of a global problem, where competition over common land and resources has left a legacy of exploitation and degradation. In Western countries, many powerful examples of strong conviction stand out amid small-mindedness: the determination of Rosa Parks and other African American activists

The Highgate Hill Gully, Brisbane

Wendy was travelling in Canada, presenting her approaches to community engagement to academics and professionals when the Highgate Hill Gully campaign exploded in August 2002. She rang her Brisbane office one morning to check in. Sam La Rocca, a member of her staff, alone in the office, answered the phone. Sam searched for words to break the news to Wendy, who asked how the business was going:

'Well ...' Sam began, 'Yollana is up a tree, Steph's been arrested and I'm just here briefly to write a letter to the local council member.'

'Oh, no,' was Wendy's muted reply.

A short silence and then... 'Gee, I wish I could pay you all for working on the Gully'.

Located a short walk from the West End office, the Gully was some of the last undeveloped land in inner city Brisbane large enough to support a wide range of local and migrating bird and other species, as well as native flora. Also a water catchment, it directed flows to the Brisbane River. Local people valued the Gully for its potential for intimate connection with Nature and the refuge it provided for native wildlife. They called it 'the heart, soul and lungs of our suburb'.[13] The five acres, in private hands since 1959, was under considerable development pressure since the 1980s, when proposals first reached Brisbane City Council. Until 2002, resident protests defeated every development proposal.[14]

When activists decided that what they viewed as the Council's 'shallow' and formal community engagement processes had failed to yield satisfactory results, Steph and Yollana decided to engage in non-violent direct action (NVDA) to bring about change in direct ways.[15] Their passion to protect the Gully from development was widely echoed within Brisbane's West End and Highgate Hill communities. However, despite hundreds of local people actively campaigning, development did take place (although only ten or so of the planned 29 houses have so far been built).[16]

> Well ...' Sam began, 'Yollana is up a tree, Steph's been arrested and I'm just here briefly to write a letter to the local council member

to overturn segregation laws in the USA in the 1950s;[17] Freedom Rides in 1960s Australia, when Aboriginal people were not considered legal citizens;[18] non-violent direct action campaigns to save Tasmania's Franklin River from damming;[19] and, more recently, the efforts of monks and supporters highlighting human rights and social justice conditions in both Burma and Tibet. Such potent examples led some to argue that human evolution can be viewed as a history of activist participation in progressing how we treat each other and nonhuman life.[20]

Why activists bypass community engagement processes

People often become involved in community activism because they believe (or experience) that government agencies lack the political will to address issues that concern them

People often become involved in community activism because they believe (or experience) that government agencies lack the political will to address issues that concern them. They've witnessed the failure of formal community engagement processes as catalysts for sustainable action. We explained some of those reasons in Chapter 3. Some activists refuse to engage at all (regardless of how participatory and inclusive community engagement processes are) for a number of other really good reasons.

In his 2005 essay, 'Six Reasons Not to Engage', community educator James Whelan summarizes global research on active community members' feelings about community engagement, focusing on Western democracies but with wider applicability. Whelan found that decision-making processes fail to be truly consensual or based on a 'reciprocal compromise' approach (where all parties prepare to give and take to achieve appropriate outcomes). Active community members complain that government and development agencies are generally unable 'to recognize and deal with conflict' and that genuine power issues within government and industry reduce the scope of power available to participating community members. In short, decision makers' agendas override community sentiment. Active community members also see community engagement processes as difficult to access and often closed to community stakeholders' involvement in all phases of the project and beyond.

His six reasons not to engage are summarized below:

1. 'Patterns in group behaviour mitigate against environmental management decisions that provide the highest level of conservation.'

2. Conflict produces results, whereas reliance on advisory committees, boards, discussions, 'polite deputations' and well researched lobbying and letter-writing rarely succeed. Radicalized conservationists can relocate the debate from private meetings and parliamentary hearings to 'the public space of civil society'.

3. Community engagement is 'a wolf in sheep's clothing'. This discourse has been applied to the decision-making processes that fall well short of the democratic ideals appropriately associated with community engagement.

4. In community engagement, some people are more equal than others. 'These and similar experiences of community engagement contribute to community sector disillusionment and "consultation fatigue".'

5. Community engagement takes energy. 'Active participation in community engagement activities requires time, stamina and considerable personal and economic resources.'

6. Community engagement rarely encompasses the full policy cycle. Processes tend to engage community groups and concerns more often at the plan-making stage and less frequently at the plan-implementation and evaluation stages of the policy cycle. This approach does not support sustainability. We need to focus on more comprehensive, long-term and holistic approaches.[21]

Active participation in community engagement activities requires time, stamina and considerable personal and economic resources

We agree with James and have found that young people, in particular, often don't embrace community engagement processes because they find them irrelevant, a waste of their time and boring and they do not directly experience results that are relevant to their concerns.[22]

Activists often turn their backs on formal processes for good reasons and take their actions into the more public spaces of the civic arena because they are sharply aware of the weaknesses of formal engagement processes

As the summary above explains, activists often turn their backs on formal processes for good reasons and take their actions into the more public spaces of the civic arena because they are sharply aware of the weaknesses of formal engagement processes. The lesson here is that community engagement practitioners need to conduct better processes in the first place. To satisfy the frequently articulated complaints of activists, they must take *the whole of the policy cycle* into account, ensure that community engagement processes are interesting and fun, that participants receive a tangible and timely 'return on investment' of their time and energy, and make genuine undertakings to ensure that diverse voices are being heard.

We also need to find creative ways to listen to voices outside of formal processes, to be genuinely inclusionary and not listen solely to identified stakeholders in 'polite' contexts. All the current research and theory about inclusion supports this view: our forums must allow for a wider discursive range. It should be acceptable to become emotional, passionate or upset without being thrown out of a meeting or workshop. We discuss this matter further in Chapter 8, Inclusion.

Contending with the status quo: How existing structures resist change

Transformative change is difficult because, more often than not, it challenges the status quo and the many vested interests (from government agencies to NIMBY activists) represented by it. Unfortunately for those seeking to advance the cause of sustainability, the status quo often favours the economic over the ecological, the private over the social and individual power over collective needs. Further, even where the regime, or 'dominant cultures, structures and practices' can see the need for change, are willing to change and take significant leaps in the right direction, inbuilt rigidity can be a powerful resisting force.[23]

In Australia, we saw a pertinent example of this when, after 11 years of conservative government, the new prime minister, Kevin Rudd, initiated an unprecedented national participatory process to engage Australians in developing innovative ideas and solutions to address Federal Government priorities. The Australia 2020 process was expansive and ambitious, initially consisting of local Community Summits, School Summits and a Youth Summit. In April 2008, this process culminated in the Australia 2020 Summit, involving 1000 'leading' Australians (professionals, politicians, celebrities, artists, industry representatives, bureaucrats, community leaders, Indigenous leaders and other notables), who engaged in two days of facilitated workshops to refine community contributions. And at each of these events, professional facilitators, recorders and organizers listened to and managed conversations and recorded comments.

Alison Croggon, a delegate at the Summit, described the process as 'a startling expression of collective goodwill' and an 'inspiring experiment in open government'.[24] This was the first time such a process had been held in Australia, capturing big-picture sustainability visioning and prioritizing actions to be implemented through national policy.

However, the day after the Summit ended, Australian newspapers began to portray a different picture. Headlines such as 'Invitees depart feeling hijacked'[25] and 'Diverse input, but little output'[26] suggested that, despite promises of an inclusionary approach to developing sustainability policy, the process had fallen short.

One of Wendy's close friends, who participated in the Summit, explained that initially everyone was thrilled and excited to be involved. When the results of the first day's work were reported back, however, they bore little resemblance to what had happened in his group of 100 people. Then, he said, participants became 'very cross'. We were shocked to hear that even the most basic facilitation rules were broken during the 2020 event. Participants claimed that facilitators at workshop tables did not properly record their comments, refusing to record or completely ignoring some ideas and changing the wording of others in overnight deliberations and during the preparation of reports.

Facilitators were accused of converting everyday language into bureaucratic and management jargon, to the point where some participants were unable to recognize their own contributions. In the report-back session, where the first and then the second days of deliberations were summarized and priorities identified, completely new ideas emerged that had never been discussed at workshop tables. These are serious, yet basic, breaches of the trust relationship that must exist between participants and facilitators if engagement is to be valued and seen as legitimate.

This example illustrates just how important it is to be vigilant to matters of detail, when designing and executing community engagement processes. The butcher's paper, flip charts and Post-it™ notes matter. A lot. As does what happens to them after the participants go home.

Why, despite all the good will and commitment to an open approach, were the basics of facilitation and accurate recording seemingly ignored?

We raise this example not to undermine the courageous intentions and genuine steps forward demonstrated by the Australia 2020 process. Rather, we want to learn from it. Why, despite all the good will and commitment to an open approach, were the basics of facilitation and accurate recording seemingly ignored? While certainly it will be months and years before we can judge the true effectiveness of the Australia 2020 process in producing sustainable outcomes, we have to ask: How can important contributions ever be implemented if they aren't accurately recorded in the first place?

When a supposedly innovative and groundbreaking process like Australia 2020 fails to get the basics of facilitation and recording right, it is no wonder that many people often despair that transformative bottom–up views have little chance of survival against the structural rigidity necessary to keep the machinery of government ticking. We see the Australia 2020 process as an example of an attempt to transform high-level bureaucratic decision making with a progressive and inclusive sustainability process: a paradigm shift in Australian governance. Yet the actual process fell short of this goal because the habitual and predictable activities of bureaucracy (including those employed to do facilitation) lacked a systemic and transformative understanding of the processes required to support that vision in practical terms.

Why unsustainable practices take so long to change

When change does occur, it can seem to be happening at a snail's pace. This can be infuriating to activists, as well as others engaged in community processes. (It can certainly be infuriating to community engagement practitioners.) So why does it seem as though so little real action takes hold? Why do unsustainable practices take so long to change? And how can paradigm shifts occur in practice?

Research on the nature of transitions reveals that there are four phases involved in a transition:

1 *Predevelopment*: lots of experimentation but nothing *seems* to change.
2 *Take-off*: the process of societal change ignites and small changes take hold.
3 *Breakthrough/acceleration*: structural changes occur as a result of reinforcing interactions across society, economy, ecology, institutions and so forth.
4 *Stabilization*: the speed of change slows down and a new balance is achieved.[27]

The challenge for community engagement processes is that *many actions are required at different levels over long periods* before we see any real evidence of those actions resulting in change. This can be immensely frustrating. Only the *breakthrough* phase is rapid. To complicate matters, when dealing with complex socio-ecological systems, we cannot predict when a transition process will flip into the breakthrough phase. This provides none of the certainty most proponents and participants involved in community engagement processes seek. Until 'real' change occurs, the participants' view is often that 'nothing is happening'.

Steph and Yollana remember attending their first year of Environmental Science together at university in Brisbane. Studying environmental policy, they spent a class discussing the meaning and implications of the term 'paradigm shift' in relation to environmental awareness and action. At that time, ten years ago, people like Steph and Yollana, who were passionate about protecting the environment, were considered to be on the fringe, perhaps obsessive. Some would even say 'weird'. Over the last few years, together with thousands of other fringe, obsessive, *weirdos*, they have watched the environment movement begin to make a breakthrough. Their observation is that environmental practitioners are no longer trying to convince everyone that there is a crisis. That has finally (mostly) been accepted. We are now trying to convince everyone that we must do something about it – and quickly.

Actions are required at all levels if sustainability is to become the dominant paradigm

This understanding of the nature of transitions demonstrates why community engagement is so important for sustainability. Actions are required at all levels if sustainability is to become the dominant paradigm. Community engagement with sustainability, well designed and managed, provides opportunities to communicate strong messages to decision makers about the need for sustainable action at the international, national and regional levels. It can also support community-initiated action at the local level.

Recipes for action to achieve transformative change

You never change things by fighting the existing reality.
To change something, build a new model that makes the
existing model obsolete.

Buckminster Fuller[28]

One of the challenges for transformative action is that most sustainability problems today exhibit a high degree of complexity and uncertainty. They involve many people with different values and priorities.[29] How should we act in this context? Which actions can address these *wicked* problems?[30] What does this mean for community engagement with sustainability?

We offer seven approaches, drawn from our practical experience and knowledge of change processes:

1 Evaluate whether or not conditions support generative relationships.
2 Ask deeper questions to frame actions.
3 Align action by 'thinking like a movement'.
4 Allow space for ongoing experimentation.
5 Network among social innovators.
6 Be aware of and learn from shadow networks.
7 Use a broad range of actions.

We discuss each of these recipes in detail below.

Recipe 1: Evaluate whether conditions support generative relationships

We need ideas and ways of working together that we cannot currently imagine

To create solutions to the Earth's sustainability problems and overcome implementation barriers, we need generative relationships that 'produce new sources of value which cannot be foreseen in advance [sic.]'.[31] We need ideas and ways of working together that we cannot currently imagine. We also need to work together collaboratively and effectively to identify them. For transformative action to occur, community engagement processes must foster generative relationships between participants, and between participants and proponents. Community engagement with sustainability has this potential. But how can we design community engagement processes to maximize the potential to develop generative relationships?

Strategic management specialists Brenda Zimmerman and Bryan Hayday have developed a tool called the 'Generative Relationships STAR',[32] which identifies four aspects of a generative relationship: *Separateness* or difference, *'Tuning'* (talking and listening), *Action* opportunities and a *Reason* to work together. Figure 6.1 illustrates these relationships.

These analysts argue that *each* point of the star must be well represented in any relationship or collaborative activity to achieve generative results.

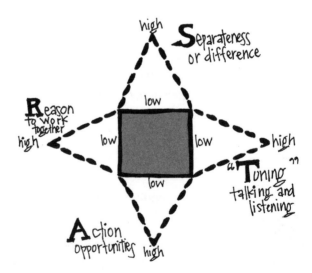

Figure 6.1 The Generative Relationships STAR
Source: Zimmerman and Hayday (1999)

In Table 6.1, we take each of these aspects and pose questions relevant to community engagement with sustainability. Whether or not you are designing, managing or participating in community engagement processes, you can use these questions to evaluate the degree to which the starting conditions support transformative action.

Table 6.1 Community engagement with sustainability: Considerations for each Generative STAR aspect

STAR aspect	Description	Considerations for community engagement with sustainability
Separateness or difference	Differences in background, skills, perspectives needed to challenge assumptions & turn fact into interpretation.	Is a diverse range of perspectives represented? How could it be broadened?
'**T**uning' (talking and listening)	Real opportunities to talk & listen with permission to challenge status quo. Opportunities for reflection (to grow and learn).	What techniques can be used to facilitate real listening? How can space for reflection be included? How can permission to challenge the status quo be demonstrated?
Action opportunities	Opportunities to act together on the 'talk' and so co-create something new.	What walk-on parts can be identified? How can actors work together?
Reason to work together	Compelling reason, mutual benefit to share resources and ideas – to be allies (even if only for a short time).	What is the promise to the public? How might that be deepened?

Source: Adapted from Zimmerman and Hayday (1999, p299)[33]

The Great Bear Rainforest story is a good example of conditions fostering opportunities for generative relationships that, in turn, enabled transformative action. These types of processes are hard work and personally challenging, as we explain when we revisit the Great Bear Rainforest story in Chapter 9, Nourishment.

Recipe 2: Ask deeper questions

There is a fundamental difference between action that 'tinkers at the edge' and transformative action that has the potential to change our 'master metaphorical templates', as discussed in Chapter 2. Community engagement processes that seek improved sustainability outcomes must ask deeper questions. They must go beneath the surface to reveal more, if not all, of the iceberg.

Richard Hames, a corporate philosopher and futurist who works for governments, NGOs and industry internationally, challenges us to question more deeply if we want to achieve transformative change. Cathy has worked closely with Richard Hames for many years. His iceberg model, shown in Figure 6.2, links levels of communication to corresponding questions and action. In community engagement with sustainability, we must aspire to deeper questioning to enhance opportunities for transformative action.[34]

Here's an example of how we could use the iceberg model. Most cities are experiencing increasing traffic congestion as car ownership rates and population growth increase. If the question remains at the 'what has happened' level, above the surface, the corresponding action is to build more roads: a 'reaction'. If questioning goes one level deeper to 'what has been happening', perhaps those additional roads would be built ahead of demand: 'anticipation'. And so on, until we realize that we are dealing with a complex problem. Building our way out of it is not an option. We need a totally different kind of questioning that leads to very different types of action: *redesign, remodelling* and eventually *transformation*.

We need a totally different kind of questioning that leads to very different types of action: *redesign, remodelling* and eventually *transformation*

142

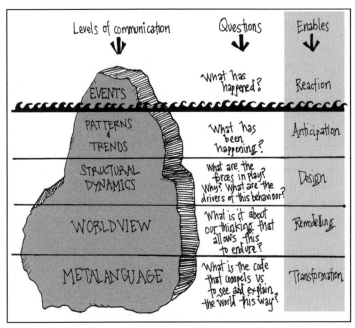

Figure 6.2 The Iceberg model: Different levels of strategic thinking, triggered by different types of questions, allow for different responses
Source: Richard Hames (2007, p287)

All processes of community engagement with sustainability do not need to operate at the deepest level of questioning. Those designing and managing these processes should be aware of the deeper levels and, wherever possible, encourage proponents and participants to delve deeper. Otherwise, resulting actions cannot be transformative.

It is clear from the Maleny case that formal public engagement processes failed because they did not ask the right questions. Early community engagement processes were designed to ask local people *how* they wanted the Woolworths site to proceed but the community wanted to answer a deeper question about whether they wanted it to proceed at all. Strategic questioning can hold a key to improving these stale and outdated processes. Activist author Fran Peavey describes this approach as 'the skill of asking questions

Asking the wrong questions

People in Maleny, a small town north of Brisbane, discovered first-hand how disempowering and frustrating it can be when proponents and decision makers ask the wrong questions of communities. In this case, the main question asked was, 'What will the supermarket look like?', rather than, 'Are we going to have a supermarket at all? Is it appropriate for our town?'

In what has been called 'the cooperative capital of Australia', a new Woolworths supermarket was proposed on the banks of the Obi Obi Creek that runs through the town.[35] The site is a known platypus habitat and an important water catchment that supported native trees, including Bunya and Karri pines. It was much loved by local residents. In sustainability-conscious Maleny, opposition to the supermarket was also about issues related to globalization of food distribution, local food security and the fragmentation of social capital and community economies.

Independent research suggested that local opposition to the development was as high as 79 per cent.[36] Despite local involvement in formal government-facilitated engagement activities and clear community opposition, the Woolworths development was approved. When public meetings failed, activist campaigns began. Through petitions and online campaigns, the Maleny Woolworths campaign spread well beyond the town, receiving the support of Steph and Yollana in Brisbane and many others around Australia. Wendy remembers attending a community renewal conference in August 2002, in Melbourne, 1775 kilometres away, where participants received hourly reports about the success of the Maleny direct actions. Residents engaged in direct action on the site to stop the development. They sat in trees, stood in front of vehicles, formed human chains around valued natural areas and wrestled with police. The Maleny Voice, a community-driven website, reported:

They sat in trees, stood in front of vehicles, formed human chains around valued natural areas and wrestled with police

The forked bunya pine, the last in Bunya Street, was saved by Daniel Jones, 28, a local landscape gardener, who climbed the tree and lived in it, with the help of locals, for 60 days. Maleny's tree-sitter drew international support for Maleny's plight.[37]

Continued

144

Overall, strong police presence (on occasions, up to 70 uniformed officers) and lack of governmental support thwarted protestors' efforts and the supermarket was built. However, it was a bitter victory for the supermarket, as The Maleny Voice explained:

> Woolworths has more than 700 supermarkets in Australia and the turnover for all but one is recorded monthly in company documents. The glaring omission is Woolworths Maleny, suggesting that residents' 'I Won't Shop There' campaign is having an effect.[38]

For Maleny and the wider activist community, on the other hand, there have been many victories. The campaign consolidated community spirit and raised awareness nationwide about the importance of supporting local retailers. It has inspired people in other small towns to take a stand against unwanted supermarkets – such as the town of Mt Evelyn in Victoria, which recently succeeded in opposing a Woolworths development there.[39]

that will make a difference' and demonstrates in her workshops that it is 'a powerful and exciting tool for social and personal change'.[40] Strategic questions aim to create a 'middle ground' unfamiliar to either participant in an argument or mediation.[41]

Strategic questioning is the skill of asking the questions that will make a difference:

- It involves a special type of question and a special type of listening.
- It is a process that may change the listener as well as the person being questioned; creates options and digs deeper.
- It avoids 'why', 'yes' or 'no' answers.
- It is empowering and asks the questions that often aren't asked.[42]

Strategic questioning is the skill of asking the questions that will make a difference

Australian community engagement specialist Lyn Carson reviewing extensive research, argues that strategic questioning proved to be a significant tool for change. It allowed new ideas to emerge and stimulated shifts in thinking and feeling – for both the interviewee and the interviewer. With its emphasis on listening and the required preparedness on the part of the questioner to change, strategic questioning may provide a model for engagement processes with the wider community.

To achieve a transition from existing unsustainable practices, actions need to be coordinated across the strategic, tactical and operational levels

Recipe 3: Act like an organization, think like a movement

The field of transition management proposes a new mode of governance for sustainable development that we briefly introduce here because of its critical relevance to identifying 'action arenas' to frame what can otherwise become isolated and unrelated actions.[43] To achieve a transition from existing unsustainable practices, actions need to be coordinated across the strategic, tactical and operational levels, as Figure 6.3 illustrates.

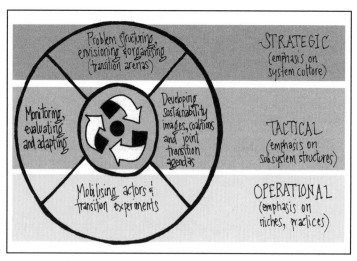

Figure 6.3 The transition management cycle
Source: Loorbach (2008)[44]

The PLAN Institute in Canada (Planned Lifetime Advocacy Network) is a good example of working across these different levels; of 'acting like an organization but thinking like a movement'.[45] PLAN was founded by parents of children with a disability who wanted to ensure ongoing quality of life for their children. Its members sought to answer the difficult question faced by many who care for a relative with a disability: 'What will happen to my relative when I'm not there?' Just as important as *what* will happen is: *Who* will be there? To address these important questions, PLAN works to create social networks and advocate for policy and regulatory reforms.[46]

From its humble origins, PLAN is now being replicated in 40 places around the world. We believe that this expanded capacity was enabled because the founders were 'thinking like a movement' from the beginning. 'Thinking like a movement' means thinking beyond our day-to-day lives or the day-to-day operations of an organization to embrace a much larger vision. It means acting in an 'intentional, conscious, strategic and systemic way to bring about structural, institutional, systemic and legislative change; and a cultural and attitudinal shift'.[47]

Thinking like a movement' means thinking beyond our day-to-day lives or the day-to-day operations of an organization to embrace a much larger vision

Some practices we encourage to support thinking like a movement are described below.

Deliberative Action Framing

As the Maleny Woolworths example shows, how we frame a project or programme and the questions we ask at its outset have a significant role in determining the nature of subsequent actions. Proponents sometimes seek to avoid conflict by not asking basic questions initially or at all. We believe this is a mistake, as it can alienate natural stakeholders and lead to more conflict, rather than including potential activists in collaborative processes.

Deliberative Action Framing is a process that helps us develop and clarify how we frame issues and projects in a collaborative manner before we develop action outcomes. We often use a *Search*

Deliberative Action Framing is a process that helps us develop and clarify how we frame issues and projects in a collaborative manner before we develop action outcomes

Conference or *Stakeholders Workshop* to determine how to frame a project or action, who should be involved, appropriate actions and evaluation processes.[48] Used with intention, deliberative processes can create active partnerships among stakeholders and bridge cultural conflicts among government, industry and community, fostering generative relationships and networks.

The Movement Action Plan

Figure 6.4 illustrates *The Movement Action Plan: A strategic framework describing the eight stages of successful social movements.* It is a tool designed by social change activist Bill Moyer to describe and identify eight stages of a social or environmental justice movement, from *Normal Times* through to the movement's *Take-off* (Stage 4) to *Success* (Stage 7) and *Continuing the Struggle* (Stage 8). Moyer argues that movements are generally in more than one stage at any time.[49] Understanding these stages helps activists situate their campaign within an overall framework.[50]

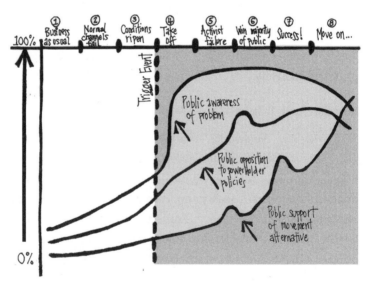

Figure 6.4 Stages of a movement
Source: Moyer (1987, p1)

Recipe 4: Allow space for ongoing experimentation and process evaluation

For decades, planners and decision makers have approached complex socio-ecological systems like cities with a 'command-and-control' mentality, assuming that they can be controlled in a linear way. But achieving sustainability in cities is not like baking a cake.[51] There is no straightforward, tried-and-tested recipe. Cities, ecologies and societies are complex systems with non-linear causal relationships. Achieving sustainability within these complex systems is difficult because the structural dynamics of change are messy. Often uncomfortably so. As social innovation expert Frances Westley and colleagues suggest, dealing with complex systems is more akin to raising a child than baking a cake![52]

Dealing with complex systems is more akin to raising a child than baking a cake!

When community engagement processes seek solutions to a particular problem, participants want to be confident that they will work. Individuals crave a certain degree of certainty. Unfortunately, sustainability problems are generally not that simple. We cannot predict reliably which action, or collection of actions, will achieve the desired shift or phase transition. We need to keep experimenting to achieve transformations for sustainability, both within and outside of formal policy actions. This need to experiment underlines why we must be vigilant about inclusivity in community engagement processes. Inclusive processes encourage diversity of views and opinions and this diversity can then inform the design of processes and the design of 'experiments'.

Experimentation is a relatively new concept for planners. It requires that we explore *unknown* territory. This can be challenging for organizers of community engagement processes, who often feel that they are required, at least to appear, to 'know the answers'. We need to embrace opportunities to experiment, however challenging, to allow new and innovative solutions for sustainability to emerge.

Cathy experienced the power of the desire for certainty when working on Melbourne 2030, the metropolitan strategy for Melbourne. 'Adaptability' is one of strategy's seven guiding principles, purposefully designed to provide an overarching framework for sustainable change. A first five-year action plan was included. This was intended to be reviewed and adapted over time, based on monitoring what was working and what wasn't. As soon as Melbourne 2030 was released, however, the dominant description in the media became 'Melbourne's blueprint for sustainability'.[53]

As soon as Melbourne 2030 was released, however, the dominant description in the media became 'Melbourne's blueprint for sustainability

This type of language prohibits experimentation. It implies that something is fixed and definite. It suggests that – like a formula – if we implement a particular action, we will see a particular result. We need to recognize that there are some things we simply don't know or can't predict. We need to develop processes that are flexible and adaptive to support ongoing active experimentation. We must have space to learn.

Formative evaluation

A supportive framework for incorporating experimentation into community engagement processes is *formative* evaluation. Sadly, evaluation of community engagement processes most commonly occurs *after* the process or project has been implemented.[54] This is called *summative* (or outcome) evaluation. This approach dilutes the ongoing responsibility of diverse stakeholders, including government, to pay critical attention to whether or not the proposed actions are being effective. In contrast, formative evaluation can occur *during* a community engagement process, as discussed in this research–practitioner dialogue:

> *There is little point in waiting to show, in an objective manner, that the process was perceived negatively after it has finished. Evaluation needs to be incorporated in the*

process as something that can provide timely direction to the overall public involvement program... Evaluation is not a hands-off data-gathering procedure, but an interactive one, which influences the outcome of public involvement.[55]

Within the framework of formative evaluation, community engagement processes with sustainability can – with experienced facilitation – often proceed with a much more flexible format than previously employed, to enable experimentation and innovation.

Recipe 5: Networking among social innovators

Social innovation is defined as 'an initiative, product or process which profoundly changes the basic routines, resource and authority flows or beliefs of any social system in a direction of greater resilience. Successful social innovations have durability, impact and scale.'[56] They are critical to achieving transformative change for sustainability. Social innovators actively pursue this type of innovation or change. They have a diverse range of roles – such as *citizen, reformer, change agent* and *rebel.* They work in a variety of settings, including government, industry, community organizations and NGOs. When social innovators team up and work together, innovative breakthroughs are often achieved, as in the case of the Great Bear Rainforest.

Community engagement processes are marvellous opportunities to link previously unconnected social innovators across various sectors. When designing processes for community engagement with sustainability, we need opportunities for social innovators to connect. After people make these connections, different players can pursue diverse actions, directly related to the community engagement process, but also outside it, in parallel. Often the most significant actions within community engagement processes are processes and relationships that that are never documented in formal reports.

Community engagement processes are marvellous opportunities to link previously unconnected social innovators across various sectors

They are the many actions pursued by committed individuals with different value sets and perspectives, who are connected in diverse ways through community engagement processes. They often have the heartfelt quality embodied by Rebecca Cotton in the Eagleby example in Chapter 10, Governance.

Social innovators are not always engaged in formal community engagement processes. Although activism has fostered many positive environmental and social changes, some activists are excluded – by choice or design – from community engagement processes.[57] Organizations such as The Change Agency (TCA) in Australia,[58] Training for Change in Minneapolis[59] and the Earth Activist Training Centre in California[60] help to link between formal and informal action. They provide activists and organizers with tools to engage with sustainability on all levels, including personally. They also help activists make the transition from being 'responsive' to 'proactive' in campaigns, focusing on linking with other campaigns and movements, identifying objectives and subsequent strategies and devising tactics based on clear understandings of roles and types of action.

We encourage you to experiment with innovative ways to involve a diverse range of social innovators – not only the usual suspects

Given the importance of achieving sustainability breakthroughs by networking social innovators, we encourage you to experiment with innovative ways to involve a diverse range of social innovators – not only the usual suspects. Having designed and managed countless community workshops, with purposes ranging from informing to collaborating, Cathy imagines an alternative type of process, where proponents and/or bureaucrats spend more time tapping into and learning from existing community networks while also managing general engagement workshops that provide access points for those not already working within recognized networks.

Recipe 6: Be aware of and learn from shadow networks

In his book *Blessed Unrest,* activist and author Paul Hawken likens the hundreds of thousands of not-for-profit organizations to humanity's immune system: a response to 'toxins like political corruption, economic disease, and ecological degradation'.[61] He argues that:

> At the core of immunity is a miracle of recovery and restoration, for there are times when our immune system is taken down...The immune system depends on its diversity to maintain resiliency, with which it can maintain homeostasis, respond to surprises, learn from pathogens, and adapt to sudden changes.[62]

We now see increasing attention to these so called 'shadow networks' across a range of disciplines.[63] These emergent informal networks, the knowledge they contain and expertise they have developed are valuable during times of crisis, precisely because they reflect experimentation in ways that challenge the dominant and unsustainable paradigm.

These emergent informal networks, the knowledge they contain and expertise they have developed are valuable during times of crisis, precisely because they reflect experimentation in ways that challenge the dominant and unsustainable paradigm

Wendy, Steph and Yollana have experienced a few players in shadow networks in their engagement work. Invariably, they were willing to 'stand up' for important community initiatives and take risks to ensure that the voices of communities were not lost in bureaucratic decision making. These actors, actions and experiments are a critical resource to help achieve regime shift, as well as to recover after such shifts.

A high-profile example of shadow networks in action is the urban agriculture movement in Cuba. In response to sanctions and the withdrawal of Soviet oil supplies, Cuba had to rethink how their whole society could be restructured to reduce oil dependence. The knowledge and experimentation of alternative practitioners suddenly moved from the periphery of society to front and centre. Today, Cuban cities produce an average of 60 per cent of their vegetables.[64] Cuban Permaculture activists travel worldwide spreading the message of their successes. (One recently visited Wendy's Permaculture community.)

Of direct relevance to community engagement processes is the example of the Stockholm green wedges, large areas of non-urban 'green' land located throughout the metropolitan area. They provide natural, cultural and communal amenities. As with most large cities, undeveloped land is under constant development pressure for housing, road expansion and buildings associated with sports and cultural facilities. Decades of activism, within and outside formal community engagement processes have focused on the protection of the Stockholm green wedge, with some great successes alongside incremental reductions in the total size of green wedges. One current activity is community gardening. Recent research shows how critical this humble activity is to maintaining local knowledge of and practices for the protection, maintenance and recovery of ecosystems.[65] Initiatives such as Food Connect in Brisbane are part of a global movement towards localization sometimes called 'glocalization'. Food Connect, a community food-distribution project operating in South-East Queensland, uses the Community Supported Agriculture approach to forge links between the consumption and production of food through closer relationships between farmers, within a five-hour radius of the city and consumers, who pay farmers in advance for a season of produce.[66]

At the moment, these sorts of activities barely register on the radar of policy and decision makers. In this sense they are shadow networks, with the people engaged holding local knowledge and practices that are currently afforded little external value. However, in different contexts, as in Cuba, these approaches could become central both to engagement processes and to our ways of viewing the natural world. How can we transform community engagement processes for sustainability to afford equal priorities to the knowledge and activities of shadow networks? Governments and industry, in particular, find it challenging to be open to these so-called 'peripheral' views, what our friend Leonie Sandercock calls 'Voices from the Borderlands'.[67] Yet the knowledge and practices expressed by marginal voices may hold the key to the 'kitchen table' common-sense action we need to address sustainability problems.

Recipe 7: A broad range of actions

As community engagement processes identify and give priority to actions for sustainability, we encourage you to cast a wide net, to look beyond the familiar, whether you are a bureaucrat, a developer or a citizen. Planning has historically relied on statutory planning as the 'panacea' action, an approach with serious limitations. There is probably no sustainability problem that can be solved by relying exclusively on one type of action.

The knowledge and practices expressed by marginal voices may hold the key to the 'kitchen table' common-sense action we need to address sustainability problems

In the Great Bear Rainforest example, participants undertook many different actions. A range of actors continue to work for sustainability, with actions such as the following:

- *Community development (including social, cultural and network capital)*: development of a human well-being plan; other ecologically appropriate businesses by First Nations and communities, with financing and infrastructure through fairer distribution of rewards from resource extraction.
- *Capacity strengthening*: retraining of forest workers.
- *Advocacy*: environmental groups building international support for ancient forest-friendly products.
- *Policy statements*: initial commitment to Great Bear Rainforest Agreement by all signatories.
- *Legislative change*: protected areas legislated; new logging rules.
- *New funding arrangements*: to support a local conservation-based economy.
- *Institutional structures*: establishment of an Ecosystem-Based Management Working Group.
- *Knowledge management*: documentation of species

diversity and monitoring achievement of milestones by www.GreatBearWatch.ca.

- *Asset management*: working towards full implementation of an ecosystem-based management approach for the Forest.[68]

While this list is by no means comprehensive, it does offer guidance for those seeking to progress sustainability initiatives.

We must be strategic and identify actions that can provide the most leverage for the problem at hand

One warning is necessary, however. When identifying actions, we must be careful to avoid a scattergun approach. We must be strategic and identify actions that can provide the most leverage for the problem at hand. It's critical to keep things manageable: we must not identify so many actions that we have insufficient space for reflection and learning.

Kitchen table conversation starters

- Which action needs to take place to make your local area sustainable?
- What sorts of actions are already taking place towards local sustainability … by government? … by community? Are there opportunities to work together?
- Who are the 'activists' in your community? How do people feel about them? Are they valued or 'demonized' for their attempts to contribute to sustainability?

What would make it easier for people in your neighbourhood to engage with community action for sustainability?

- What would make it easier for people in your neighbourhood to engage with community action for sustainability?
- What community infrastructure exists locally? How is it used? How could it support creating more sustainability actions?

For more opportunities to continue the conversation about community education for sustainability, please visit www.kitchentablesustainability.com.

Final thoughts

Without action and activism, we cannot achieve sustainability. This chapter has focused on the deeper context within which both occur, as we are committed to supporting a wide spectrum of actions and actors to foster transformative change. None of this work can occur or be effective, however, without the magical ingredient of *trust*. It is the cornerstone of community engagement and especially important in navigating the complex territory of sustainability. In the next chapter, we explore ways in which trusting relationships strengthen community connectivity and networks. And how new ways of working in community will depend on trust. Only when we trust can we open ourselves to the possibilities of creating local and global sustainability through community engagement.

7

TRUST

> ... as we
> move forward with our good
> work on and for the land, let us
> remember: We are all in this together. We
> are all on the same wavelength. We are all
> indivisible in our respect for and connection
> to the earth – reaching out in the gathering
> darkness, fingers spread wide to touch and
> understand our place in the family of things.
>
> Robert Perschel,
> 2002, p160

Remember that terrible meeting in the community hall, when you told us all that bad news about how our whole community was going to be torn down? I couldn't believe it. After 26 years living here, I was being turfed out. But after it was finished, when you came and sat beside me and you held my hand when I was crying ... then I knew that I could trust you.

Muriel, age 75, Sydney resident, 2005

When you came and sat beside me and you held my hand when I was crying ... then I knew that I could trust you

Introduction

We believe that trust is the factor that determines whether community engagement with sustainability succeeds or fails. It's vital to the success of such important projects. Muriel, quoted above, relied on her intuition when Wendy held her hand. Wendy turned out to be trustworthy. Trust means assured reliance on the character, integrity, strength or truth of someone or something. The adage that trust is 'earned by the drop and lost by the bucketful' has direct relevance in community engagement contexts. This chapter offers some stories about hopefulness and breaches of trust.

How does trust relate to kitchen tables? It is about levelling the playing field to foster understanding. When we show up at the table, face-to-face, where we can see and hear each other, each person is as powerful as the other. If we can hear each other's stories, laugh and cry together, we can learn to trust. Trust is also about power. Empowered people can trust others because they trust themselves to meet the challenges that others – and life – might throw at them. They know whom to trust and who is untrustworthy so that they can head off betrayal at the pass. Community engagement with sustainability, done well, creates the effect of the kitchen table. Easy to lose and difficult to regain, trust takes time to develop. And yet we cannot undertake engagement with sustainability without it.

Easy to lose and difficult to regain, trust takes time to develop

Why is trust important in engaging communities and achieving sustainability?

Trust is the basis of all community engagement work. It is central to the *EATING* approach and foundational to all the other *EATING* components because, without trust, we cannot create anything deep, substantial and long-lasting. Trust is subtle and essential, like yeast. Without yeast, bread won't rise. And, just as natural yeast makes for better bread, trust cannot be fabricated. It can't be artificially created. We advocate building long-lasting trust, as opposed to trust simply for the purposes of engaging about a single plan or project.

Hope: A delicate commodity

For people living in extreme conditions of dysfunction, poverty and alienation, hope can be a survival tactic that keeps the prospect of better times alive

Trust often involves hopefulness for a better future and therefore relies on follow-up action. And hope is a valuable and delicate commodity. For people living in extreme conditions of dysfunction, poverty and alienation, hope can be a survival tactic that keeps the prospect of better times alive. It is increasingly important for everyone, as we face the challenges of the planetary crisis. In the face of despair, hope encourages us to continue to engage with the issues and seek solutions. Authors like David Suzuki (*Good News for a Change: Hope for a Troubled Planet*), Jonathan Sacks (*The Politics of Hope*), John Forester ('planning as the organization of hope') and the author of our Foreword, Peter Newman (*Case Studies in Environmental Hope* and *Hope for the Future: The Western Australian State Sustainability Strategy*) describe hope as a rallying point for engaging people in our ongoing sustainability challenges.[1]

As community members engage with sustainability, their hopes for a better future directly relate to their levels of trust

As community members engage with sustainability, their hopes for a better future directly relate to their levels of trust. Discussing contested issues surrounding sustainability, community members need to know that they can trust community engagement people and processes, because they are depending on them.

Trust: A prerequisite for 'dialogue'

Community engagement processes are about communication. As we learned in Chapter 3, different types of communication have the capacity to generate vastly different outcomes. 'Dialogue' is one type of communication where people suspend judgements and listen to what others are saying.[2] This is the arena where generative relationships develop – constructive collaborations where participants can genuinely transcend differences and work together to generate creative innovations and solutions. However, the gap in the continuum between 'conversation' and 'dialogue' can seem like a barrier at times. Bill Isaacs, a leading authority on the theory and practice of dialogue, explains that as 'conversations' move to deliberations where differing worldviews and perspectives are expressed and challenged, people can often feel frustrated.[3] This process gives rise to discussion and debate in which people defend their individual views. To make the transition to 'dialogue', we need to move through the inevitable crisis points and periods of anxiety.

Without the yeast, the bread won't rise. Without trust, we cannot elevate the level of communication from 'discussion' and 'debate' to generative 'dialogue'. Thus trust is an important key to achieving sustainability outcomes through community engagement processes.

> Without trust, we cannot elevate the level of communication from 'discussion' and 'debate' to generative 'dialogue'

Why most community engagement processes with sustainability fail to support trust building

Community engagement processes with sustainability fail to support trust building for many reasons. Like Maisie, whom we met in Chapter 5, some people can feel shy or embarrassed about their lack of knowledge or understanding. Or their communities may have already experienced untrustworthy 'environmental' projects. So-called 'consultation' processes may not have been transparent, accessible or inclusive, as the folk of Eagleby point out in

We are often dealing with material that people do not understand and many fear deception and betrayal

Chapter 10. Poor-quality or inappropriate processes, a diversity of interests and activities negotiated by different bodies remote from communities can exclude some people.

Community engagement with sustainability raises additional problems for trust. We are often dealing with material that people do not understand and many fear deception and betrayal. Further, some people still choose to deny the realities of peak oil, climate change and environmental problems. There is a lack of trust in information provided in the media and by 'experts'. Some prefer to trust NGOs or community groups, rather than government or industry. Some have an instinctive trust in organizations working for social and environmental justice because they see them as less secretive and more worthy of their trust.

When the environmental issues discussed extend beyond the 'local', community members often comment that their trust has been broken by the major players on the global playing field. Many, including well informed activists, believe that governments collude to keep accurate information from reaching the general public. Some players, with primary responsibilities to shareholders and boards of directors at *board* tables, rather than *kitchen* tables, engage in explicit campaigns of misinformation about global environmental issues. Shocking misinformation campaigns like the 'Great Global Warming Swindle' aimed at discrediting NGOs (such as Greenpeace and the Sea Shepherd) result in further confusion and loss of public trust. In that so-called 'documentary', documentary-maker Martin Durkin presented arguments of scientists and commentators who do not believe that CO_2 produced by human activity is the main cause of climate change.[4] Activist and community artist Graeme Dunstan argues that because *betrayal* of trust has often been on the agenda in the past in community engagement processes, the deeper issue that needs to be healed is the *expectation* of betrayal. He argues in favour of 'sustainable resistance' in such situations.[5]

Because *betrayal* of trust has often been on the agenda in the past in community engagement processes, the deeper issue that needs to be healed is the *expectation* of betrayal

At the end of this chapter we provide many recipes for addressing both the *expectation* of betrayal and providing the foundation for authentic trust-building processes. But first, we offer a summary of some of the ways that trust-breaking occurs in community engagement processes with sustainability.

Promising and not delivering

In a small, remote Queensland community, using a creative visioning process, Wendy and Yollana helped local service providers develop a functional architectural brief for an expanded facility to accommodate 12 separate community services. Unfortunately, the brief did not extend to supervising the final architectural brief or helping the workers negotiate with the architects. While Wendy and Yollana felt they had done an excellent job, anecdotal evidence revealed that the community members were bitterly disappointed with the outcome, feeling that their dreams had not been realized. The community members felt betrayed. Wendy and Yollana were heartbroken.

Inaccurate reporting

In another example, the trust issue related to the public record of a community SpeakOut in a conflict-ridden inner Sydney suburb. Wendy and colleague Sophia van Ruth were overly conscientious in reporting, being careful not to 'mess with the record'. The report appendices upset one highly committed local resident, who was identified by this statement by a participant: 'Bill is a wanker'. There was only one 'Bill' (we've used a pseudonym here) participating in our community events and he was a high-profile player. Our heartfelt apology was accompanied by a comment that at least this demonstrated that we did not alter the workshop transcripts. Bill apologized months later and more or less admitted that he had been acting as the SpeakOut participant described.

'Messing with the butchers' paper'

Another example of inaccurate reporting occurred at the Australia 2020 Summit described in the previous chapter. The most obvious weakness was 'messing with the butchers' paper' or changing the record without the permission or knowledge of participants. This led to a major breakdown of trust, with some participants (who were initially enthusiastic) feeling 'very cross'.

Withholding support

In the 1980s, when Wendy was working as a consultant for the New South Wales Housing Commission in Alexandria, Sydney, she sought the assistance of the powerful local community develop-ment organization in planning the first community workshop. Explaining that they respected her but did not trust her client (the Commission) because of insensitive and heavy-handed tactics used with the local community in the past, the organization withheld their support until Wendy held the first workshop – their bellwether of the Commission's good faith.[6] Following a successful workshop, a much more trusting and collaborative working relationship was possible between the consultants and the community organization. They did not change their opinion of the Commission, but they did assist Wendy and her colleagues in their efforts to deliver a fair and open engagement process.

Blaming the wrong people

Often in community engagement contexts, the very fact that one is a consultant can create mistrust. In a project with a somewhat ironical outcome, Wendy and Karl (assisted by community activist Kevin McMillan) were working in a small village in southern New South Wales to help the local community decide among several housing development options proposed by a private developer. The community did not trust the consultants because the developer was paying the fee (which, incidentally, he never did pay). The community leaders vehemently resisted help and effectively sabotaged their best interests. Unable to earn their trust, the consultants were unable to protect their village from inappropriate development.

Lack of transparency

Personal and group agendas (or at least the perception of agendas) mean that community people generally operate from their own value bases, advocating changes they believe to be appropriate. Event organizers and decision makers may believe otherwise. When we do not attempt to identify and reconcile these differences in explicit processes, conflicts can arise with the potential to generate mistrust. Further, many community processes are far from transparent, outcomes are rarely binding and specific actions aren't always an outcome. While all of these trust-busting activities are difficult for most participants or would-be participants, they are particularly distressing to low-income people, who may be victims of unfair welfare practices. They are already likely to expect betrayal.

Withholding information

Proponents often do not trust community engagement practitioners or the communities they work with and may keep them in the dark, withholding critical information. When Karl first began working with Wendy in Perth in 1993, he was appalled, as a former union organizer, at the many excuses proponents used for withholding information. And he was equally appalled by the negative effects this had on community trust. Proponents often miss the point that building trust is a major component of any community engagement activity. Fast-tracking (or intolerable delays) are often accompanied by limiting access to information, with 'commercial-in-confidence' used as an excuse. Rarely have we found authentic commercial reasons to withhold information from communities. The results are invariably fractured relationships and bitter disappointment.

> **Unable to earn their trust, the consultants were unable to protect their village from inappropriate development**

> **Fast-tracking (or intolerable delays) are often accompanied by limiting access to information, with 'commercial-in-confidence' used as an excuse**

Lack of a heart space

We now know a great deal about how activists experience burnout working for environmental causes at the community level.[7] Their problems are exacerbated by a lack of a 'heart' space – a safe space where they can express what they are feeling – within families and households. This is reflected in how people engage more broadly. Activists often feel uneasy about revealing their emotional states or trusting others to reveal deep feelings or their dreams of community and sustainability. Further, a lack of coordination and strategic organizing among activists sometimes means that they work at cross-purposes. Thus, a cycle of mistrust evolves: as proponents lose trust in the community, the community loses trust in the activists. Sometimes planners and consultants are caught in the middle.

Thus, a cycle of mistrust evolves: as proponents lose trust in the community, the community loses trust in the activists

Absence of 'soft skills'

The humble community planner often lacks the skills, confidence or influence to convey community sentiments to the right people (that is, those in power). Planners, often the ones conducting engagement processes, receive little or no training in community engagement and almost certainly no formal opportunities to develop emotional intelligence or the soft skills of community engagement. Government planners probably will not receive professional debriefing regarding the outcomes of processes, especially in terms of their emotional content and impacts.[8] It can be seen as a sign of weakness to 'wear your heart on your sleeve' or 'let them (community members) get to you'.

It can be seen as a sign of weakness to 'wear your heart on your sleeve' or 'let them (community members) get to you'

Wendy's research into the intelligences and learning styles of planners revealed that many believe their work has nothing to do with emotions and relationships.[9] Emotional intelligence is rarely on the workplace agenda. Planning education and workplaces reinforce rationality, objectivity and detachment. It's not surprising that planners may lack trust and be unable to communicate their own trustworthiness to others. Further, planners are rarely lauded for building trust and relationships within communities. While we see some evidence of a shift to embrace more enlightened approaches, the changes are still not widespread. For example, planning education lags behind in teaching emotional intelligence and some high-profile planning schools still have no dedicated courses to teach community engagement skills. We suspect that this applies to other sustainability professionals as well.

Short-term thinking

To complicate an already sorry tale, community engagement is usually handled on a project-by-project basis, rather than by building ongoing relationships with community members and organizations. We've lost count of the times we have been told that the municipality has no list of community organizations, that the planner who just resigned took all the files, that there is no record of previous processes and no community engagement policy. The ubiquitous short-term thinking problem is compounded as government employees and elected members (particularly in municipalities) work to the deadline of their term in office, rather than building longer term relationships of trust.

Trust: An essential ingredient in (and outcome of) building social capital

Social capital is widely regarded as the most critical component of social sustainability. Nick Wates, a prominent community engagement theorist and author of two books in this Earthscan suite, refers to social capital as the 'ability of social structures and institutions to provide a supportive framework for individuals; includes firms, trade unions, families, communities, voluntary organisations, legal/political systems, educational institutions, health services, financial institutions and systems of property rights'.[10] The United States Centers for Disease Control and Prevention has another helpful definition: '...the individual and communal time and energy that is available

> We've lost count of the times we have been told that the municipality has no list of community organizations, that the planner who just resigned took all the files, that there is no record of previous processes and no community engagement policy

for such things as community improvement, social networking, civic engagement, personal recreation, and other activities that create social bonds between individuals and groups'.[11] This type of capital also includes our decision-making processes, access to and conduct of governance and how we implement policies for our own management. In this context, we need to envisage what sustainability might look like and how it could be implemented, as well as how we could collaborate to implement such strategies. The quality of our collaboration in communities will rely solely upon levels of social capital.

We need social capital development 'because changes of the magnitude necessary for sustainable development require collective mobilization of people in communities worldwide'.[12] Social capital emerges from interactions and resulting relationships among people. It is a property of groups rather than of individuals.[13] For our purposes, social capital is about more than merely building community on a broad scale. It involves building interpersonal connections among people within communities. It can be both inclusive and exclusive and takes several forms, which we describe briefly below.

The challenge for community engagement is to facilitate the growth of these networks and to create contexts for people to connect and develop relationships

The challenge for community engagement is to facilitate the growth of these networks and to create contexts for people to connect and develop relationships. Social sustainability is about people's contributions to local and regional projects and, on a broader scale, about meeting, developing ongoing relationships and collaborating to develop community responses to sustainability challenges.

Bonding is a form of social capital that describes exclusive relationships formed between close-knit groups of people. *Bridging* social capital refers to the links among such small groups, while the third type, *linking*, connects these interlinked small groups to the wider community, as well as to other communities.[14] Linking social capital is characterized by an initial focus on accepting difference and a move to inclusion from which trust arises. Social capital is a constantly evolving and devolving process of community integration and relationship forming. It's important that communities, supported by community engagement, move beyond *bonding* and *bridging* to *linking* with the wider world.[15] An essential ingredient for supporting this transition is diversity. In diverse communities, we are constantly confronted by new ideas and approaches that can transform how we relate to and manage our communities. Trust and reciprocity must underpin the growth of social capital. We know this and the experts agree.[16]

In diverse communities, we are constantly confronted by new ideas and approaches that can transform how we relate to and manage our communities

Recipes for trust: Approaches that work

Despite the sad stories and challenges chronicled above, we *have* experimented with approaches for building trust that *can* be applied to community engagement with sustainability. We provide some recipes below.

Recipe 1: Starting out the way you want to end up

First impressions are important. People make judgements about other people based on a few seconds' perception of them. When engagement processes begin with a commitment to open discussion of sustainability issues and the inclusion of all voices, they establish the foundations for building people's trust from the start. On the other hand, it's easy to form a negative initial impression. A high standard at the start helps everyone to respect the issues being discussed.

It's dangerous to ignore first impressions. Early in a contentious project, Wendy received the following memo from Steph:

It's dangerous to ignore first impressions

> *Wendy: I've just had another bizarre visit from Daryl, our developer client. This time he handed me $3000 in a brown envelope. Karl told me that's the second time this has happened. Same brown envelope the last time, too. And the same amount. It's nowhere near what he owes us. What should we do? I'm feeling very uncomfortable about this.*

This project was dear to our hearts because of its strong sustainability underpinnings: it was to be a high-density, innovative, transit-oriented development inside a new town centre in a suburban community. It had encouraging green credentials; some of Australia's most competent sustainability and design professionals were working on it. Nevertheless, the local municipality withdrew their support because they distrusted the developer. The developer went bankrupt, the community felt betrayed and we felt sad that we had wasted community members' time (as well as our own).

Recipe 2: Demystifying the professional

Heather, an Eagleby resident, worked with Wendy in a community renewal process in her neighbourhood for several months before she found it in her heart to address Wendy about a personal matter. 'Wendy', she said, 'I've only known you for a short time but I have to tell you this. You must stop wearing that terrible purple dress. It makes you look like the mother of the bride.' Slowly, Heather (now a close friend) came to see the unusual 'Dr Wendy' merely as a person with her own foibles and (apparently) appalling dress sense. It was during a community workshop in another community, where Heather was facilitating, that she offered her advice. For Wendy, it was a sign that Heather trusted her enough to make such a comment. (Wendy took the purple dress to a charity shop the following day.)

It's important to be open to feedback (regardless of its validity or the eloquence with which it is phrased) and encourage further constructive and negative feedback

In our experience, initially, the professional 'expert' will often be seen as the leader of a community group. It is essential, therefore, that early in the life of the group, people are given an opportunity to challenge the expert role so that the group can progress to a more collaborative and cohesive stage. It is also important that professionals react positively to such a challenge. It's important to be open to feedback (regardless of its validity or the eloquence with which it is phrased) and encourage further constructive and negative feedback.

Recipe 3: Taking the community's pulse: The Energy Wheel

The field of neurolinguistic programming emphasizes the import-ance of visual, auditory, kinaesthetic, verbal and energetic rapport to facilitate productive communication. Before any engagement process begins, leaders and advocates need a solid understanding of the community and its dynamics. If not, our efforts may not be well received. At worst, we can create fragile relationships not based in trust and put future engagement prospects at risk. We need to understand the general group or community characteris-tics, energy and morale so that we can build rapport and communi-cate effectively. Rapport facilitates communication, communication engenders understanding, and understanding promotes trust. The Energy Wheel, shown in Figure 7.1, helps us understand where a community is *at a feeling level*, so that we can meet them there for, as others have noted, 'true rapport creates an atmosphere of mutual confidence and trust'.[17]

Rapport facilitates communication, communication engenders understanding, and understanding promotes trust

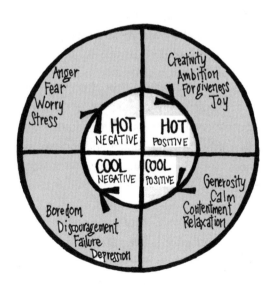

Figure 7.1 The Energy Wheel
Source: Richmond (1999, p22)

The Energy Wheel is a simple but elegant diagnostic tool that Wendy, Yollana and Steph use to support their engagement work with communities. It defines four types of emotional states: *hot negative, hot positive, cool positive* and *cool negative*. When we encounter communities, we always find that they are located somewhere within this circle.[18]

To give an example, 'cool negative', often present in communities with an expectation of betrayal, can sometimes come across as disengaged apathy. In *Psychology for Peace Activists*, David Adams explains that apathy is born of fear, which can be paralysing. Fear is an impediment to engagement and definitely no good for sustainability.[19] Anger, on the other hand, is active: it can play an important role in motivating people to engage. As we come to understand these relationships, we can design engagement processes to help transform apathy into anger (cool negative to hot negative)

From a place of creativity and joy, a community may move into contentment and calm

and anger into creativity (hot negative to hot positive). From a place of creativity and joy, a community may move into contentment and calm (hot positive to cool positive). Using the Energy Wheel, we can help communities make changes more easily. We have found that this is far more effective than attempting to 'shift them' from apathy to calm in one step.

Wendy experienced this natural flow of energy when she worked with the local community on the *Stories in a Park* project in Eagleby, Queensland (see Chapter 8 for a further description). The consultants challenged and supported residents as they moved though those four stages, For example, Lynn, a longtime resident, explained:

> *People seemed to think that Eagleby residents were a hopeless bunch of no-gooders and we would be tarnished by saying we lived here. This was just another Housing Commission area where people (single mums mostly and unemployed) who didn't fit elsewhere ended up.*[20]

And Peter, another resident, explained how things had changed in Eagleby:

> *This time around it was different... The community actually had their say and the bureaucrats had to listen, not to tell them what they are going to do. And ... people who went to all these community consultation processes were actually realizing ... I can tell them what I want and then they say, 'Here's a bundle of money. Now you need to prioritize what you want first.' And these people actually sat together and talked about it.*

After nearly a year of work, the community held a dramatic cele-bration to 'light a fire' under a huge cardboard representation of Eagleby's negative self-perceptions or 'stigma'. The stigma engulfed in flames is shown in Figure 7.2.

Figure 7.2 The Eagleby stigma on fire, 2000

Recipe 4: Taking enough time

The Eagleby community engagement processes reveal that *building trust takes time*. Wendy did not weave any magic in Eagleby. But Wendy and her colleagues, including husband Karl and activist-artist Graeme Dunstan, spent long hours listening closely to local people's stories. As Graeme explained, in telling Stories in a Park, a new story had to be created about Eagleby's parks and to do that someone had to listen respectfully to all the bad old stories.

Graeme and Karl devised a creative way to refashion some of the inaccurate and disparaging stories about Eagleby's parks by 'occupying' a large, central park. They camped in Cec Clarke Park for three weeks, Graeme in his van and Karl (an unpaid volunteer) in his hatchback. There they worked in two shipping containers during the day helping local people, especially primary school students, who came with their teachers, to make lanterns and cardboard art for the forthcoming community celebration. But, equally important, they listened and demonstrated trustworthiness by their continued presence.[21]

Inclusion was made possible by the earlier Reconnecting Ceremony (described in Chapter 8, Inclusion) and Graeme's trust-building

Figure 7.3 Artist, storyteller and activist, Graeme Dunstan, Eagleby Celebration Day, 2000

activities over several months. Further, the two campers discovered that the drug and alcohol abuse that supposedly characterized the park after dark was merely an urban myth. Later, during the Celebration, the community 'took back the park' (not from crime but from fear) at sunset with an emotional lantern-lit children's' parade into the centre of the park. Many of the most powerful components of this process were able to emerge only because of the time commitment by the consultants, the client group and the community.

Many of the most powerful components of this process were able to emerge only because of the time commitment by the consultants, the client group and the community

Recipe 5: Being generous

Graeme's approach could be described as 'non-instrumental'. He could not predict the outcome of his listening, sharing and open-hearted 'occupation'. Trained as an engineer and high school teacher, he provided educational opportunities so that local people could understand the project without the project being 'sold' to them. We have found that there is no substitute – from a trust-building perspective – for gestures of generosity and dedication. So, when local people needed to understand Crime Prevention through Environmental Design (CPTED) to assess the safety of their parks, Wendy and Melbourne-based planner Andrea Cook conducted a free CPTED workshop for them.

We must emphasize that there are always limits to time, money and generosity. As we were working to a set budget, our generosity could have been seen as totally impractical. But we fell in love with the Eagleby community. And we were eager to demonstrate to them that they could trust us. They let us into their hearts. It was a truly humbling experience. It always is – when we allow ourselves to understand someone and find we can trust them. Even an 'unreliable' person, once known, can be trusted to be unreliable. Trust is very much a matter of conforming to expectations. When you truly trust, you can't help but love. Trusting is a heart-opening experience. It transcends the physical, practical, pragmatic side of community engagement. It is something you can't see, touch or hear. And it transforms everything.

There is no substitute for clear and reliable information in building community trust in engagement processes

Recipe 6: Sharing information openly and transparently

There is no substitute for clear and reliable information in building community trust in engagement processes. Using trustworthy sources and inviting NGOs and activists to share information and data build trust. Involving trustworthy academics in action research projects can also be an effective approach. Developing sustainability indicators can also nurture trust. Framing a project by clarifying what is on the table and what is not is critical to enabling trust. The scope of any community engagement process must be clarified and clearly communicated from the beginning. The International Association for Public Participation (IAP2) 'Promise to the Public', introduced in Chapter 3, should be appropriate to the level of predicted community impact and the promise should be honoured.

Contrary to a popular view in government and private enterprise, we do not need a final plan before speaking with the community. Often, as in the Alexandria case discussed in Chapter 3, it's wise to approach a community and ask for advice, rather than flourishing what appears to be the 'final plan'.[22] In the Alexandria case, the 'plan' presented at the first public meeting was a huge drawing of a blank site that filled an entire wall. Then appropriate questions could be asked for such an initial stage: 'What could happen here?' If we do not do that, 'consultation' is easily, and often rightfully, seen as a manipulative, symbolic gesture.

How information is presented can nurture or shatter trust. If a proposal or plan *is* available, it is critical that more than one option be presented, to communicate a desire to explore alternatives rather than 'selling' one preferred option. Most communities are wise to what Wendy calls 'the dead duck option'. It's important to have more than one viable option to select from. Where a plan is far from complete, it's good to be clear about that, too. Conveying the true status of a plan builds trust and encourages further engagement.

Recipe 7: Building ongoing relationships beyond a project-by-project approach

We spoke above about the importance of strengthening social capital as part of community engagement processes. Because of the complexity of many sustainability initiatives, communities are likely to regard short-term approaches to community engagement with distrust. A relationship-building approach means that all players are searching for sustainable solutions for the long term. This requires the direct involvement of senior managers, such as our colleague Kelvin Walsh, shown in the photograph below, so that they can carry back to their organizations not only information gathered in engagement processes, but also requests for adequate

Because of the complexity of many sustainability initiatives, communities are likely to regard short-term approaches to community engagement with distrust

Figure 7.4 Kelvin Walsh listening to community feedback, SpeakOut, Footscray, Maribyrnong, Melbourne, 2004

funding and other feedback. The woman shown in the photograph below is good-naturedly 'getting stuck into' Kelvin, as Australians say. Importantly, he's listening attentively.

Providing financial and other resources to community organizations is another trust-building activity that helps them collaborate and contribute effectively. One approach is to establish a community trust and a community trust fund to go with it. More than a play on words, this 'trust' structure supports the transfer, sharing and management of community assets such as knowledge, insight, resources and practices. It can also be a pool of funds managed by the community to implement projects, engagement, training, community development, capacity strengthening and administration. This *coproduction* model demonstrates commitment by proponents, as it specifies that they have a say in how resources are allocated and money spent.[23] Trust can be greatly enhanced when those in charge not only allocate funding to community engagement but also engage the community directly in decisions about the specifics of resource allocation.

Trust can be greatly enhanced when those in charge not only allocate funding to community engagement but also engage the community directly in decisions about the specifics of resource allocation

Recipe 8: Working with community facilitators, recorders and researchers

Working with community researchers, facilitators and recorders has been a hallmark of our practice for many years, beginning in 1999 with the establishment of the Flying Eagle Facilitators in south-east Queensland. We have chronicled the success of this group in other publications.[24] When we worked with the Flying Eagles in other communities, participants repeatedly reported that facilitators who understood their problems because they were 'community people' and not outside 'experts' helped to build trust. They seemed to relate better to them than to the more 'polished' professional facilitators from middle-class backgrounds.

Recipe 9: Embracing cultural diversity

Involving representatives of the whole community can build confidence that we are genuinely interested in listening to a wide variety of community views. Connecting people from different backgrounds and ages helps build trust among them and shows that we do not need to give priority to one dominant voice or seek to control the discourse in any way. Focusing on intergenerational outcomes demonstrates commitment to the future and confirms that children and young people are citizens – and are trustworthy sources.

We can build trust by encouraging expressions of people's core issues in safe environments. Sometime these can relate to a deeply held fear or trauma. Near the end of a powerful community visioning workshop in Bonnyrigg, Sydney, in 2005, the large speakers attached to the public address system blew loudly. It sounded like a drive-by shooting (unknown in this community but not out of the question). While everyone reacted differently, many members of the refugee communities hit the floor. Immediately after, all the older Vietnamese women left the workshop. They sent a message back that they were intending to leave in any case and that we should not worry because they were already fully involved in the community engagement process. We guessed that they had been re-traumatized. We felt grateful that they trusted us that their departure would not be misunderstood and that they would be welcomed in the next processes. And they were.

A similar issue arose with the Khmer refugees in the same community. In that case, explained in Chapter 8, Inclusion, as we were building trusting relationships and focusing on listening, we were able to uncover (and subsequently address) the rumour that the Khmer people believed they would not be rehoused if they did not attend all meetings.

> Connecting people from different backgrounds and ages helps build trust among them and shows that we do not need to give priority to one dominant voice or seek to control the discourse in any way

Recipe 10: Using self-disclosure and demonstrating a sense of humour

Also in Chapter 8, we meet Kevin McMillan, a local activist who used the term 'the latte set' to describe those people who work in communities but relate poorly to them and do little to engender trust. This is a common problem. Wendy and Kevin developed a workshop presentation for a community-strengthening workshop in Melbourne in August 2002, involving an ancient ritual called 'The Stone Ritual'. The idea was that senior bureaucrats at the community-based conference would engage in this ritual in front of the participants as a way of showing that, even though they might be considered members of 'the Latte Set', they had feelings, were aware of the exclusionary potential of their roles and were willing to relax and have a little fun.

Sophia van Ruth, with many years' community engagement experience, has uplifted many a tense community workshop with her skilled and lighthearted laughter-based icebreakers

Our colleague and friend Sophia van Ruth, with many years' community engagement experience, has uplifted many a tense community workshop with her skilled and lighthearted laughter-based icebreakers, as we illustrate in Chapter 9, Nourishment.[25]

We describe a powerful example of the power of self-disclosure in Chapter 9 in the story about the Great Bear Rainforest. There we relate how environmental activists with a Buddhist background brought the approach of 'owning their shadow' to highly charged negotiations with forestry industry, government, First Nations people and scientists. Researchers evaluating the project concluded that this single act played a major role in allowing diverse interests to develop collaborative – and hopefully sustainable – solutions.[26]

Recipe 11: Helping people strengthen their trust in themselves

Although she demonstrated natural confidence, Eagleby resident Heather was not always confident about community engagement. When she began working with Wendy as a founding member of the Flying Eagle Facilitators, Heather lacked experience in community engagement. However, as a single mother of a profoundly disabled daughter, she did have lots of experience with bureaucracies. Working with Wendy's facilitation team, Heather came to trust her own judgement about community engagement processes. Wendy remembers one remarkable telephone conversation in 2000 that went something like this:

Heather: 'Hey, Wendy, I've just attended one of those disability services forums – you know, the ones I have to go to because of Naomi.

Wendy: Okay, how was it?

Heather: It was a nightmare, Wendy. An absolute nightmare. I'm so upset. I'm in the middle of writing a letter of complaint right now but I just had to ring you. You wouldn't have believed it. There was no agenda. There were no recorders. Nobody seemed to be taking notes. Honestly.

And when I asked them, do you know, nobody could tell me what they were going to do with the information that all of us – all us parents of disabled kids – were giving them. They had no plan for sending us the report. No plan. And do you know, they didn't even record on vertical surfaces with those big pens for everyone to see? I told them that *we* would never do that.

I think they were very surprised to hear me say all those things. Not that I'd been a mouse or anything before. But yesterday, honestly, Wendy, I just *knew* what was the right thing to do and they weren't doing it!

This story reveals how quickly Heather transferred the learning from community renewal processes to another aspect of her life and strengthened her capacity as a community member.

Recipe 12: Following through with collaborative action, evaluation, review and feedback

It goes without saying that inclusive processes that build trust need to demonstrate trust *throughout* the process It goes without saying that inclusive processes that build trust need to demonstrate trust *throughout* the process. This is particularly important as the end of the project nears and the final report is being prepared. And unfortunately, in our experience, this is where things often fall apart. In the case of the Eagleby project, Stories in a Park, with the funding exhausted and the loss of two critical project managers, we had to organize our own debriefing session and write the final report. We involved as many participants as we could in a hard-hitting debriefing workshop and all were given the opportunity to review the final report. Later, community volunteers, assisted by Wendy and Karl, prepared a video documenting the process. Community involvement in developing assessment criteria, using action research methods and formative, as well as summative, evaluation approaches can reinforce trust and establish a firm foundation for future engagement processes.

Kitchen table conversation starters

- What are our experiences of trust and betrayal in relation to community engagement and sustainability?
- Is there an 'expectation of betrayal' in your community? How does it show up?
- Community relationships are strengthened by trust. If we were to draw a 'trust map' of our community, where are the lines of trust already established? Where are they broken?
- Are there any 'neutral' relationships in our community trust map that lend themselves to strengthening through trust building activities like listening, understanding, or generosity?

For more opportunities to continue the conversation about community education with sustainability, please visit www.kitchentablesustainability.com.

Final thoughts

What is the outcome of trust building in community engagement with sustainability? At the risk of sounding tautological, it's trust. This is because, as the bread-making metaphor suggests, without yeast and time, the bread of community engagement cannot rise. Without the foundation of trust, all our efforts to achieve education, action, inclusion, nourishment and governance fall short. In the next chapter, Inclusion, we look at who might be sitting at our kitchen tables – and all other tables where sustainability issues are being discussed. And we explore ways in which inclusion can strengthen community engagement with sustainability.

Without the foundation of trust, all our efforts to achieve education, action, inclusion, nourishment and governance fall short

8

INCLUSION

Just as
biodiversity is an essential
component of ecological sustainability,
so is cultural diversity essential to social
sustainability. Diverse values should not be
respected just because we are tolerant folk,
but because we must have a pool of diverse
perspectives in order to survive, to adapt to
changing conditions, to embrace the future'.

Jon Hawkes,
2001, p14

Out beyond ideas of wrongdoing and rightdoing,
There is a field. I'll meet you there.

When the soul lies down in that grass,
The world is too full to talk about.
Ideas, language, even the phrase each other
Doesn't make any sense.

Rumi[1]

The year was 1998. I noticed the middle-aged woman sitting in the front row in the small, shabby room. As our meeting was in an Aboriginal community, I wondered if she were Aboriginal. I couldn't tell. She looked strong. Sophia and I had just got the meeting underway, working with the local community, trying to define a set of principles to guide the development of a derelict factory into a space for community use. We were holding this workshop after several months of consultation in the Redfern community – trying to negotiate agreement about community uses for the site. John, the landscape architect, was keeping an eye on things, as meetings were often stormy in Redfern.

Our job was not to consult with Aboriginal people, as Kevin, an Aboriginal architect, was handling that as a separate task and we were coordinating our efforts.

Many local Aboriginal people and their advocates wanted to redevelop the building for services for Aboriginal people and others. The local residents' group said they wanted a park – but there was suspicion that that was not really what they wanted. They didn't want facilities for Aboriginal people on the site because, they said, they didn't feel that it was appropriate for public space to be used for facilities specifically for Aboriginal people, as they were only one sector of the community. I doubted their motives. I felt that they just wanted to protect their property values. The real estate agents were on their side. Anyway, there were strongly polarized views in Redfern in 1998.

To break the impasse, in a workshop that was just beginning, about 40 of us were focusing on principles, rather than individual or group positions. I thought some

Anyway, there were strongly polarized views in Redfern in 1998

Continued

> As I was completing my introduction, I noticed tears streaming down the cheeks of the strong-looking woman sitting at the front, just to my left

assessment criteria might make it easier to assess the plans later on. I was facilitating the meeting. As I was completing my introduction, I noticed tears streaming down the cheeks of the strong-looking woman sitting at the front, just to my left. She stood and faced me.

'How dare you! Do you imagine that you can make up for 200 years of suffering, annihilation and the destruction of our culture, in one workshop?' she cried.

I stood breathless.

What to say?

The dingy room shuddered with sadness.

Finally, I found some words.

'Sister', I whispered. 'I would never expect to make good such terrible wrongs in such a short time, in our process here. I cannot begin to understand the depths of suffering you and your people have endured.'

I drew breath and steadied myself.

Then more words came out:

> My experience is that when people of goodwill come together to try to sort out a difficult problem, sometimes – only sometimes – their desire for healing is so strong that people do come to an agreement

And I have also experienced something here in Redfern what has happened in other places. My experience is that when people of goodwill come together to try to sort out a difficult problem, sometimes – only sometimes – their desire for healing is so strong that people do come to an agreement. Something magically seems to shift; you can feel it in the room. I've seen that in meetings here in Redfern maybe ten years ago, when I was working for the Aboriginal Housing Company. In my experience, the urge to heal can be very strong – stronger than the need to keep on arguing. I'm hoping that might happen here. That's all.

I held out my hand. I didn't know why. I called her sister. I didn't know why.

The sobbing woman gathered up her belongings and quietly left the room. When she reached the door, she turned. Our eyes met. I saw something different in her

Continued

face. Perhaps it was nothing more than an acknowledgement that I had spoken my truth in this painful and highly charged situation. What I saw was not hatred or disdain. Something travelled across the space between us.

The woman left the room.

Shaking, I resumed my introduction. We held the workshop. The participants developed the criteria.

Six years later, a community centre was opened on that site. A compromise design: half park and half restored building. We were all crying when the doors opened and people flooded in.

After the official opening festivities, I was talking with some of the Aboriginal participants and the conversation turned to that workshop years before. They'd heard what happened.

'You did well', they said. 'Did you know who she was?'

I said I didn't but guessed she was powerful.

'She's a local storyteller', they said. 'A very influential person in our community. That was a tight spot you were in. You did well to tell her *your* story.'

> We were all crying when the doors opened and people flooded in

Introduction

In this chapter, we explore how the principle of inclusion in community engagement is instrumental to achieving sustainability. Inclusion has a strong theoretical foundation in political science and community engagement theory. And as Western communities become more diverse and complex, the practical relevance of inclusion is highlighted. It encompasses issues of cultural and linguistic diversity in today's intercultural cities. It has been a hallmark of our professional practice for many years. If we fail to be inclusive, we risk the derailment of sustainability outcomes. However, being truly inclusive may not be as easy as it seems. In this chapter we:

> If we fail to be inclusive, we risk the derailment of sustainability outcomes

- explain why inclusion is important in community engagement for sustainability
- share anecdotes of inclusive and non-inclusive community engagement practice
- offer recipes and ingredients for an inclusionary model of community engagement.

Inclusion is essential in community engagement with sustainability, to ensure that *decisions that affect all are not made by only some.*

Why inclusion is important in community engagement with sustainability

The reason we are so concerned about inclusion in this book is that most community engagement processes are so shallow that they offer few opportunities to address the challenging issues related to sustainability. Community engagement to achieve sustainability will be effective only if everyone is involved, as we all have a stake in the future of the Earth and its life. Further, inclusionary processes will be most effective when everyone is educated about sustainability and understands its dimensions. A central reason for inclusion is that we have difficult problems to address and so will need all hands on deck if we are to achieve ownership of decisions and outcomes. People need to feel a sense of agency in shaping their future, especially as global ecological and social circumstances deteriorate.

In current engagement processes, we often see non-inclusive approaches. For example, we have seen: exclusive reliance on identified stakeholders; advocates speaking on behalf of children and people from diverse backgrounds; culturally offensive processes (such as the Australia 2020 Summit, convened on Passover weekend); gender and power issues generally ignored; and little attention to what the experience of the community has been and what their energetic 'state' might be (see Chapter 7, Trust).

Inclusionary processes will be most effective when everyone is educated about sustainability and understands its dimensions

The need for a broader definition of who is an expert?

In this book, we focus on community engagement to counter the risk of making decisions about sustainability by relying exclusively on experts. Those people may have limited perspectives and may not be representative of the wider community. Further, those who are excluded may be unlikely to embrace the advice and recommendations of the selected people (particularly if they do not align with their values and desires or if the recommendations involve restraint or self-sacrifice).

Cathy remembers the framing statement Australian-based community engagement practitioner Penny Coombes used to start many community workshops: 'Each and every one of you here today is an expert in your own life. It is that expertise we are interested in today.'[2] Unfortunately, many community engagement processes don't treat community knowledge in that way.

As we explained in Chapter 2, while scientific, technical and professional experts have much to offer community engagement with sustainability, they can tend to constrain the debate to what is known (by them) and exclude opinions not based on research (such as emotional and intuitive understandings, for example).[3] They often undervalue local knowledge, preferring opinions that don't challenge the status quo. Some cling to their status-based 'power', but fail to recognize the power of facilitating education and empowerment of others. When conveners of community engagement processes declare the costs of participatory approaches as major barriers to implementation, we often believe that they misunderstand the benefits of engagement – and the costs of non-inclusion. While specialized or technical knowledge is important in achieving sustainability, landscape architect and academic Randy Hester warns against what he calls 'exclusionary professionalism':

When conveners of community engagement processes declare the costs of participatory approaches as major barriers to implementation, we often believe that they misunderstand the benefits of engagement – and the costs of non-inclusion

> *Some designers argue that citizens are capable of setting goals and stating their wants but that the technical analysis*

*and form making should be left to professionals. This is
nonsense. Such exclusionary professionalism undermines
the most impelling aspects of ecological democracy... There
should be a place at the table for everyone. This requires a
diversity of table settings.*[4]

**We need
scientists,
technicians and
people who
know things
that others may
not. However,
what needs to
change is the
'trump value' of
this knowledge
over other
forms**

We need scientists, technicians and people who know things that others may not. However, what needs to change is the 'trump value' of this knowledge over other forms.

British planning theorist Patsy Healey calls the systematic reliance on technical experts to address issues like sustainability *instrumental rationality*. We've seen this in our practice: technical 'experts' undertake analytical and evaluative work in their offices, relying on scientific or technological approaches. They separate discussion of 'facts' from discussion of 'values', which encourages a separation of the activity of technical analysis (the province of experts) from that of setting values (seen as the province of politicians representing the 'public interest').[5] We are left asking, what is the province of the community? And of sustainability?

Jane Jacobs' remarkable *Death and Life of Great American Cities* (1961) provided classic descriptions of community life in Greenwich Village and argued that communities themselves needed to take responsibility for their children, their streets, their safety and their futures. As the need for sustainability increases, localization and community-based solutions become even more important. Community engagement processes can support these solutions,

**Communities,
themselves,
have the
capacity
to identify
solutions and
act on them**

not only by being inclusive with respect to who is involved, but also by *expanding the range of decisions* in which communities can be involved. Communities, themselves, have the capacity to identify solutions and act on them. Landscape architect, participatory design specialist and academic Randy Hester sees these as matters of *fairness* and asks further:

Who has information? Who does or does not understand and have access to local government agencies? Who typically participates in the design process, and who doesn't? Who lacks power to influence decisions that affect locality?[6]

Avoiding 'othering': Learning to 'listen across difference'

In our modern communities, diversity is the reality and our task is to take on, truly face, manage and embrace that reality in community engagement. In Canada and Australia, two countries we know well, we increasingly see polarization and disadvantage. We must be particularly vigilant to avoid what some people call 'othering': separating ourselves from other people because of what we see as their different origins, cultural practices, attitudes, values, perceptions or behaviours. We make them 'other' and thereby exclude them from discussions about sustainability. This may be because we believe they cannot understand, are too young (or too old), are not literate or intelligent enough or because we think they will not care about the outcomes. Or we may believe that they are simply not 'eligible' to be included in our discussions. Perhaps they are not citizens? Not permanent residents? Not owner-occupiers? Not rate-payers? Richard Sennett's *The Uses of Disorder: Personal Identity and City Life* (1971) argues that we have to be willing to relinquish cultural purity and develop tolerance of ambiguity, uncertainty and disorder. Implicit is the notion that societies need to tolerate difference and include everyone. We agree.

We must be particularly vigilant to avoid what some people call 'othering': separating ourselves from other people because of what we see as their different origins, cultural practices, attitudes, values, perceptions or behaviours

Social exclusion is a problem being addressed in all Western countries. Excluded people can be unemployed, with low or no income, under-educated, under-resourced, without access to goods and services, information, education, facilities, of low literacy, marginalized or on the periphery of communities, people with a disability, people in locationally 'isolated' communities and those with cultural, linguistic, conceptual and psychosocial differences. Sometimes, people simply cannot afford to participate: to pay for child care, transport or to take a day off work. And because of the technical and scientific nature of many of the issues we need to discuss in sustainability debates within communities, people without formal training or education are likely to be excluded unless we take specific measures to include them. Already, we exclude people because of their age, ethnicity, literacy levels, geographical disadvantage, culture or social class. In fact, most community engagement processes typically round up stakeholders known as 'the usual suspects' and rarely expand the net to include others.

Another problem is the inaccurate (but common) assumption that sustainability issues are beyond the comprehension of children and young people

Another problem is the inaccurate (but common) assumption that sustainability issues are beyond the comprehension of children and young people.

In planning our multicultural cities, towns and villages, we need an explicit commitment to and resourcing of inclusion to respect diversity, not to achieve homogeneity. For Iris Marion Young, a good society is one with a differentiated and culturally plural network of contemporary urban life. She argued for group-differentiated policies because she did not believe in the notion of a homogeneous public. She felt that we needed expanded arrangements for including people who are not culturally identified with the same 'norms of reason and respectability' as white European males.

We also seek that transformation, as communities begin to take more responsibility for bringing about sustainability outcomes

Theory and policy should affirm, rather than suppress, social group difference.[7] It's important to note that for Young, a politics of difference was more than 'identity politics'. It meant maximizing opportunities and resources presented by diverse groups so that they could contribute their concerns. She saw a potential opportunity to transform the outcome of ongoing negotiated relationships with city governance structures. We also seek that transformation, as communities begin to take more responsibility for bringing about sustainability outcomes.

Another powerful analyst of the multicultural city is our friend and colleague, Leonie Sandercock, whose poetic writings and films (with Italian colleague, Giovanni Attili, an engineer/planner, self-trained in theatre and anthropology), portray a multifaceted and multi-cultural 'Cosmopolis',[8] marked by people's willingness to engage respectfully and fearlessly with 'the other', to learn and change by 'transgressing' communal and cultural boundaries in 'spaces of urban negotiation'. Leonie's 'integration-in-plurality' advocates long-term processes and mediation with groups that celebrate common culture (that is, communities). We need to learn to work democratically in culturally diverse associations and forums; we need to listen to the 'voices of difference' and develop 'a productive politics of difference' in theory and practice. Leonie believes that practitioners must recognize multiple publics, develop multiple ways of knowing and being and value cultural difference. We must negotiate with 'the other', *not by transcending difference but by acknowledging and fully engaging with it*, to help us become more aware of ourselves as well as the unfamiliar 'other'. This can lead to mutual creation of new understandings and meanings.[9]

We need to learn to work democratically in culturally diverse associations and forums; we need to listen to the 'voices of difference' and develop 'a productive politics of difference' in theory and practice

Leonie's most recent project is a powerful documentary directed by her Italian colleague, Giovanni Attili. It is about the Collingwood Neighbourhood House in east Vancouver.[10] In a neighbourhood that experienced serious interethnic conflicts 20 years ago, Collingwood is now a welcoming place for everyone. Leonie and Giovanni's film asks, 'How did this happen? How do strangers become neighbours?'

A welcoming and safe place at the table for all

We use the metaphor of the kitchen table throughout this book to characterize those spaces and places where communities come together – to despair, care and share – in order to engage in community processes for sustainability. The success of these community engagement processes depends on the 'kitchen table' being a welcoming and safe place for all. This section provides inspirational examples of how participants we often ignore can be included (e.g. children, young people, Nature). We also tell some

The success of these community engagement processes depends on the 'kitchen table' being a welcoming and safe place for all

not so encouraging stories that illustrate how community engagement processes can (sometimes inadvertently) exclude by not being welcoming or safe.

A welcoming place that does not 'other'

We've found that because processes of debate and decision making can often marginalize individuals and groups, we need a broad palette of flexible and creative approaches and ways to validate *listening across difference*.[11] Iris Marion Young points out that less privileged people may feel put down or frustrated, either losing confidence in themselves or becoming angry. In community workshops and processes, we have observed the 'norms' of behaviour, speech and articulateness she identified:

- Speech that proceeds from premise to conclusion in an orderly fashion.
- Dispassionate and disembodied ways of speaking and acting.
- The tendency to presuppose an opposition between mind and body, reason and emotion.
- The tendency to falsely identify objectivity with calm and absence of emotional expression.
- The assumption that expressions of anger, hurt and passionate concern discount the claims and reasons they accompany.[12]

Norms of assertiveness and combativeness and 'speaking by the contest rules' can be powerful evaluators and silencers of speech

Norms of assertiveness and combativeness and 'speaking by the contest rules' can be powerful evaluators and silencers of speech. We need community engagement processes that overcome these problems.

The latte set

Wendy's friend Kevin McMillan is a community activist in Eagleby, Queensland, with wide experiences of community engagement, as several large community renewal projects have occurred in his community over the past decade. Kevin coined the term 'the latte set' to describe a certain type of person who made the people in his low-income community feel 'other'. He includes in the latte set people (often bureaucrats) who, in Kevin's words:

- exhibit snobbery and distance
- will use their superior education to make you feel uncomfortable (using words that aren't understood)
- rely too much on pomp and ceremony
- tend to overemphasize their importance and will talk over the top of you
- speak bureaucratically (using acronyms and words we cannot understand) and talk far too quickly (they understand it and they expect us to as well).

We have seen these sorts of people trying to engage with communities about sustainability issues and several classic cases in Kevin's community. In one appalling display of bad manners, after the new residents' association invited senior State Government officials for lunch to meet their new board, the bureaucrats arrived from Brisbane 45 minutes late, having stopped en route for lunch. Looking at the uneaten sandwiches, Wendy predicted it would take years to undo the effects of such an insult. And it did.

Kevin has ten challenging questions to help us remember that to be truly inclusive we have to relax and have a sense of humour about all the discouraging things that will occur on our journey towards sustainability. The last of these challenges us all: 'I do what I do because I'm passionate about my suburb. So why not mix my passion and your knowledge instead of doing it "by the book", which seems to me to be lifeless crap?'

In one appalling display of bad manners, after the new residents' association invited senior State Government officials for lunch to meet their new board, the bureaucrats arrived from Brisbane 45 minutes late, having stopped en route for lunch

The boilermaker's temper

Sometimes people are made to be 'other' by virtue of their communication styles, which may not accord with local norms Sometimes people are made to be 'other' by virtue of their communication styles, which may not accord with local norms. Wendy and her husband Karl (trained as a welder-boilermaker, who first attended university at age 46), live in an eco-community where residents are expected to participate in community meetings and workshops. Recently, Karl lost his temper in a community meeting, arguing loudly that some community members were bullying older and less outspoken residents. His anger (or what some might call his emphatic 'discursive style') was apparently too strong for one woman, who complained bitterly that he had 'frightened the children'. Karl had not frightened the children (who were pre-teenagers) but had acted in a way that separated him from others and created an opportunity for people to make him 'other'. Not surprisingly, he stopped attending those argumentative meetings. (We would hope that others would continue to engage, despite, or even because of, conflicts like this one.)

A safe place for all – at the community engagement table and in the community

For many of us, living in relatively affluent Western communities, 'safety' is somewhat taken for granted. It may not be foremost in our minds when we are participating in community engagement processes. However, for some people it is, as the following stories illustrate.

Speaking for 'Milton Queers'

About the same time that Kevin McMillan was developing his views about the latte set, Wendy was managing community engagement processes in a higher income community in Milton, inner Brisbane, where the expansion of a large football stadium was being discussed. She'd established a storefront office in a central location and was staffing it alone one winter day when a young man came in. She complimented him on his spiky haircut and he complimented her on hers and they had a cup of coffee. He was in his mid-20s, maybe a bit older. As they settled down to chat, he announced, 'I'm here representing Milton Queers.'

Wendy thought, 'I'm glad I'm here for you', reflecting that some of her more conservative colleagues might have found that a shocking introduction. She bent forward to hear his story, which went something like this:

As they settled down to chat, he announced, 'I'm here representing Milton Queers

> I've lived in this neighbourhood for five years with my partner, who is Korean. We love living here, with all the bars and cafés, in a community that is tolerant of gay people. Everything is fine except for when the football games are on. Then, life is so shocking and frightening we can't face going out of the house. With all the hooligans and drunks throwing up and pissing in the letterboxes, we have to stay inside to avoid the homophobic and racist abuse that always comes with the football games. My partner's been abused and attacked in the street in broad daylight.
>
> If you make this stadium any bigger so that there will be concerts and entertainment several days a week, as well as more and bigger football games, we will simply have to move out of this neighbourhood. I think that's really unfair because we love it here but we will just not be safe.

What could Wendy say? She took a detailed record of the young man's concerns and reported them to the project manager and in her final report. Predictably, the stadium was expanded. Wendy does not know what happened to the young man and his partner. At least, in that moment she found a way to listen to his voice and communicate his views. But what could a more inclusive engagement and decision-making process have looked like?

But what could a more inclusive engagement and decision-making process have looked like?

'The Department is not the Khmer Rouge'

Wendy worked from 2004 to 2006 in a community renewal project in Bonnyrigg, an outer suburb of Sydney, where it was necessary to translate all material into eight local languages, as 50 per cent of residents did not speak English at all or well, by their own assessment. Despite energetic attempts to involve culturally and linguistically diverse groups, most did not participate in mainstream processes. These appeared to be the main reasons: messages were not communicated accurately; some groups were insular and did not communicate much with their neighbours; some knew little about sustainability issues (such as housing density); there were culturally diverse attitudes about fear and compliance; and stereotyping of some ethnic communities.[13]

Nevertheless, Bonnyrigg *is* a sustainability project, as it aims to increase housing density, reduce stigma, improve employment opportunities and strengthen public transit, as well as incorporate water-sensitive urban design and solar passive housing design features. When Wendy began working in Bonnyrigg in late 2004, the enthusiasm of the Khmer people impressed her. They attended meetings in the local temple in large numbers (for a small community) and graciously welcomed bureaucrats and consultants with delightful Cambodian food. They seemed very interested in everything that Wendy had to say about the community renewal project.

Many believed that, as public tenants, if they did not attend *every* meeting, they would be refused housing and would therefore be homeless

Later Wendy discovered a strong rumour in the Khmer community that may have contributed to their strong participation – but for the wrong reasons. Many believed that, as public tenants, if they did not attend *every* meeting, they would be refused housing and would therefore be homeless. Suddenly, Wendy remembered hearing the words 'Khmer Rouge' in an earlier session. When she had asked the interpreter to explain, she heard that an older woman had said, 'Remember, the Department of Housing is not the Khmer Rouge.'

There was laughter as that was interpreted back to Wendy and then again to the small group of refugees.

On a more serious note, the engagement practitioners were horrified by the communication breakdown and the depth of the misunderstanding, as the authority had promised to rehouse every tenant in a dwelling of their choice. The inclusionary processes had failed – at least until the Department hired a Cambodian-speaking community worker in 2005.

A place at the table for children

Many planners avoid community engagement processes with children, arguing that children – especially young children – have nothing to offer. We have had the opposite experience, having used a variety of methods. Because children do not vote and often cannot voice their dissatisfaction with engagement processes, we must be careful to ensure that processes that involve them are equitable, authentic and appropriate. Roger Hart in a brilliant Earthscan book, *Children's Participation* (1997), outlines six principles for working with children in community engagement contexts:

1. Ensure children understand the intentions of the process and volunteer for the project after these are explained to them.
2. Make clear the organizational structure and power relations at the beginning. Rules should be established through dialogue at the start of the project and amended by dialogue throughout.
3. Offer all children equal opportunity to participate if they wish in all phases of a project, even if this may mean that, because of age or experience, a child is initially simply observing the work of others.
4. Always try to make the entire process of any project transparent to participants. Bringing children into a

Margin notes:

Many planners avoid community engagement processes with children arguing ... children – especially young children – have nothing to offer [handwritten annotations: REFLECTIVE PRACTICE]

Bringing children into a project at the last minute is a classic error, guaranteed to lead to only token involvement

project at the last minute is a classic error, guaranteed to lead to only token involvement.

5   To the extent of their intellectual ability, fully inform children of the history and complete scope of the project and where they are currently in the process.

6   Ensure that the facilitator explains the importance of all phases and that no children are excluding themselves because of a sense of incompetence.

Transparency and the establishment of democratic principles within the group are essential ingredients.[14] Many other practitioners and academics work in this area. A forthcoming Earthscan book and other recent publications also address these issues.[15]

The Ladder of Children's Participation

Roger Hart (1997) developed the *Ladder of Children's Participation*, shown in Figure 8.1, that specifically addresses community engagement programmes involving children and young people.

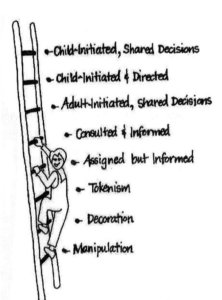

- Child-Initiated, Shared Decisions
- Child-Initiated & Directed
- Adult-Initiated, Shared Decisions
- Consulted & Informed
- Assigned but Informed
- Tokenism
- Decoration
- Manipulation

Figure 8.1 The Ladder of Children's Participation
Source: Roger Hart (1997, pp40–45) (Drawing by Andrea Cook)

Hart warns against the pitfalls of 'decoration' and manipulation of children, as Sherry Arnstein did (for adults) in 1969 with the 'Ladder of Citizen Participation'.[16] We're always on the lookout for the odious 'decoration' approach, where children's work is displayed on the cover of an organization's annual report but the child artist is neither acknowledged nor the purpose or content of the artwork explained.

Storytelling and face painting to uncover children's environmental values

One simple but effective method for engaging young children involves storytelling while facepainting. Landscape architecture students developed this process in 1989 for a community workshop in Melbourne. The new community, which now houses 25,000 people, was to be developed on a greenfield site, requiring us to engage with the neighbours. We used face painting to gain information about young children's activities and perceptions of their everyday environment.

One simple but effective method for engaging young children involves storytelling while facepainting

It is important to select facilitators with face-painting, storytelling and facilitation skills. The facilitator (the face painter) engages the child individually in a conversation about an environmental or sustainability issue and gains inspiration from the conversation. In effect, the face painter paints aspects of the environment that the child wishes to display or embody. The conversation can be directly recorded on a digital recorder. The process takes about 15 to 20 minutes, including discussion. The method is particularly successful because we can individually care for the children. Two photographs (Figures 8.2, 8.3) show the process.[17]

The sensation of paint applied to the face helps the child relax and engages the child's imagination. We generally use this method as one component of a larger participatory process.[18] It works well with children as young as three to seven years.

The sensation of paint applied to the face helps the child relax and engages the child's imagination

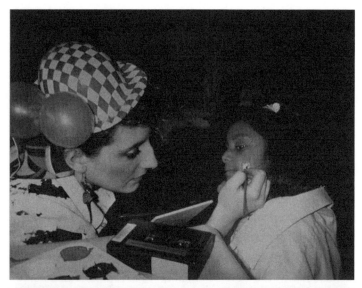

Figure 8.2 Painting a butterfly that flies close to my house
Figure 8.3 Embodying 'wildness' in my neighbourhood
Photographs: Kelvin Walsh

A place at the table for young people

Young people require opportunities to participate and contribute to a sustainable future. If anyone has a stake in the future and a concern about long-term consequences and the sustainability of communities, it is young people. Working directly with young people can be practical evidence of our commitment to intergenerational equity. Nobody knows better than today's children and young people what it is like to be young today. Young people themselves are most knowledgeable about their own lives. We believe that outside 'experts' should facilitate, not dominate, democracy. Importantly, considering children and young people, our position must be that that they are citizens and not citizens-in-the-making.[19]

Nobody knows better than today's children and young people what it is like to be young today

Young people are not always easy to reach, as they are a complex, individualistic, busy and media-savvy group. We have found them to be open to a variety of engagement methods and most likely to respond to small group face-to-face situations. They are looking for a sense of trust in the process, as well as a serious commitment from organizers to listen to their views and to respect and value their views. Anything we can do to avoid wasting young people's valuable time will send a strong message that we care about them and understand their needs. Good ways of working are not very different from good ways of working with adults. Respect and autonomy are key factors. For example:

Young people are not always easy to reach, as they are a complex, individualistic, busy and media-savvy group

- Be direct and candid with young people.
- Be authentic in your message.
- Establish a creative and supportive atmosphere.
- Let them decide about how they want to work.
- Make it easy for them to find out more about the process or the project.
- Develop options that allow flexibility in levels of involvement.
- Make the contact clear – develop a communications plan and communicate openly and frequently.[20]

An inclusive environment for children and young people

When considering how to include children and young people in community engagement with sustainability, it is important to honour the children's level of development and skills, and make sure that the environment and arrangements are appropriate and accessible. We have often experienced that small changes to the physical environment can make a big impact on the psychology of participants and the degree to which they feel included. Yollana experienced this same effect recently at home:

> We have just had an epiphany at our house about 'including' Erin at our kitchen table. She's only one and a half years old. Until now, she has variously eaten in her highchair, which has its own 'table', or at a little table separate from ours. With Will working nights, we found it hard to have dinner together, anyway, and often I would get a job done like cleaning the kitchen while she was engaged with eating.

> Then we realized we could take the little in-built table off her high chair and pull her in at the kitchen table with us (we discovered this during our candlelit dinner for Earth Hour[21] the other night). Wow ... what a difference! She loves eating at the big table with us and we love including her.

A place at the table for Nature: Widening our ethical community

Cathy will never forget the first time she met Wendy in March 2007. Both were participants at a 'Faith and Spirituality in the City' colloquium at Durham University. At the start of Day 2, after no reference to Earth-based spiritualities whatsoever, Wendy interrupted proceedings to offer an abalone shell, which she carefully unwrapped and placed in the middle of the table, to remind participants of the fundamental importance of Nature and the need to listen to its voice. She was symbolically offering Nature a seat at the table.

This was no idle gesture. Because of the seriousness of the planetary emergency we all face, we need to widen our ethical community to include the other-than-human or more-than-human species: what we call the nonhuman realm. This is because all our current approaches to community engagement with sustainability are weakened by their *anthropocentrism*, or human-centredness. Anthropocentrism means that we only see our world – the natural world around us and in which we are embedded – from *our* perspectives as humans. That's not surprising, as we are humans. But to consider all those communities – or as the Native American Indians say – 'all our relations' to be 'other' or 'less than' constrains the scope of our caring. That's a step in the wrong direction. Now is the time to widen the scope and expand the boundaries of our caring. This position – putting humans at the centre of our worldview or philosophy – is so prevalent in our societies that many philosophers refer to it as the 'default ethic'. Like the settings inside a new computer, it's invisible. We have to actively find it and change it; otherwise, invisibly, it continues to influence everything we do.

Now is the time to widen the scope and expand the boundaries of our caring

Donella Meadows captures the essence of an expanded sense of a caring self:

> *Living successfully in a world of complex systems means expanding not only time horizons and thought horizons; above all it means expanding the horizons of caring... No part of the human race is separate either from other human beings or from the global ecosystem.*[22]

True inclusion to achieve sustainability means confronting our basic anthropocentrism. We must ask, 'Who are these other beings and how can we take them into account?' Further, 'How can we take them into consideration as part of our ethical community?'

Asking the question, 'Who or what deserves consideration in community engagement with sustainability?' requires us to define the criteria of deservability. Consider for a moment, the range of

Asking the question, 'Who or what deserves consideration in community engagement with sustainability?' requires us to define the criteria of deservability

entities in Table 8.1 below. How can we move from anthropocentric to ecocentric, to make 'a place at the table' for those whose voices are never heard in human discourse – for nonhuman Nature?

Table 8.1 Who or what is worthy of consideration as part of our ethical community?

Only humans	*All sentient beings*	*All biotic entities*	*Inanimate entities*	*All entities*
Human beings at the centre of one's worldview (anthropo-centrism)	... who have the capacity to suffer (feel pleasure or pain)	... who are alive	Air Water Soil Mountains Beauty in landscapes	Wildness Aesthetics Ecosystems and species

What we are advocating is something greater: a place at the table for nonhuman Nature so that ordinary people, sitting at their kitchen tables or in community meetings and workshops, can hear those voices directly without the intervention of human advocates

We hear you reply that humans always speak on behalf of nonhuman Nature: Greenpeace, the Wilderness Society, conservation groups, the Department of Natural Resources, the Environmental Protection Agency, numerous advocates and activists. What we are advocating is something greater: a place at the table for nonhuman Nature so that ordinary people, sitting at their kitchen tables or in community meetings and workshops, can hear those voices directly without the intervention of human advocates. We are calling for an expansion of what Iris Marion Young calls 'enlarged thought', moving from a narrowly subjective, self-regarding perspective to a more socially inclusive view.[23] We would term it 'an ecologically inclusive view'. Then all can be present and accounted for. While this is challenging, we have had some success in listening to the voice of Nature in community engagement. One example is described below.

The Reconnecting Ceremony, Eagleby, Queensland (27 May 2000)[24]

Wendy and Graeme Dunstan, assisted by Karl and other helpers, undertook this process in 2000 in Eagleby, a low-income Queensland community, as a component of a health promotion project called *Stories in a Park*.[25] The focus was to explore ways in which Eagleby's parks and public places could be safer, more welcoming and contribute to wider community sustainability. The Reconnecting Ceremony was designed to contribute a new nonhuman perspective to deliberations about Eagleby's parks. Participation was offered to 21 self-selecting participants, who were told that this was sensitive work to be approached with respect. Based on the Deep Ecology ritual, *A Council of all Beings,* the powerful day-long Ceremony provided opportunities to reconnect with the natural world.[26]

In the morning, participants arrived by boat after travelling along the river from a central gathering point to private land, favoured by local Indigenous people as a place for gathering. The Ceremony structure involved three approaches: *Mourning, Remembering* and *Speaking from the perspectives of other life forms.* The most powerful component of the day was when participants elected to be chosen to embody a nonhuman life form. Individually, they went out into the landscape to discover which aspect of it might call to them and ask them to represent them in the Council. In the next part, each person made a simple mask to represent their nonhuman being. The participants sat, masked, in the Council to discuss Eagleby's parks. They represented *Fire, Wind, the Rivers,* an Egret, various other animals and birds and the Eagle of Eagleby. It was a passionate discussion, with a fair amount of blame sheeted home to humans for spoiling the beauty of Eagleby's natural environments.[27]

The most powerful component of the day was when participants elected to be chosen to embody a nonhuman life form

The debriefing session revealed the following outcomes:

- new and creative insights and ideas for design of Eagleby's public spaces

- widened anthropocentric worldviews to include the rights and needs of nonhuman Nature
- focus on the primacy of the natural world in sustaining all life on Earth
- opportunities for people with different backgrounds and experiences of the natural world to see their commonalities and build bridges between different perspectives

she remembers Liz's whispered words, as they were leaving: 'Don't despair of small beginnings'

Wendy remembers Mike's heartfelt plea – as The Rivers – for humans to clean up the rivers and allow humans to appreciate their beauty and beneficial powers. She heard herself – as Egret – speaking in support of the Rivers – the source of her strength, nourishment and power. And she remembers Liz's whispered words, as they were leaving: 'Don't despair of small beginnings.'[28]

Figure 8.4 At the Eagleby Reconnecting Ceremony, 2000

Recipes for an inclusionary model

We've based our community engagement practice on extensive research, reflecting a model called *inclusionary argumentation*, documented in the academic literature by British academic and practitioner Patsy Healey. Her inclusionary model asks us: Who could have a 'stake' in any situation? To answer, we need to cast the net as widely as possible, as there is really no objective way of identifying the complete 'universe' of eligible stakeholders, still less of reaching all of them. As Healey explains, 'The focus is on the process through which participants come together, build understanding among themselves, and develop ownership of the strategy, rather than the specific production of decision-criteria or an attractive image'.[29]

In concocting the recipes below, we draw heavily on Healey's 'inclusionary argumentation' model. Wendy, Steph and Yollana have been using these recipes for some years, perhaps calling them by different names. They have a universally attractive flavour, however, as do the ingredients of the inclusionary model listed below.

Four recipes for inclusion

Recipe 1: Accept that there will be fractures and chasms and work with them

Communities often contain deep fractures and chasms that represent realms of disagreement, cultural difference, struggle and misunderstanding. These often stem from – or are compounded by – breaches of trust in community engagement (see Chapter 7). We cannot 'paper over' these cracks. Rather, we must see them as opportunities to collaborate across differences, forming truly generative relationships where people can acquire different frames of reference and develop new systems of meaning. This time-consuming work requires extreme care, as people attempt to shift power bases and create new relationships of collaboration

Communities often contain deep fractures and chasms that represent realms of disagreement, cultural difference, struggle and misunderstanding

and trust. Yet it is worth the effort, as generative collaborations will be far more productive than attempts to homogenize diverse worldviews.

Recipe 2: There is no privileged, correct rationality

There *is* a place for expert knowledge and a place for practical consciousness and local knowledge

There *is* a place for expert knowledge and a place for practical consciousness and local knowledge. However, the 'expert' view should not be given top ranking in collaborative discourse. Particularly when the experts are not the ones who will have to live with the consequences of the decisions in their communities.

Recipe 3: Consensus cannot be uncovered; it has to be created

Wide practical experience reveals that there is no objective 'answer' lying hidden in the minds of community members that need only be unearthed to achieve consensus. Rather, consensus 'has to be actively created across the fractures of the social relations of relevant stakeholders'.[30] We have found that such work strengthens the capacity of the community and of the proponent, not only through its impact on participants but also through its impact on institutions.

Recipe 4: A new discourse needs to be created

We have found that developers and their technical advisers often shy away from the deeper aspects of conversations about sustainability

Storylines develop where there are parts for most people. Many can play a part in a multifaceted process. Some suffer more and some benefit more as the story proceeds. We must pay attention to the languages used and the stories told. John Forester reminds us to pay explicit attention to those whose needs have been neglected, to what cannot be achieved, what the costs of this may be and for whom, as well as what can be done.[31] For Patsy Healey, 'the work of discourse creation is therefore both the most important and the most dangerous part of the process'.[32] Not surprisingly, we have found that developers and their technical advisers often shy away from the deeper aspects of conversations about sustainability.

Twelve ingredients for inclusive community engagement

Ingredient 1 INCLUSION: Cast a wide net (all present and accounted for)

We must ask, 'Who are members of the stakeholder community? How are they to get access to the arena in such a way that their points of view can be appreciated as well as their voices heard? And how can they have a stake throughout the process?' And we must involve *all* individuals and groups who might be affected by any decision, including those individuals and groups who are often systematically marginalized from decision making: children, young people, people for whom English is a second language, older people, people with a disability and Indigenous people. We also need to consider how members of the stakeholder community are 'called up', as they have much more to do than simply 'represent the stakeholders'. Ultimately, a few will play key roles in shaping discussion, sorting out arguments and developing strategies, but others do not necessarily have to be marginalized.[33]

We must involve *all* individuals and groups who might be affected by any decision, including those individuals and groups who are often systematically marginalized from decision making

Processes should include *everyone* (including those who may feel differently from the way we do – the ones whom we'd often prefer to avoid). Regardless of what the most politically correct engagement practitioners tell you, in our honest moments we'll admit that certain people are difficult to include. Even the best 'inclusionary' processes exclude some people. The secret is to identify everyone who has a 'stake' in a decision and then actively work to include them. Our *Easy-to-Hard Continuum* provides a suggestion of how to identify those who might be excluded (see Table 8.2).

Table 8.2 The easy-to-hard continuum of inclusion in community engagement

Exceptionally easy to include	Easiest to include	Harder to include	Even harder to include	Harder still to include	Hardest of all to include	Beyond our imagining
• Proactive people who probably tend to dominate most processes unless actively countered • Some activists • Professional engagement specialists • People with a direct stake in a directly relevant issue	• Hard-to-reach people • Children • Older people • Women • Low-income people • Geographi-cally isolated people	• Unaffiliated people • 'Apathetic' people • Angry betrayed and disaffected people • Impolite people acting inappropriately • 'Losers' from previous engagement processes	• Homeless people • Young people • People from culturally and linguistically diverse (CaLD) communities • People with a disability	• Faraway people, places and societies you can't imagine • Dramati-cally different cultures	• The nonhuman realm • Animals • Plants • Landscapes • Bioregions • Mountains	• All life, everywhere

Ingredient 2 TIMING: Provide plenty of time and handle timing carefully

In engagement practice, the saying 'time is money' presents a skewed version of reality because inclusionary processes require more time than developers, proponents and governments often prefer. This does not *always* mean that they cost more, particularly when social and ecological externalities are taken into account. Further, non-collaborative, non-inclusionary processes can lead to increasing lengths of time and costly delays. We need enough time for all participants to be fully involved. Importantly, some communities – notably Indigenous Australians and many other Indigenous peoples – may have different conceptions of and relationships with time.

Community time frames, as well as commercial and political ones, are important. We must seek public involvement *before* a decision has been reached. And in each stage participants need adequate time to receive, integrate, reflect and respond to information. Sometimes this is a difficult balance to achieve: we must maintain momentum and ensure feedback from respective stages occurs as quickly as possible. For participants whose lives will be affected, it is unfair to 'leave them hanging'. Wide experience has taught us that communities always greet rushed timetables with suspicion. A little more time spent demonstrating openness and building trust always pays off.

Ingredient 3 RESPECT: Practise respectful listening and speaking

An inclusionary model emphasizes respectful speaking and listening to encourage mutual listening. This is the open-hearted listening discussed in Chapter 5. This ingredient involves facilitators and proponents listening deeply to community members, trying to hear what is underneath their expressed views and doing so in a way that helps build consensus. Such 'situated learning' requires an ethical stance of listening for more than content and interests.

We are listening for values and cultural references; listening with our third ear We are listening for values and cultural references; listening with our third ear.

Ingredient 4 INTEGRATION: Take a holistic approach

For any system to be sustainable – especially an engagement process – it must be considered holistically, taking into account the multiple layers and components of social systems. They are similar to ecosystems. We must consider *all* the components collectively, as well as individually. These ingredients combined equal more than the sum of their parts.

Ingredient 5 PROCESS TRANSPARENCY: Speak openly about ethics

Sometimes we feel as though we are working in 'a moral vacuum' brought about by a cultural obsession with objectivity, rationality and detachment.[34] But increasingly, ethical issues surface in community engagement with sustainability. This new inclusionary moral sense requires us to maintain close scrutiny of the ways people exercise power. It can transform policy discourse.[35]

For many years, our friend and colleague Andrea Cook, a Canadian-born community planner based in Melbourne and co-author of one of the books in this Earthscan suite,[36] has explored the ethical positions of Australian planners. Andrea's work focuses on unpacking planners' views of the ethical dimension of planning. She interviewed and worked with a wide range of urban, regional and remote area planners, whose disciplines include land-use planning, social/community planning, environmental and economic planning. She found some common ethical themes, which show how important it is to speak openly about ethics:

- general professional confusion regarding planning's roles and responsibilities
- appreciation of competing ethical discourses: professional, organizational and personal

- absence of ethical literacy, particularly concerning meta-ethical issues
- inertia: confusion about how to resolve ethical dilemmas as planners
- the need for a professional 'moral voice' and professional ethical guidance

Ingredient 6 ACCESSIBILITY: Pay attention to the 'rituals of discussion'

John Forester uses the term 'the rituals of policy discussion' to describe the many processes employed in community engagement: how people prepare themselves; how rooms are arranged; how communicative routines are set up (who speaks when and how); and how discussion is concluded.[37] In an inclusionary model, we must also pay attention to *where* engagement occurs. By using different arenas, ranging from formal to informal, we can make processes comfortable, convenient and accessible to a range of participants.

In an inclusionary model, we must also pay attention to *where* engagement occurs

John and Wendy enjoy stimulating conversations about the importance of the fine details of welcoming and making people feel comfortable. Not everyone agrees, however. Recently overheard were two postgraduate planning students attending one of Wendy's workshops on the SpeakOut model. It had been a long morning of details: setting up, welcoming, signs, catering, handouts, lighting, technology, displays, what to do when things go wrong...[38]

'I can't believe she's talking about Velcro dots', one complained. *'Surely **we** are above **that**!'*

*Had Wendy been there in person, she would have replied: 'Surely, we are **not** above that.'*

I can't believe she's talking about Velcro dots', one complained. 'Surely we are above that!'

Sometimes people are excluded because of the ways we design our engagement processes. The format may be intimidating, the time inconvenient for women with children or people who work during the day, the location may be inaccessible, inconvenient or even unsafe. And these language barriers keep people from participating. All of these are issues that concern community engagement practitioners, and we have written at length on this topic.[39]

To achieve sustainability, we must emphasise that *everyone* needs to be included for decisions to be made based on wide community understanding. This means that if an older person feels that a night-time meeting is dangerous, we have to rethink the timing, or find a way to include her by helping her to feel safe and confident to participate. Technology is often a barrier. In British Columbia, Nancy reminded us that some First Nations people recognized that they were disadvantaged in some community engagement processes because they had difficulty reading maps.[40]

Some First Nations people recognized that they were disadvantaged in some community engagement processes because they had difficulty reading maps

Ingredient 7 COMMUNICATION: Pay attention to language

Particularly in the complex arena of sustainability, we must pay attention to the various 'languages' people use and how these affect their ability to communicate and build consensus. Because we want to include participants from a variety of backgrounds, we have to be careful that our language does not confuse them or turn them away. We have found that policy and planning information is generally discussed in 'the language of consequences, grounded in economic reasoning or scientific evidence'.[41] For example, in a complex project discussed in Chapter 10, Governance, Wendy explained to her developer client, a former banker, that the language of finance and development (her preferred mode of communication) would not work in public forums.

The languages commonly used by convenors of community engagement processes often serve to confuse

The languages commonly used by convenors of community engagement processes often serve to confuse. Some community members are more comfortable with the language of belief, or the political assertion of rights. Others may be more comfortable with the expression of fears and dangers. The 'challenge' in an inclusionary

220

model, Patsy Healey says, 'is to accept them all, but to recognize that translation between them is a complex, delicate and powerful task…'[42] We must avoid exclusionary language at all costs.

Ingredient 8 OPENNESS: Keep things open

In all our processes, we try to keep initial discussions open, fluid and focused on sharing, understanding and building meaning, rather than on a particular outcome. This is very difficult for some of our clients to tolerate! Yet, as participants develop confidence in talking and listening to each other, we can then move on to more formal discussions and settings. Healey calls this moving from discursive 'opening out' to consolidation around particular ideas and consequential actions. The challenge, she reminds us, is to experiment with, and test out, ideas in initially tentative ways, and to 'open out' possibilities for both evaluation and invention of better alternatives, before allowing a 'preferred' discourse to emerge and 'crowd out' the alternatives.[43] Facilitator Sam Kaner illustrates this progression in 'The Diamond of Participatory Decision Making', shown in Figure 8.5. The Diamond progresses from divergent thinking, through 'the groan zone', to convergent thinking and decision making.[44] Again, the style and ethics of the discussion setting are critical ingredients in an inclusionary approach.

The Diamond progresses from divergent thinking, through 'the groan zone', to convergent thinking and decision making

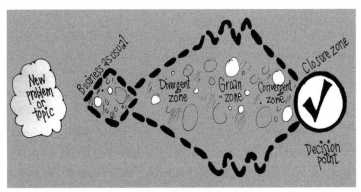

Figure 8.5 The Diamond of Participatory Decision Making
Source: Kaner et al (1996, p20)

Ingredient 9 INFORMATION TRANSPARENCY: Keep the information flowing

Information flow is vital to inclusionary engagement with sustainability because the more open and transparent a process is, the more effective it can be. Thus, we need to inform participants of opportunities and constraints so that they can form knowledgeable opinions and seek useful areas of consensus or dissent. For community members to build their understanding of the complex components of sustainability, they need regular opportunities to review information *as it emerges*. While it is often unlikely that the same people will continue to be involved at all stages, advisory bodies can review emerging concepts and policies and their members can communicate back to their individual constituencies. Inclusive information flow does not only benefit community participants; staying open to information coming in from community members and other stakeholders can also build the institutional capacity of the proponent, government and other relevant agencies. In this way, proponents can expand their 'expert' knowledge and come to understand sustainability issues from the enriched perspective of community members. This has the benefit of greater general understanding, hopefully leading to less interpretive distortion and better decisions.

For community members to build their understanding of the complex components of sustainability, they need regular opportunities to review information *as it emerges*

Ingredient 10 REFLEXIVITY AND ACCOUNTABILITY: Engage in evaluation and regular reviews

Chapter 5, Education, emphasized the importance of reflection and critical thinking in evaluating sustainability options. The same holds true for community engagement. Many past engagement processes depended on a 'rationalist methodology', where proponents and their agents regarded review as retrospective 'monitoring' of outcomes to ensure they were implemented. This old-fashioned approach alone does not reflect leading practice. We are aware of three types of evaluation, each with a different purpose:

1 *Summative or outcome evaluation*: to ensure accoun
-tability at the completion of a process by judging
its effectiveness according to predetermined criteria.
2 *Formative evaluation:* to provide ongoing information for
refining and improving engagement processes as they
occur.
3 *Evaluation for knowledge*: to contribute to a general body
of literature, rather than a specific project.[45]

The inclusionary model is concerned more with reflection, evaluation and refinement, than with monitoring progress toward a
specific goal. One of the benefits of this reflexive critique is that it
helps us keep an eye on whether the emerging plan or policy still
'makes sense' in sustainability terms.

> **One of the benefits of this reflexive critique is that it helps us keep an eye on whether the emerging plan or policy still 'makes sense' in sustainability terms**

Ingredient 11 TRANSFORMATION: Look for the discursive key

When we listen and pay attention to culturally constructed meanings, we make space for the emergence of new understandings
and concepts. Sometimes participants can then completely reframe
the plan or project and come to a shared vision that is dramatically different from anyone's original vision. Maarten Hajer calls this
the *discursive key*, which 'turns' the discussion from one conception to another, shifting the storyline from one account to another
and performing the critical transformative work so an issue can be
reframed.[46]

A brilliant example of the 'discursive key' occurred in a community
cultural development project, discussed in Chapter 7, which Wendy
undertook in 2000 with artist-activist, Graeme Dunstan. It went
something like this:

> *Everybody had been talking about stigma and from the very
> beginning people were saying, 'Eagleby's a nice place and
> it's a nice place to live, but our biggest problem is that other
> people look down on us.' There was the classic problem:*

'You have to give a different address when you are applying for a job,' and *'You don't admit that you live here.'*

Graeme began working directly with the residents in a widening circle of probably 30-odd people. He was asking what this Eagleby stigma looked like. Finally someone said, 'It's an eagle that's lying down, and the thumb of other people's judgement is holding it down so it can't fly.' We had asked for months, 'What's the bloody stigma?' and they finally said, 'Well, this is what it is.'[47]

Once everyone started talking about stigma in 'embodied' terms, community conversations about sustainability were transformed

Graeme had discovered a discursive key for Eagleby. Once everyone started talking about stigma in 'embodied' terms, community conversations about sustainability were transformed. And they have been since that time. They eventually built a huge cardboard representation of the stigma to be burned (see Figure 8.6) in a dramatic community ceremony (see Chapter 7), and a new story was created.

Figure 8.6 The Eagleby stigma

Ingredient 12 PROFESSIONALISM: Hold yourself to a high standard

How to achieve inclusion in community engagement with sustainability when so many forces seem to work against it? Community engagement facilitators require professionalism and rigour to allow participants – from the proponent to the local shopkeeper and resident – to relax, to trust and to participate effectively. This is even more important in politically sensitive arenas and with complex topics such as sustainability. Professionalism includes paying careful attention to detail in the implementation stage. Contrary to what Wendy's workshop students believed, if the font on a poster is too small for older eyes, the Velcro to hang the poster boards is forgotten or the facilitator appears to favour one comment over another, participants will be quick to notice 'inaccessibility' or lack of neutrality. Professionalism often evaporates in the analysis and reporting stages, sabotaging efforts to achieve inclusion. Often, after a day-long weekend workshop attended by hundreds of participants, Wendy has answered the telephone on Monday morning to hear a client asking, 'Wendy, do you think we could have a draft report by Tuesday?'

> Often, after a day-long weekend workshop attended by hundreds of participants, Wendy has answered the telephone on Monday morning to hear a client asking, 'Wendy, do you think we could have a draft report by Tuesday?'

Kitchen table conversation starters

- Is there anyone in your community whom you have seen as an 'other'?
- Is there anyone who might think of you this way?
- What would it take to bridge the gap between you and 'others'?
- How are harder to reach groups included in your community at present? And how could their inclusion be improved in the future?
- Does Nature have a say in your local neighbourhood? If it did, what might it communicate?

For more opportunities to continue the conversation about community education for sustainability, please visit www.kitchentablesustainability.com.

Some final thoughts

Inclusion is a great challenge in today's fragmented societies. Inclusive community engagement with sustainability is very complex and time-consuming, complicated by the technical issues that communities now must address. This delicate work requires us to take an 'enlarged view' of our moral or ethical community and include others whom we might not have considered in earlier processes. It requires tailor-made tools and the time and resources to 'translate' technical matters into simple, jargon-free language. Different cultural groups require different types of forums for community engagement. Intergenerational styles require specific attention.

This delicate work requires us to take an 'enlarged view' of our moral or ethical community and include others whom we might not have considered in earlier processes

While this is complex work, help is at hand.[48] It's critical that we do not 'despair of small beginnings'. Nourishing ourselves and our immediate communities is a powerful way to strengthen our resolve and strengthen and support our competence. We discuss that aspect of community engagement with sustainability in the following chapter.

9

NOURISHMENT

Care flowing through your system gradually reconnects you with your spirit and vitality. Care enough about yourself to go to your heart to get peace, clarity, and direction before you act.
True self-care has to come first.

Sara Paddison, 1992

[It's time to] ... embrace a 'new bottom line' in which corporations, social practices, government policies and individual behaviors are judged rational, efficient or productive not only if they maximize money or power, but also to the extent that they maximize love and caring, kindness and generosity, ethical and ecological sensitivity, enhance our capacity to treat others as embodiments of the sacred and to respond with awe, wonder and radical amazement at the grandeur of the universe.

Rabbi Michael Lerner[1]

Introduction

This chapter explores how we can nourish ourselves, our communities and Nature in sustainable way; and the role of nourishment in community engagement with sustainability. As peace activist Rabbi Michael Lerner suggests above, acts of nourishment – the 'maximization of love and caring' – have implications for every level of society, the Earth and beyond.

The Latin root of the word nourish is *nutrire*: to feed. To nourish means to 'supply with what is necessary for life, health, and growth'.[2] It also means to 'cherish, foster, keep alive' and to 'strengthen, build up, promote'.[3] Each of these meanings can apply to community engagement with sustainability. If we're not nourishing ourselves with what we need for life, health and growth, how can we build up and strengthen our communities or cherish and sustain the Earth? Nourishment involves balancing active engagement with learning and reflection, rest and rejuvenation, time alone and time with others. Spending time in Nature is also important because Nature can be deeply nourishing. Nourishment is about cultivating healthy habits on a personal level, as well as nourishing systems and routines within our communities.

If we're not nourishing ourselves with what we need for life, health and growth, how can we build up and strengthen our communities or cherish and sustain the Earth?

The importance of nourishment to ongoing engagement with sustainability

The process of creating a sustainable world will not occur in a moment or even in our lifetimes. The complex patterns of social inequality, environmental imbalance and conflict reflected in every sphere of modern life have taken generations to weave. To unravel them completely will also take generations. That does not mean, however, that we should abandon this quest. Many milestones on the road to sustainability are well within our reach – in this lifetime. Perhaps even in this decade. Now, more than ever, we have the reasons and resources to draw our chairs to the table of engagement with sustainability.

Many milestones on the road to sustainability are well within our reach

Throughout this book, we have emphasized that we all need to engage with sustainability. We all need to be nourished in the process, as well. Whether you are an activist or community organizer, sustainability professional, planner, student, academic or government officer, community engagement practitioner or developer, we all need nourishment. And we all need the specific kinds of nourishment that support us to engage with sustainability.

We all need nourishment. And we all need the specific kinds of nourishment that support us to engage with sustainability

The challenge of coming to, staying at and returning to the table

Cathy's son, an active, energetic four-year-old, is like most children his age. He finds it incredibly challenging to stay at their kitchen table during mealtimes, let alone stay focused on the eating task. And so it is for many participants involved in community engagement. For many reasons, we find it difficult to come to, stay at or return to the community engagement table we describe throughout this book.

Sustainability is complex and a challenge for everyone – whether experienced or new to the conversations. It's difficult to understand issues and then engage in sustainable ways. Most people fall into one of two camps. Either we've found it a bit overwhelming and have shut down from engaging with the 'alarming realities' of sustainability. Or we've recognized the crucial nature of the situation, dived into working as a professional, practitioner, bureaucrat or activist and ended up flirting with, or falling into, burnout. Sadly, many of us strike an uneasy balance: engaging with some issues but holding back from others. Whatever our process – pulling back from engagement, or throwing ourselves in far too deep – a key to finding a balance is within our reach. That key is nourishment.

Nourishing ourselves, our communities and Nature are essential to engagement with the crucial issues that comprise sustainability. We have directly experienced the journey from engagement to being overwhelmed, despair, disillusionment, denial and back. We have experienced some of the barriers to engagement with sustainability that individuals and communities face. And we have discovered ways to nourish engagement, while acknowledging those barriers.

We have directly experienced the journey from engagement to being overwhelmed, despair, disillusionment, denial and back

The Great Bear Rainforest

We introduced the inspirational story of the Great Bear Rainforest in British Columbia, Canada in Chapter 6. After decades of conflict over how to manage a pristine coastal rainforest, interest groups achieved a breakthrough and a solution. Cathy heard Frances Westley tell this story at the 2008 Resilience Conference in Stockholm. Her description of how the 'environmentalists' deliberately nourished themselves at one stage in the intensive process illustrates the message of this chapter.

And in May 2007, the World Wildlife Fund presented a *Gift to the Earth* Award to the leaders who crafted the agreements for protecting the Great Bear Rainforest.

'What happened here? How did they go from people lying down in front of logging machines to the kind of break-through solutions they were able to achieve? (How did people stay at the table?)... The organizers, who were the environmentalists, brought a whole different attitude to the negotiations that they called "Facing the Shadow". They said everybody hated them... Forest workers thought they were "cappuccino sucking urban enviros". The First Nations called them eco-colonialists. The forest companies said, "They are trying to destroy us and the province we care about." There were duelling scientists who did not want to work with anybody. There was the Government saying they were irresponsible and the "enemies of British Columbia." Other environmentalists thought they were corporate sell-outs. It's pretty easy to get your "back up" in this kind of environment.

'But a number of these environmentalists were Buddhists. So they decided to bring their personal faith into this practice ... to own their shadows. They had to agree that some of this was true... They did suck cappuccinos down and they did have eco-colonial tendencies, etc. And they worked together to stay centred. They were passing notes to each other saying: "Breathe", "Stay centred." And they would literally sometimes run out of the room when they thought they were going to explode, and meditate, so they could come back in. By the testimonials of other people in the group, this fractal sense of them being prepared to transform themselves in an effort to transform these rela-tionships ... actually had a transformative effect. It made people stay at the table. And gradually they began to shift their positions.'[4]

And they would literally sometimes run out of the room when they thought they were going to explode, and meditate, so they could come back in

The nourishment recipe: To enable sustained and sustaining community engagement

The three main ingredients of our nourishment recipe involve nourishing Nature, community and ourselves. Because each of us is already engaged in reciprocal, interdependent relationships – a circle of giving and receiving – we can engage consciously with that circle to feel nourished, energized and to express our willingness to do so with others. Figure 9.1 illustrates how we see this relationship.

Because each of us is already engaged in reciprocal, interdependent relationships – a circle of giving and receiving – we can engage consciously with that circle to feel nourished

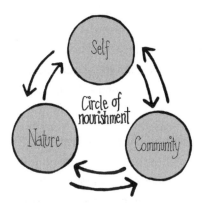

Figure 9.1 The Circle of Nourishment

Engagement with Nature and with community are two ways of nourishing and being nourished. In each case, the returns are twofold. When we nourish Nature, we are rewarded with a natural environment that is cared for *and* is nourishing for us. By engaging with and supporting our communities, we develop resources to help each other. When we allow ourselves to be *nourished by* our communities, we support the interdependent patterns of relationship that constitute community. Similarly, when we nourish ourselves, we have more to give to our communities and to Nature and we receive more from them in return.

When we nourish ourselves, we have more to give to our communities and to Nature and we receive more from them in return

The first ingredient: Nourishing Nature

We cannot win this battle to save species and nature without forging an emotional bond between ourselves and nature as well – for we will not fight to save what we do not love.

Stephen Jay Gould[5]

Stephen Jay Gould is correct in identifying the emotional component of caring for Nature. 'Nourishing Nature' is a *double entendre*. Initially, nourishing refers to the activity of nourishing the natural environment around us. It is also an adjective referring to the ability of an environment to nourish – or be nourishing to – us. While we can nourish Nature in many practical ways – like planting trees, recycling, turning off the lights – we also need deep-seated philosophical and emotional shifts to support 'healing the Earth'. At the most fundamental level, we must be *in* Nature and experience ourselves as *part of* it.

> **At the most fundamental level, we must be *in* Nature and experience ourselves as *part of* it**

A long Western tradition has emphasized controlling Nature, not loving or caring for it. Nowhere is this more evident than in our cities. Over half the world's population is urban; by 2030, nearly five billion people will live in cities.[6] Research reveals that ecologically impoverished metropolitan areas contribute to increased 'environmental amnesia' among city dwellers.[7] However, as the brilliant palaeontologist Stephen Jay Gould reminds us, *love* is the key.

> **In Nature, an individual can be open to healing on a deeper level than is possible within human contexts**

In 1996, following a year of solitude in the Australian bush, Wendy developed a curriculum for teaching an ethic of caring for Nature to planning students. She argued, supported by many educators, that human relationships with Nature could be healed by direct experience. In Nature, an individual can be open to healing on a deeper level than is possible within human contexts. Wendy sees this 'experiential invitation' as a critical first step towards an 'ecological and social healing process' for the wider human community.[8]

Arne Naess, the Norwegian philosopher and father of Deep Ecology, explains that, with sufficient maturity, '...we cannot help but "identify" our self with all living beings; beautiful or ugly, big or small, sentient or not'.[9] Naess calls this the *ecological self,* an expanded sense of self that goes beyond the individual ego to include not only our society and relationships, but also Nature. He argues that the desire to care for Nature emerges naturally (via a process he calls 'self realization') when we fully experience *being* with Nature. Naess distinguishes between ontological and deontological ethics: In the latter, we act out of a sense of moral duty or obligation. In essence: *we do the right thing, because it's the right thing to do.* Naess contends that ontology precedes ethics, by which he means that the action of caring flows from the *feeling* of caring, rather than the other way around. With *ontological openness,* we have both a sense of deep relatedness and intense participation in experience. While Naess and other Deep Ecologists have been expressing these views for decades, there is extensive recent research to support Naess' views.[10]

Encouraging children to nourish Nature

People who do not experience Nature early or regularly are less likely than those who do to develop sentiments to motivate much needed environmental protection efforts. Thus, regular experiences of Nature during childhood are essential for nourishing community engagement with sustainability. For those of us with children, it is important to encourage them to experience Nature directly. We need the next generation to love Nature so deeply and passionately that they will protect it with their lives. Human evolution depends on our fostering a deep understanding and respect for Nature. Without that understanding, we destroy the Earth and, ultimately, ourselves. By encouraging children to engage with Nature, we can embed in their neural pathways an understanding of the preeminence of the natural world – and its primacy and power. If this occurs in childhood, the recognition of the importance and power of Nature may contribute to actions that protect and nourish the Earth.

We need the next generation to love Nature so deeply and passionately that they will protect it with their lives.

Human evolution depends on our fostering a deep understanding and respect for Nature

Scandinavia has a long tradition of daily connection with Nature. In the extremely cold climate of Swedish Lappland, where Cathy now lives with her family, that was initially something of a culture shock. At kindergarten, her two-year-old daughter sleeps outside in her pram irrespective of weather. It can be raining, snowing or minus 20 degrees Celsius. Children as young as 18 months are accompanied by their teachers on regular walks through the forest.

Together with her children, Cathy has come to delight in this closeness to Nature. Like many homes in her small town of Luleå, her property has no fences. Forest becomes back garden. Autumn brings a bounty of wild blueberries. After Cathy and her friend discovered their sons hacking apart an anthill, her neighbour was inspired to organize a weekly 'forest play' activity for local children. Now both boys are learning to tell whether a mouse or a squirrel has eaten the fallen pinecone, the names of the different berries, which ice is safe to walk on and to track the busy work of the ants as they rebuild their home.

Figure 9.2 'Forest play' in Luleå, Sweden: Weekly measurement of the height of an anthill

How community engagement practices can nourish Nature

To nourish Nature, we must understand it. As explained in Chapter 5, Education, citizen science is a participatory process that brings together community members, government and industry to develop and conduct public-interest research to bridge gaps between science and community and between scientific research and policy, decision making and planning. Bridging these gaps involves a process of social learning through sound environmental research, full community engagement, adoption of adaptive management practices and the development of democratic values, skills and institutions for an active civil society.[11]

To nourish Nature, we must understand it

Meaningful involvement of all stakeholders occurs through a commitment to social learning. Hands-on, practical processes undertaken in a natural environment can help build skills and encourage participants to care for Nature. In the Australia-wide *Cooperative Research Centre for Coastal Zone, Estuary and Waterway Management* (the Coastal CRC) example, below, we see how citizen science can support community members and other stakeholders to learn about and care for their local environment by volunteering with local environmental groups.

Hands-on, practical processes undertaken in a natural environment can help build skills and encourage participants to care for Nature

A capacity-strengthening case study from Queensland[12]

One example of effective citizen science learning, reported by the Coastal CRC, occurred not far from where Steph and Yollana live. Interviews with long-term members of the Norman Creek and Gowrie Creek catchment groups reveal how participation in catchment research and care can strengthen community capacity to nourish and care for Nature in their local area. These comments, extracted from interviews, illustrate this:

> *Iain: I have vastly expanded knowledge and appreciation of issues in waterway restoration.*

Barry: There has been a profound change in my feelings about waterways... I have got a quiet determination to fix our creeks.

Helen: I think that earlier we were very dependent on professionals. We didn't know that, between us, we already had the skills we needed.

These stories hold great lessons for community engagement practitioners. In repairing and recreating natural places, questions arise that deepen participants' understanding of ecological processes. We can bring these questions into community conversations about sustainability. Community service and restoration projects can provide opportunities for people to regain value in themselves by combating the experience of alienation and isolation and by strengthening our capacity to nourish Nature.

Being nourished by Nature

The key to being nourished by Nature is to get up close

The key to being nourished by Nature is to get up close. After her year in the bush, Wendy realized that, 'all Nature wants to do is heal us. This is all the rest of nonhuman life wants – for us to be healed!'[13] You just have to go there to experience it. Several decades of research support this statement, revealing how strongly and positively people respond to open, grassy landscapes, scattered stands of trees, meadows, water, winding trails and elevated views.[14] The theoretical basis for these results is developed in E. O. Wilson's *biophilia* theory. Wilson argues that for 'human survival and mental health and fulfilment, we need the natural setting in which the human mind almost certainly evolved and in which culture has developed over these millions of years of evolution'.[15]

Author and ecologist David Rain Wallace supports this view, describing the healing effect of his experience in Nature in this way:

When I reached the trailhead and started walking through
the harmonious association of huge ponderosa pines,
incense cedars, and white firs with its apparently endless
diversity of wildflowers, shrubs, grasses, songbirds, and
insects, I experienced a novel sense of rightness. Growing
up in the suburbs had been an experience of fragmentation
as roads and buildings dissected the landscape. The thought
that this harmony would continue for dozens of miles
without interruption was like relief from a headache so
habitual I hadn't known I had it.[16]

Encounters with Nature do not always require 'wilderness'. Yollana, **Encounters with**
who lives in the inner city, had a surprise encounter with Nature **Nature do not**
when her family participated in Earth Hour in 2008. Earth Hour is **always require**
an international initiative that encourages homes and businesses to **'wilderness'**
turn off their lights for one hour to raise awareness about global
warming.[17] Here's what happened…

As we turned out the lights and sat down to a candlelit
dinner in our small dining room, I felt my whole being begin to relax in a completely different way. I felt rejuvenat-
ed by the dark. The flickering candles didn't eradicate it
as electric lights did. Instead, the flame danced within the
night. It gently drew me into its ancient and wild rhythm,
triggering ancestral memories of the nourishing power of
Nature embodied in the element of fire … and in the spa-   **As I sat there**
cious darkness of night.   **at my kitchen**

table, I was
As I sat there at my kitchen table, I was shocked to realize   **shocked to**
that – in places where electricity is just a flick of a switch   **realise that we**
away – we experience the natural dark of the evening only   **experience the**
when we are asleep. We turn our lights on well before sun-   **natural dark**
set and the last thing we do, as we get into bed, is to turn   **of the evening**
them off. We have successfully extended our days by many   **only when we**
hours, but we have lost something precious, found in the   **are asleep**
conscious engagement with natural night.

The second ingredient: Nourishing community

The healing of our present woundedness may lie in recognizing and reclaiming the capacity we all have to heal each other, the enormous power in the simplest of human relationships: the strength of a touch, the blessing of forgiveness, the grace of someone else taking you just as you are and finding in you an unsuspected goodness.

Rachel Naomi Remen[18]

How community engagement can nourish communities

Like nourishing Nature, nourishing community works both ways Rachel Remen reminds us that, like nourishing Nature, nourishing community *works both ways*, nourishing both the wider community and the individuals within it. Formal community engagement processes can play an important part in fostering the interactions that nourish communities. Approaches that facilitate learning, trust and engagement include:

- helping communities develop a clear vision of their preferred futures
- providing a safe and supportive environment for discussions and negotiation
- fostering understanding and opportunities for participants to express their opinions by providing opportunities for deep listening
- encouraging everyone to speak in plain language
- allowing adequate time for processes to unfold
- being patient with people as they grapple with sustainability issues.

For community engagement practitioners to be effective in providing these approaches, *they* need to be nourished by access to adequate resources However, for community engagement practitioners to be effective in providing these approaches, *they* need to be nourished by access to adequate resources. Then practitioners can help create opportunities for members of fragmented communities to reconnect with each other so that they show up, share their gifts and learn from each other.

240

A clear vision for the future: A Welcome Home in Timbarra

Wendy experienced how support can be generated through community engagement processes in 1990 when she worked with community artist/activist Graeme Dunstan in Timbarra, a new suburban community in Melbourne. Wendy, Graeme and a team of 'heart politicians' whom you met in Chapter 5, Education, designed a workshop for residents who had recently bought house lots in a new suburban estate. As a play on words, they called the workshop, 'A Welcome Home'. Graeme developed a detailed prospectus to ensure that facilitators, recorders and architects helping at the workshop would have a felt sense of the new residents they were welcoming because his initial research (he spoke to all registered participants by phone) revealed that some were likely to feel somewhat vulnerable. They were mostly first-time land buyers, a bit shy and unsure about the place and people that would become their new community. Having bought the land, they were now dealing with the financial and practical realities – and risks – of designing and building their homes. The well-known concept of 'buyer's remorse' had set in for some.

They were mostly first-time land buyers, a bit shy and unsure about the place and people that would become their new community

So that they could provide the best support to them, Graeme invited the staff team to *play the roles* of the registered participants. They were asked to put themselves in the shoes of the new lot buyers – a Sri Lankan family of nine, empty nesters moving from a neighbouring community, a couple expecting their first child – so they could viscerally experience the people and their energy and then be able to support them. Many of the facilitators were therapists so this approach was familiar to them. Graeme's vision for the Workshop was that:

> Lot buyers would read the personalized invitation and realize it was in their best interests to attend. As they arrived, they would quickly feel at home and affiliated with the people they would meet. There would be lots of good talking,

advice freely given and openly received, and introductions and meetings between neighbours open to explore with each other for the common ground that they would share in the future. The children would creatively engage in processes of planning and house design and share their work with their parents at the end of the session.

The Workshop session would finish as daylight faded. New neighbours would stay for supper and conversation. Some would leave because their children were tired and they had come a long way. Others would stay and continue talking with the architects, facilitators, recorders and their new neighbours. Food and lively music (provided by a bush band) would invite people to dance.

People would notice that the seeds of community had been planted because they would not hurry away. Rather, they would linger to talk and to hold contact with people who had been strangers only a couple of hours earlier

People would notice that the seeds of community had been planted because they would not hurry away. Rather, they would linger to talk and to hold contact with people who had been strangers only a couple of hours earlier.[19]

After they had envisaged the participants' feeling welcomed and supported, the workers found that they could easily imagine the appropriate environment for the workshop.

We were therefore not surprised to learn, as the years passed, that the modern-day Timbarra community boasts both strong community organizations and an enduring activist presence. We hope that the 'seeds of community', consciously envisaged, planted and acknowledged through the Welcome Home workshop, contributed, in some way, to those qualities.

A supportive environment: Sandwiches and tablecloths!

We have found that if we manage processes, from the moment when people first arrive 'at the workshop door' to our last contact with them, giving and receiving feedback well after the event, our efforts are more likely to be effective and satisfying for the participants (see Chapter 3). Literal nourishment – food and drink – is part of this. Cathy remembers one community engagement consultant carrying on endlessly about the importance of sandwiches. Sandwiches! 'Nothing will be achieved if we have hungry participants, facilitators or support crew.' It might seem obvious, but in a context of tight budgets, it was yet another cost Cathy had to justify to the authorities. Feeding thousands of participants and a large support crew does cost money. Looking at it from the perspective of nourishment and support, it is not expensive. It is a small part of an invaluable investment.

Sandwiches! 'Nothing will be achieved if we have hungry participants, facilitators or support crew'

In 2005, Wendy and Yollana facilitated a workshop for residents and government stakeholders in a redevelopment project in Minto, a public housing estate in south-western Sydney. The project had a troubled history. Residents and their advisers felt that the Department of Housing had begun the process of demolition and relocation without adequate social impact assessment or guidelines for fair and consistent treatment of existing residents. An independent study showed that 90 per cent of residents surveyed felt they had no involvement in the redevelopment and 9 per cent felt they had no power or say over the consultation process or outcomes.[20]

As so many community consultation activities were already underway (in response to resident action), our very specific role was to help participants create a vision of how the relationship between the community and the Department could be improved. Our workshop, entitled 'Imagining Our Common Purpose', focused on continuing to build strong and resilient relationships among participants in the redevelopment process. Our conversations with residents and other stakeholders revealed a strong and enduring sense of betrayal within the community. In particular, residents reported that they didn't feel respected or cared about by decision makers. Even the drab community meeting room where we held our workshop seemed to reflect this feeling. It featured barred windows, institutionally painted walls and shabby furniture.

Residents reported that they didn't feel respected or cared about by decision makers. Even the drab community meeting room where we held our workshop seemed to reflect this feeling

Continued

We played relaxing but joyful music for the participants' arrival

To bring care and respect into the process, we took great care to design a supportive environment that engaged all the senses. We came early and cleaned the room, bought flowers, a colourful tablecloth and an aromatherapy vaporizer. We played relaxing but joyful music for the participants' arrival and – of course – made sure that participants received wholesome and satisfying refreshments with morning tea, lunch and afternoon tea.

We remember the satisfied grin we gave each other when the first participant walked into the room, stopped for a second, looked around and said, in a light-hearted voice, 'This feels different!'

Figure 9.3 Minto workshop participants commit to working together, 2005

The workshop was an unqualified success. Careful attention to 'the little things' was a big part of the nourishing process. The photograph (Figure 9.3) shows the participants joining hands at the close of the workshop to symbolize their commitment to a harmonious working relationship.

Deep listening and speaking in plain words

In a 1991 workshop for public housing tenants in Alice Springs, which Wendy conducted with her colleague Ann Forsyth (who helped to design and develop the Minnesota Block Exercise discussed in Chapter 4), participants were invited to draw and describe the advantages and disadvantages of their housing. Responding to the exercise, one elderly participant shyly whispered, 'I don't have anything to say about my house'. Ann took a seat beside her and listened to her story. As the woman responded to her gentle questions, Ann was able to draw the house, and eventually produce several pages of notes working with a participant who originally claimed she had 'nothing to say'.[21] At the end of the workshop, the woman thanked Wendy, saying how much she'd enjoyed talking with 'that nice young girl from a small country town in New South Wales', who listened so carefully to all her ideas, however silly they might have seemed. Eighteen years ago, the woman who has become a professor of planning at Cornell University unobtrusively demonstrated the powerful – and understated – skill of listening across difference.

> **Careful attention to 'the little things' was a big part of the nourishing process**

> **As the woman responded to her gentle questions, Ann was able to draw the house, and eventually produce several pages of notes working with a participant who originally claimed she had 'nothing to say'**

Figures 9.4, 9.5 Ann Forsyth helps a public housing tenant describe the features of her house, Alice Springs, 1991

Adequate time and patient facilitation

Community engagement is time-consuming, especially when we are dealing with complex issues. We need to be patient throughout. Nourishing community engagement processes give participants, including experts, time and space to mull over ideas before making a decision. In community engagement with sustainability, this quality is particularly important. As we learn about the extent of our unsustainable actions, we need time to address personal dilemmas and identify hopeful alternatives before we can move on to global socio-economic analyses, and identify opportunities for individual and collective action. Often in community engagement this process can be facilitated by simply having the patience to listen and give community members the attention they need to feel safe and empowered.

Community engagement is time-consuming, we need to be patient throughout

Yollana remembers a wise monk-in-training inducting her into the care of 100 potted plants in a conference centre where she was working some years ago. 'The key to making anything shine', he whispered, 'is to help it feel love. And the key to feeling loved is *time.*'

Given enough time and attention, plants, people and processes can all transform and blossom.

Given enough time and attention, plants, people and processes can all transform and blossom

Nourishment by community

> When people realize that the community is there to sustain them, they have the most secure feelings in the world. The fear starts to leave, and they are imbued with hope.
>
> Jeanette C. Armstrong[22]

Asking people for help is one of the keys to fostering a community where people feel safe, secure and nourished, where people feel that others will sustain them. Many of us have learned to wear a mask that communicates, 'I'm okay. I have it all sorted out. I don't need any help, thanks,' telling ourselves that it's better not to 'burden' anyone with our problems. Yet one of the greatest gifts we can give is to ask for help when we genuinely need it. Asking demonstrates vulnerability. Others are given permission to show their vulnerability. Asking can also empower others to find solutions.

Communities are the heart and hands of the sustainability movement

Martin Prechtel is a leading writer, thinker and teacher who lived for many years within a community of Tzutujil Mayans. In the Epilogue to his eloquent memoir, *Long Life Honey in the Heart* (1999), Prechtel tells how, after he had served as a village chief for a year, the responsibilities of keeping the village alive left him financially destitute. Shortly after he concluded his work as chief, he sold a number of paintings to outsiders who turned up 'miraculously and unsolicited' to buy his work. He decided to use the money to pay back the ex-chiefs, their wives and chieftesses who had helped him financially in the past year. His offers were met with great hostility: bitter scolding, hateful insults and missiles of pebbles and wood.

Taking refuge in the house of his friend and mentor, Prechtel struggled to understand their reactions. In a persuasive and impassioned speech about the mutual indebtedness and interdependence that sustain the village, his friend explains how the whole point is to 'get so entangled in debt that no normal human can possibly remember who owes whom what, and how much'.[23] He revealed:

> *Everything comes into this Earth hungry and interdependent on all other things, animals, and people, so they can eat, be warmed, and not be lonely. I know you know this, but why do you push it all away now? We don't have a word for that kind of death, that isolation of not belonging to all life...*[24]

Being nourished by community means accepting our dependence on others as a blessing, rather than a curse

Being nourished by community means accepting our dependence on others as a blessing, rather than a curse, and embracing the opportunity that it gives us to participate in community life.

The third ingredient: Nourishing ourselves and the Personal Sustainability Action Plan (PSAP)

The authors of the book *Worldchanging* (2006) recommend that we develop a *Personal Action Plan* to support us individually to make 'smart choices' toward sustainability. The Personal Action Plan suggests that we take climate change seriously and ask ourselves questions, like:

- What kind of stuff do I buy?
- What do I do for a living?
- Where do I live?

They also suggest we check our carbon footprint and consider using personal carbon trading and carbon offsets.[25]

Our experience in community engagement with sustainability is that it is important not simply to plan what we can do externally, but also to know how we are going to nourish ourselves in that process so that we can sustain engagement. Successful professionals and activists know that to make a difference, they need to give, to work and to take action. They also need to pace themselves, to rest, reflect and receive. When our own cup is full, we cannot help but let it overflow to our communities and the natural world.

Successful professionals and activists know that to make a difference, they need to give, to work and to take action. They also need to pace themselves, to rest, reflect and receive

We have developed the *Personal Sustainability Action Plan* to support personal and community engagement with sustainability and help avoid overwhelm and burnout. The *Plan* helps us align our personal passions with our visions for sustainability. Thoughtful, heart-centred planning can keep our passion flowing so that it continues to inspire action over the long term.

The four steps of the PSAP are *discovering vision*, *identifying values*, *engaging passion* and *developing practices*. Each step is important in motivating, supporting and structuring individual action toward creating a sustainable world. These brief definitions explain how they fit together:

1 *A vision* simply states what we want and where we are going. Like a beacon, it shines so we can steer toward it. A vision helps keep us moving forward.

2 *Values* provide a guide for our journey, giving it personal meaning. Like a rudder on a boat, our core values align us with our purpose and help keep us on track.

3 *Passion* refers to our unique affinities, talents and skills: what we love to do and what comes easily to us. Engaging passion is like engaging a motor that drives a boat forward. Yet without a suitable channel, passion can exhaust itself.

4 *Practices* are the daily habits that keep us nourished. Like steering, practices require constant vigilance and attention. Yet as they become habits, attention becomes easier. Practices provide a structure that supports us as we pursue our vision, aligned with our purpose and passion.

Practices provide a structure that supports us as we pursue our vision, aligned with our purpose and passion

In another publication, we expand on how we can discover our vision, embrace our purpose and engage our passion.[26]

Discovering vision

For both personal and community engagement with sustainability, we need to have a clear (and evolving) vision of what we want

As discussed above, for both personal and community engagement with sustainability, we need to have a clear (and evolving) vision of what we want.[27] According to *Worldchanging*:

The bravest and most important thing any of us can do is to actively imagine a much better future: not to imagine it in the casual sense of daydreaming about it, but to imagine it in the way an architect imagines a house she is planning to build – to imagine it as a reality, to try to see it whole, to lovingly dwell on its details, and to see ourselves walking through it one day.[28]

When Yollana wrote out her personal vision for global sustainability, she found that it gave her increased clarity and motivation to engage with sustainability. It also helped her to prioritize subsequent actions and avoid wasting time on activities not aligned with her vision. Her vision is fourfold:

Spiritual Connectedness: Where all people can feel at home in themselves; feel self-love, self-respect and hope for the future.

Social Justice: Where all people are empowered to overcome limiting factors in their lives and are free to pursue their dreams in wholesome and sustainable ways.

Environmental Balance: A global sense of respect for Nature, grounded in practical actions and sustainable lifestyles for all cultures.

World Peace: Ending the senseless fighting for resources by creating global communities united in peace, love, creativity and all-gain situations.

Social change consultant Katrina Shields reminds us that, while there are many reasons why it is important to envision our preferred future, we must also remain flexible. A truly sustainable vision is flexible and inclusive to accommodate and integrate the dreams of others, and allow for individual diversity.[29] When we clarify our own vision, Shields suggests that we also ask:

A truly sustainable vision is flexible and inclusive to accommodate and integrate the dreams of others, and allow for individual diversity

- How does my vision also allow for individual diversity?
- Who is left out of my ideal world?
- Is there room in my dreams for all kinds of people?
- How will there be space for all other life forms with whom I share the Earth?[30]

A vision creates a compelling context for our values, our passions and our practices.

Identifying values

Our values can be deeply sustaining and become an important yardstick by which we can judge whether an action, project or task is likely to be personally or communally sustainable

Values stem naturally from a clear vision. As ecological economist Robert Costanza points out, we 'cannot state a value without stating the goal being served'.[31] Yet once we discover our vision, it is important that we *do* identify the values that are informed by, and inform, it. This allows our vision to maintain the necessary flexibility without compromising our core values.

Values can provide a sense of purpose and meaning and can inform the many activities and roles that we choose to play in personal and community engagement with sustainability.[32] Clearly identified, our values can be deeply sustaining and become an important yardstick by which we can judge whether an action, project or task is likely to be personally or communally sustainable.

Engaging passions

> If we are to achieve a richer culture, rich in contrasting values, we must recognize the whole gamut of human potentialities, and so weave a less arbitrary social fabric, one in which each diverse human gift will find a fitting place.
>
> Margaret Mead[33]

If we were to ask what we can do within our communities to support sustainability, an infinite number of 'jobs' (both paid and volunteer) cry out for someone to fill them. Even if we have the skills, we cannot do all of them. However, each of us *can* do something. And, as Mead implies, the sum of our 'somethings' can make a big difference. We believe that *if we want to do something sustainable, we must find ways to do what we love*. Many, many tasks are required to make the world a better place. Our engagement is likely to be more effective if we use our energy where it is naturally inclined to go. When we engage in ways that are aligned with our personal vision and values and where we already have talent or passion, our activity is also likely to be sustained for a longer time. People are more productive when they are having fun.

Our engagement is likely to be more effective if we use our energy where it is naturally inclined to go

Developing practices

Sustainability on a personal level is about the cultivation of habits that are stable and supportive. Habits that nourish both our communities and ourselves can generate personal energy and improve our effectiveness.[34] We can use the practices below within and outside of formal community engagement processes to help us remain nourished – to come to, stay at and return to the table.

Practice 1: Attuning with your energy source

In *Blessed Unrest*, leading environmentalist and social activist Paul Hawken describes how the entire sustainability movement is driven by the invisible impulses of human energies:

> *The movement ... is the most complex coalition of human organizations the world has ever seen. The incongruity of anarchists, billionaire funders, street clowns, scientists, youthful activists, indigenous and native people, diplomats, computer geeks, writers, strategists, peasants, and students all working together toward common goals is a testament to human impulses that are unstoppable and eternal.*
>
> Paul Hawken[35]

The entire sustainability movement is driven by the invisible impulses of human energies

Although poets, mystics and others in the wisdom traditions have described this energy as the essence of humanity for centuries, it is difficult for scientists to quantify. Whether you call it a quantum field, energy, lifeforce, *prana*, *qi*, inspiration, creation, Nature, the Universe, holy spirit, God or Goddess, there is a source of personal inspiration and energy that is unexplainable, beyond the reaches of science or our rational minds. It influences every aspect of life. It must be respected because of the large numbers of people who believe in and value this ineffable quality. In the words of the beloved 13th century Persian poet, Rumi, 'There are hundreds of ways to kneel and kiss the ground.' There are many ways to attune with this energy.

A variety of methods can help us: meditation, reflection, music, dance and time in Nature are all 'ways in'. We have discovered that it is not so important *what* you do, as that you make a conscious effort to do *something*. Then, as Rabbi Lerner argues, we must 'enhance our capacity to treat others as embodiments of the sacred and to respond with awe, wonder and radical amazement at the grandeur of the universe'.[36]

Practice 2: Learning to work 'with the flow'

This quality can make a considerable difference to our effectiveness. Knowing what it feels like when everything is flowing makes being 'out of the flow' much more uncomfortable. Athletes call it being *in the zone*. When we are in that space, we are naturally effective, efficient and productive and everything feels effortless. Attuning to this quality in engagement processes can make a huge difference to our effectiveness in working for sustainability. Our activist-artist colleague Graeme has taught us much about that.

In our experience, there are three keys to re-entering the flow when things are not going smoothly:

- *First, it's important to pause*, just for a moment. Too often we push on with a task, thinking, 'I don't have time to take a break', when a moment away to re-energize or get a fresh perspective will help us to think more clearly, be more productive, avoid mistakes and ultimately give us more time, not less.
- *A second key is to move.* Physically moving our bodies around will inevitably help shift our attitudes and our energy. To get up and walk outside is a simple act that involves a thousand subtle changes that make a big difference. Our experience is that changes in physiology, visual perspective, light, temperature and colour can subtly affect our mood and trigger different thought patterns.

- *Finally, a simple ritual* like lighting a candle, taking a deep breath or touching the Earth can help us reconnect with a greater source of energy that energizes and inspires us.

How long will these three steps take? A minute? Three minutes? Ten minutes? It is different every time and for each person. We experience that it will usually take less time to stop, move and feel and then come back to what we were doing if we take a break, rather than keep banging our head against that darn wall! The Great Bear Rainforest story, presented earlier in this chapter, clearly illustrates this point.

Practice 3: Working with the shadow

The *shadow* is one side of our personality (or culture) from which we turn away. It is 'dark' because it is usually unconscious or unintegrated.[37] Strong emotions such as despair, shame or fear can cause us to avoid our shadow sides. However, left unchecked and unexplored, our unconscious personal motivations and psychological issues can sabotage our conscious purposes towards sustainability.[38]

In their group environmental science masters thesis, Cathy and her colleagues explored ways to navigate nihilistic responses to the 'alarming realities' of the environmental and social destruction we face.[39] They found that when we deny our shadow side, individually or as a community, we give it more power. Only when we delve deeper, beyond the initial 'feel-good' reaction, can we move below surface-level responses to sustainability problems, which are often merely quick 'technological fixes'. To avoid this, they suggested that we 'search honestly within ourselves for all our motives in a situation, as well as for disowned or difficult emotions or destructive attitudes'.[40] They recommended that we ask:

Left unchecked and unexplored, our unconscious personal motivations and psychological issues can sabotage our conscious purposes towards sustainability

- What is really going on in this situation?
- What might I be denying or avoiding in terms of my insights or feelings?
- What would they demand of me if I didn't deny them?
- And how could I respond constructively to this demand?[41]

Using these approaches, we can avoid deluding ourselves about the negative impacts of our daily actions upon the Earth and open ourselves up to greater feeling and insights. The environmentalists in the Great Bear Rainforest story drew on this practice to great effect by being prepared to own their shadows while suspending negative or alienating judgement of the other actors. Their willingness and ability to do this hard personal and collective work dramatically transformed the engagement space.

Practice 4: Attracting and receiving support

Support enables both external and internal transformation

It is vital that we practise receiving support: learning how to ask for and accept help, to listen and to communicate our needs

Earlier in this chapter, we emphasized just how much support an engaged community can provide and how important that is for sustaining the life of the community, as well as individuals within it. Psychologist David Adams reminds us that support enables both external and internal transformation.[42] To attract support, we must be clear about our vision and values so that we can find people, tools and resources to help us achieve them. Our colleague Graeme Dunstan clearly demonstrated that approach in the Timbarra Welcome Home workshop described above. Willingness to support others in their visions and to work across differences is also important. And it is vital that we practise receiving support: learning how to ask for and accept help, to listen and to communicate our needs. More difficult than it sounds, receiving support means showing our vulnerabilities and admitting our dependency, as illustrated in Martin Prechtel's experience in the Tzutujil Mayan community.

Accountability and support groups, such as Wendy's Heart Group discussed in Chapter 5, Education, can function as important structures for supporting engagement with sustainability.[43] Finally, many of us draw support directly from Nature.

Practice 5: Allowing grief

'After the Al Gore training, I didn't sleep for a month', exclaimed Mary Maher, our Australian planner colleague. Learning the science behind climate change and its predicted consequences had affected her personally. 'When you finally know all the facts like that, you can't help but be changed by them', she exclaimed. 'You stop taking things for granted. After that, I would just kiss the Earth every day with gratitude at the opportunity for being here.'[44] As Mary spoke, tears welled up in her eyes. Engaging with sustainability is deeply challenging. We must face all that has already been destroyed, desecrated and lost. From years of working with her and observing her tireless activism, we know Mary to be an enlightened professional, one who can allow a few tears in public without shame. Unfortunately, in the quest for objectivity and 'reason', many of us have lost the common sense and repressed the common humanity that would allow us to shed tears of sadness for what is lost and tears of joy for what remains.[45]

Avoiding feelings of loss can suppress our sensitivity. While this may appear to be a strategy for avoiding pain, in the short term, it may also disconnect us from compassion and ultimately prolong our experiences of pain. We cannot help the Earth, or ourselves, if we are disconnected from our feelings.

Practice 6: Including humour

Humour is a powerful friend in the journey of life and it's particularly valuable in community engagement with sustainability. A good sense of humour is related to 'muscle relaxation, control of pain and discomfort, positive mood states and overall psychological

Humour allows a healthy degree of emotional 'distancing', which enables us to get perspective and perhaps think more clearly about a stressful situation

health including a healthy self-concept'.[46] It allows a healthy degree of emotional 'distancing', which enables us to get perspective and perhaps think more clearly about a stressful situation. Although some types of humour present a danger of trivializing serious events, thus discouraging action, at best humour 'can increase the likelihood of conscious efforts at seeking alternative perspectives to problems'.[47] Our colleague Sophia van Ruth, an expert in laughter, has initiated many community workshop participants into her hilarious laughter routines, which serve as surprising and effective icebreakers.

Figure 9.6 Workshop participants laughing, directed by Sophia van Ruth, Bonnyrigg, Sydney, 2005

Practice 7: Joyful service

The act of giving can, in itself, be a source of nourishment

The act of giving can, in itself, be a source of nourishment. Wendy explains that one of the qualities of an ethic of caring is joy. In contrast to the belief that associates pleasure with immoral action, '[t]he emotional responses in practising an ethic of caring may be compared to an embodied state of grace'.[48] This is the law of reciprocity: when you give to a good cause, you receive much in return.[49]

The story below, penned by a journalist with a background in the environment movement, reinforces this principle:

A few years ago I attended a news conference for the Dalai Lama... He was in Melbourne speaking to tens of thousands of people on the subject of happiness, and one thoughtful journalist put up his hand to ask a question. 'Your Holiness,' he said, 'how is it possible to be happy when one knows that so many people around the world are suffering so terribly? How is it possible to have compassion and happiness at the same time?'

The Dalai Lama's reply demonstrated that when it comes to finding the recipe for sustainable activism, wise old Tibetan Buddhists have a lot more in common with Western behavioural psychologists than we might have imagined. 'If you focus only on your own suffering,' he said, 'you cannot be happy, because this leads to paralysis. But if you are focusing on the suffering of others, and if you are doing something about it, you will be energised, and you will be able to find happiness.'[50]

Practice 8: Finding cause for celebration

When we do the best that we can, we never know what miracle is wrought in our life, or in the life of another.

Helen Keller [51]

In 1978, Wendy had the privilege of spending time with Margaret Mead shortly before her death, discussing what she saw as the futility of some of her activist work. Mead shared with her that, 'Every good deed has a value in its own right. You may never be able to see the consequences, but there is a value in it.' As a mentor and feminist, she encouraged Wendy to practise celebrating her achievements, however small. Wendy began a daily ritual: at the end of each day writing down what she had achieved – no matter how small. This simple process helped her realize that she did not always need to see visible outcomes or 'results' from activist work. Similarly, sustainable agriculture practitioner Michael Abelman argues that keeping hope alive requires 'focusing on the small

Every good deed has a value in its own right. You may never be able to see the consequences, but there is a value in it

successes: on local and incremental change; one handful of seeds, one child, one garden at a time'.[52]

Kitchen table conversation starters

- What does nourishment mean to you in the context of engagement with sustainability?
- Who do you know who has avoided engagement with sustainability issues because of burnout, being overwhelmed, or fear of these? And what kind of nourishment might they need to engage?
- What kinds of activities nourish you? Do you make time for these activities, or do they end up low on your list of priorities?
- How have you been nourished by your communities? Are there ways you could be *more* open to receive this nourishment?
- What kinds of nourishment does your community need? Who could provide this? And how would your community be different if it was nourished in this way?
- How have you been nourished by Nature? Are there ways you could be more open to receive *this* nourishment?
- How are the natural areas in your community nourished or neglected? How could this be improved? If your local Nature could speak, what would it say?

For more opportunities to continue these conversations about community engagement with sustainability, please visit www.kitchentablesustainability.com.

Final thoughts

We hope that this chapter has demonstrated the vital role of nourishment for self, community and the Earth in supporting community engagement with sustainability. Nourishment must be physical, emotional and interpersonal. Ultimately, it is about caring. With Rabbi Michael Lerner, we envisage a world where we measure productivity in terms of caring, kindness and generosity, ethical and ecological sensitivity. This caring for self and others underpins the recipes already discussed in the **EATING** model: *Education, Action, Trust* and *Inclusion*. It should underpin good *Governance* as well, which is an expression of care for citizens and for the Earth. We need to be reacquainted with all of these components. Yet with regard to governance, of all the social systems, we probably have the longest road to travel. Still, we have taken enough first steps to know that it is possible. In the following chapter, we explore the opportunities to move forward from these first steps to create truly sustainable and engaged systems of governance.

Note: A complimentary *Personal Sustainability Action Plan* Workbook is available for download at our website: www.kitchentablesustainability.com. It provides detailed and systematic guidance and examples.

10

GOVERNANCE

The primary imperative for
sustainability governance
is the acknowledgement that society is
only as healthy as its individual members,
and that these members are healthiest when
they have a say in the functioning of
their home environment.

Maged Senbel,
2005, p72

'Your input will be taken on board': Wendy's reflections

Often during a community engagement event, like a meeting or a workshop, a senior person (planner, developer, their consultant, a bureaucrat) will thank participants and tell them (always in the passive voice), 'Your input will be taken on board.'

But where does this information go? What is this ghost ship that sails away into the mist carrying a cargo of comments from community engagement processes? I have never seen this ship on the ocean or entering a port. Nobody I know has, either. To my knowledge, it has never docked and unloaded its treasures of community comments or the plans that evolved from community 'input'.

I see this ship in my mind's eye, lying on its side somewhere, rusted beyond recognition. That 'somewhere' is a very long way from the place where my neighbours and I contributed our ideas. Long ago, all our heartfelt and passionate contributions slid off the deck into the ocean and were washed out to sea. Some perished on the rocky beach. Tiny shreds still cling to the rotting timbers. Vestiges of our passionate words echo weakly inside the rusted hull…

So, if you don't mind, if you can't tell me where the ship is headed, who is steering it and how its precious cargo is to be handled, I don't want my ideas 'taken on board', thanks very much.

So, if you don't mind, if you can't tell me where the ship is headed, who is steering it and how its precious cargo is to be handled, I don't want my ideas 'taken on board', thanks very much

Figure 10.1 Your input will be 'taken on board'

Introduction

'Your input will be taken "on board".'

How many times have you heard this phrase during community engagement processes? For us it always rings warning bells. It makes us question, 'How will that be taken on board?', 'How will differences of opinion be resolved?', 'Who will make the final decisions?' and 'Who will be responsible for implementation?'

After 40 years of hearing this mantra, Wendy, in exasperation, began carrying around a photo of a rusted, beached cargo ship lying abandoned on a forsaken beach at a ship salvage yard. Her call to action: That is where community contributions will end up unless we challenge the 'that will be taken "on board" approach'.

Governance – the final ingredient in our *EATING* approach – is often overlooked in community engagement processes. Musings about housekeeping and imagining better futures will remain simply that unless we roll up our sleeves and address the nitty-gritty details of how to transform ideas and energy into sustainable action. *For that we need governance.* There is much hard work that goes on (often behind the scenes) to enable a great meal to be shared at the kitchen table – leafing through recipe books, deciding on the menu, taking allergies, cultural requirements and food preferences into account, selecting and buying ingredients or preferably picking them from the garden, finding the appropriate beverage, setting the table, preparing the meal, enjoying it, discussing it, clearing up afterwards. We could go on. And so it is with community engagement with sustainability. To transform ideas into action, we must address the *how*. This is essentially what governance is about in the context of community engagement with sustainability.

Governance – the final ingredient in our EATING approach – is often overlooked in community engagement processes

Governance at the Redland Youth Plaza

One of Steph's projects is a good illustration of the importance of building in governance approaches at the very beginning. And this was a project that involved young people, who are not always renowned for housekeeping or doing the laundry! Construction of the Redland Youth Plaza began in 2007, while Steph was working with cultural planning agency Plan C in Brisbane. The Youth Plaza, located 15 kilometres east of Brisbane, features a world-class skate and BMX bike facility and live performance infrastructure, co-located with a basketball court and playing fields. The site was designed to become a highly supported and supportive youth space attracting young people from throughout South-East Queensland.[1] The Council's project manager was committed to ensuring that the facility was relevant to the needs that local young people had expressed for years. Collaborative work with them focused on involvement in engagement activities to shape its planning and design and to determine management and activation principles and approaches.

Early on, governance issues were raised. While the Plaza was being constructed, a Plaza Advisory Crew (PAC) was established. The PAC was a community group responsible for activating the facility, involving the broader community and working with the local council to resolve management issues before they could become problems. Steph worked with a diverse group of local skaters, BMX riders, artists, musicians, event producers, business owners, sponsors and council officers to develop the PAC's structure and protocols. He also proposed governance protocols. The long process was tolerated by the young people only because they had a direct commitment to the success of the facility. They knew from experience that management problems can plague skate parks. The PAC, facilitated by Plan C, met weekly for three months to resolve meeting protocols, decision-making processes and conflict-resolution procedures. They also collaboratively designed the launch event and learned event-production skills. When Wendy heard about this governance process she nearly wept, as her local Nimbin Skate Park, completed but unopened, has sat unused for several years because management and acoustic issues were not resolved early on. In a small rural community with little recreation opportunities for young people, this is regarded locally as a massive failure of governance. It did not have to be this way.[2]

Back in Redland Shire, despite wide acknowledgement of the importance of establishing group operating processes from the beginning, many PAC members felt the 'governance' work was tedious. Members were keen to discuss the launch and the fun they would have when the facility was completed. Governance was an intangible 'something', especially to the younger members. When Steph reported that all regular PAC meetings would incorporate a 'governance session', a teenaged member of the PAC asked, 'What is governance, anyway?' It's a good question.

What is governance, anyway?

Governance includes 'all "collective action" promoted for public purposes'[3] and describes how the 'whole system of interrelated actors performs these actions'.[4] In the context of community engagement with sustainability, governance includes practical matters like those the Redland Youth Plaza PAC addressed: capacity building and strengthening, conflict-resolution procedures, decision-making processes, evaluation and monitoring mechanisms, meeting protocols, process design and so forth. Later in this chapter we provide some recipes for good governance which offer practical suggestions.

Throughout *Kitchen Table Sustainability* we've emphasized that sustainability problems are not simple or even complicated. They are complex. They are 'wicked' problems that demand innovative approaches. Governance is a critical part of any solution. Table 10.1 presents a typology of societal problems and corresponding strategies. Most sustainability problems exist at the *complex* end of the spectrum. The typology suggests that these types of problems require a governance approach, diffuse decision making and ongoing learning. We need to remember that when designing community engagement with sustainability.

Table 10.1 Typology of societal problems and strategies

Problem/ Solution	Simple to Complex			
Type of approach	Technical	Market	Stakeholder	Governance
Decision making	Expert elite	Cost–benefit analysis	Consensus building	Diffuse
Policy process	Regulations	Negotiation	Pacification	Learning

Source: after Hisschemöller (1993); Dirven et al (2002)[5]

Considerations of value and power are central to resolving governance issues.[6] We argue that it is very difficult to resolve governance questions unless the community engagement goal and 'promise to the public' are both clear. This brings us back to Chapter 3, where we presented the IAP2 Spectrum of Public Participation. If the goal is 'empowerment', very different governance mechanisms are required than if the goal is simply to 'inform'. Substantial research into participatory governance has expanded our understanding of the benefits of participatory, rather than representative, governance. Nevertheless, our sad experience is that most engagement practices in the countries we know still resist these innovative approaches, as Wendy's story below illustrates.

Considerations of value and power are central to resolving governance issues

One terrible day I had to present a draft report to my clients, senior planning bureaucrats in Sydney. They asked for a short presentation so I came with only a few notes.

'Nothing fancy,' they said on the phone. 'Just tell us the highlights.'

We'd been working on the report for nearly four months and had conducted a massive review of Australian and international research. Our client wanted to know what 'leading practice' looked like and we were keen to find out, too. The topic was one aspect of community engagement. We felt privileged to be giving advice to such senior people. We hoped our research and our experience would make a difference. They had a huge project on their hands and seemed desperate for our advice.

Steph, the activist, had his reservations as he saw me off at Brisbane airport. Yollana was more sanguine: 'Tell them all about it and don't forget to tell them how important it is. Good reports *always* see the light of day, Wendy.' she offered.

I smiled, knowing that she was probably wrong but not wanting to disappoint her. Yollana was always reminding me to watch those negative 'seed thoughts'.

But later that day when I was ushered into the small meeting room and looked at the ashen-faced men who greeted me, I knew that things were not going to turn out the way Yollana had dreamed.

The project manager got straight to the point while his other three colleagues looked at their hands.

'Give us your summary, please, Wendy,' he requested, somewhat formally.

I reviewed the principles we had drawn from our research and experience and the guidance we felt would help his department with their project.

There was a long silence when I finished. Then one of the other men spoke. His voice was small for his size. He kept looking down.

Continued

'Look, Wendy,' he said, shuffling his papers. He picked up my report and held it gingerly, as though it might burn his fingers. 'We know you put a lot of work into this study and it's a really good job. Truly it is. Your recommendations are right on the money. We can see how much thought you've put into it.'

He put down the report.

'And you have to know that we will never be able to implement a single one of your recommendations. I could bet my life on it. Not a single one.'

I stared at him, breathless, heat rising in my body. 'Not a single one.'

'Yes,' the project manager spoke up where the other man had left off. He fixed his eyes on a point on the wall behind me. 'I'm afraid that's right. *Totally* right. Please don't blame us for this. Our Minister would never allow us to do *any* of the things you've recommended. We have no budget to do anything properly – in consultation terms – on this project. And I am afraid there's more bad news: your report will never see the light of day. We can't let it get loose in the system, so you must promise not to release it, either. Is that understood?'

I nodded.

'I'm really sorry. Honestly, I am,' he continued. 'Please don't have a bad opinion of us, Wendy. We just can't do anything else.'

We settled the reporting arrangements. I confirmed that my invoice would be in the post.

I rang my office from the coffee shop downstairs.

'Oh dear,' Yollana said. 'I'm so sorry. At least they told you the truth. *That* part was good.'

'Please let me speak to Steph,' I said.

'I'm sorry too,' he mumbled into the phone. 'It's a great report. I wish I had been wrong.'

Unfortunately, these sorts of outcomes often accompany community engagement processes. Now, as we face the most serious problems we have ever faced as an Earth community, we need to do better. We need to think ahead to the governance implications of not acting.

Good governance practices are based both on local sustainability needs and active engagement by the local community to meet those needs. The expression, 'If you're not part of the solution, you're part of the problem', coined by *Chicago News* columnist Sydney J. Harris in the late 1940s, reflects our belief that maximum involvement in community engagement processes and consequent actions are required to achieve sustainability. We are interested in exploring governance that enables collective responsibility for the outcomes of community engagement. From practice there is ample evidence that the results of community-led collaboration are vastly superior to processes kept behind closed doors. *Participatory governance* is a valuable approach that has generated much research and experimentation in practice.

From practice there is ample evidence that the results of community-led collaboration are vastly superior to processes kept behind closed doors

Exploring how people can engage actively with sustainability and how to enable it are the primary purposes of this book. Community governance is the ultimate embodiment of participatory democracy. Without authentic local access to decision making, our communities are at risk and will grow and develop in ways that do not accurately reflect the diversity of existing local knowledge, needs and interests. Participatory governance diversifies the range of interests and perspectives from the narrow focus currently expressed through government and industry's management of governance practices. Ensuring that those seated at the table represent a diversity of voices and perspectives and using good governance approaches increases participation by those who might otherwise be marginalized or ignored. We recommend a very different paradigm from the one in which we are currently embedded. In that model, as we explain in Chapter 8, Inclusion, those outside of the mainstream are often forced to battle to have their perspectives listened to by decision makers, who often appear preoccupied with what they believe to be the concerns of the dominant group.

Locating our views about participatory governance

When we were preparing this chapter, we had many conversations about participatory governance. What do we mean by it, how do we locate our views and why does it matter to community engagement with sustainability? Karl, the only one of us formally trained in sociology, downed tools in his makeshift kitchen, left his kitchen table, moved to his desk and undertook to provide an explanation, a summary of which follows.

In this book, we use a working definition of participatory governance, based on research and practice. Participatory governance is one of the foundation planks of participatory democracy and civil society's engagement in reshaping not only the institutions of governance, but also the reformation of democracy. This approach aims to empower the voices of civil society in decision making by maximizing accountability and transparency. As Kohler-Koch, a presenter of a European Union Commission research paper, explained, 'Both political discourse and normative theories of democracy attribute civil society a key role in reinvigorating democracy'.[7]

Kohler-Koch's paper, as well as others,[8] explores the tensions between the system of governance, the bureaucracy and external political disaffection. Governments in Western democracies face increasing pressures regarding this potential issue of legitimacy and mandate. Not surprisingly, increasing the perception of participation and inclusion is high on the agenda in many countries, as evidenced by newly elected Australian Prime Minister Kevin Rudd's Australia 2020 workshop to explore ideas for Australia's future and communicate them to the Federal Government.

Governments in Western democracies face increasing pressures regarding this potential issue of legitimacy and mandate

Continued

It reflects a principle of our practice: to provide opportunities for even the smallest and softest voices to be heard

This approach, it is hoped, will somewhat insulate governments and institutions from blame for policy failures in what is an increasingly complex economic, environmental, as well governance, environment. While acknowledging a degree of cynicism for such perceptions, we also see this as an opportunity for added momentum to a practice we have advocated throughout our work. It reflects a principle of our practice: to provide opportunities for even the smallest and softest voices to be heard.

Our approach in our community engagement work and in writing this book is grounded in the theoretical writings of Jürgen Habermas (communicative action theory) and Paulo Freire's educative work with poor people in South America. We believe that both theories are applicable to the problems confronting modern-day communities. We have found that institutions and the people who operate in them are as protective of their official territories as they are self-protective. Not surprisingly, many resist change and are far from transparent in their decision making. Often they tend to obfuscate, causing serious problems for communities trying to engage with them. Nevertheless, those institutions need to retain their functions while we work to rebuild them. We need competent people to operate them. We need to find a way to repair the ship while keeping it afloat. But these gatekeepers must change if communities are to have real influence in addressing the planetary crisis. We, our neighbours and professionals everywhere, must find ways to help them change while the 'ship of society' remains afloat.

This is where the educative processes and strategies at the heart of Freire's work join the insights of the Frankfurt School.[9] Our experience reveals that only through facilitating the empowerment of individuals to represent themselves and their communities in the company of their neighbours, by strengthening their own capacities, asking informed questions and aiming for institutional accountability in their dealings with functionaries in those institutions, is there hope for the future. We believe that sinking the ship is not an option.

Five good governance principles for community engagement with sustainability

Many characteristics of good governance are advocated by existing research and practice. These include approaches that are empowering, transparent, responsive, consensus-oriented, participatory, accountable, equitable, inclusive, effective, efficient, coordinated, flexible, strategic, information-rich, persistent and so on. In previous books in the *Community Participation in Practice* suite of books (1994–2003), Wendy and colleagues teased out many of these approaches in illustrative case studies from their practice. This is well tilled ground. Alarmingly, however, many proponents and practitioners ignore the advice and warnings that are readily available.

We have identified five principles that we consider essential for designing governance approaches for community engagement with sustainability. We outline them briefly below before sharing two cautionary tales: a tale of a community engagement process that fell by the wayside and a tale that demonstrates these principles in action.

Principle 1: Accountability

Accountability is vital to developing new paradigms of governance. It provides an ongoing openness and responsibility regarding how governance occurs, ensuring that relationships based on trust and collaboration can emerge. Governance structures must be accountable to the community and to supporting local, regional and global sustainability on all levels. Creating accountability in governance requires a transparent, multistep approach that focuses on diverse engagement, action to flow from this engagement, evaluation to follow action and review of the overall process to emerge from this evaluation. If at any stage the doors are closed and the process stops being accountable, governance opportunities are lost and the community ceases to have the influence that it needs to be effective.

If at any stage the doors are closed and the process stops being accountable, governance opportunities are lost and the community ceases to have the influence that it needs to be effective

Principle 2: Transparency

Transparent governance practice requires full community access to decision-making processes, legal and statutory information (and that bugbear 'commercial-in-confidence' material). Transparency requires that this engagement be grounded in realistic power dynamics so that those involved are clear about levels of influence in decision making and policy forming. Governance practices also need to be consistent with the effective rule of law that produces and protects fair legal frameworks and guarantees community access to good governance practice, enforced impartially through an independent judiciary and an incorruptible police force.

Principle 3: Strategic adaptability

Strategic governance must begin with the collaborative develop-ment of shared future visions involving government, community and industry participants. Adaptive, strategic approaches can then be produced based on these visions, while focusing on action outcomes to achieve sustainability for community management. Strategic and sustainable governance requires shared decision making and management practices. Governance *structures* must reflect the diversity of interests of all stakeholders, encourage collaboration and integrate diverse views. This means we need succession strategies, intergenerational collaboration processes and knowledge-management systems to ensure that some people or groups do not dominate governance processes.

Governance *structures* must reflect the diversity of interests of all stakeholders, encourage collaboration and integrate diverse views

Principle 4: Participation

In developing new participatory governance structures, inclusive-ness must become our overriding mantra. This requires involve-ment of those often neglected or ignored in the decision-making process, including young, older, marginalized people, young people and people from culturally and linguistically diverse backgrounds. It depends upon authentic access to information about how decision making occurs, including use of adaptable, consensus-based processes that ensure a diversity of stakeholder representation in resulting policy and actions. These processes also need to acknowledge that different agencies have different time frames, processes and understandings. We must design governance practice to accommodate these localized needs.

Engagement in governance also needs to be empowering on both personal and community levels. This means that processes should strengthen social capital and social networks and create opportunities for relationships, particularly between and among stakeholders whose needs may seem to conflict. As we have discussed, current approaches to governance tend to prioritize *economic* outcomes and marginalize those who seek to broaden the discussion to encompass social, cultural and environmental issues. How the discussion is framed, as demonstrated in Chapter 6, Action, and Chapter 8, Inclusion, can limit participation. Developing new approaches to governance, based on sustainable, participatory practices, requires providing more authentic access to the processes of governance and decision making. We must employ appropriate structures and focus on fairness and equitable representation. This means access to the highest level of policy development and decision making, not simply tinkering at the edges of implementation and evaluation. Once again, the distinction is the difference between influencing what a development should look like and deciding whether it should happen at all.

Accountability groups, reference groups, citizen action groups and other forms of governance groups are valuable in different contexts. Membership issues are very important, as 'stacking' is always a concern and representativeness needs to be vigilantly monitored. Any group with governance responsibilities – for carrying a plan or policy into fruition – must reflect the diversity of the local community, as well as affiliated stakeholders. We are convinced that facilitation is the key to successful participation: groups need to

We are convinced that facilitation is the key to successful participation: groups need to be facilitated equitably so that everyone has an equal opportunity to participate, to have their perspectives heard and to contribute both the decisions and the way they are made

be facilitated equitably so that everyone has an equal opportunity to participate, to have their perspectives heard and to contribute both the decisions and the way they are made. Importantly, those involved in governance groups also need to be clear about how much influence they are going to have over the final decisions.

Principle 5: Persistence and patience

In the transition to a participatory model, we must acknowledge that some people will be jaded, cynical and unsure about how they can participate in governance practice. Further, redefining governance relationships to include community, government and industry participation will take time and resourcing if we want to facilitate new dialogic structures. Given these considerations, the transition to a new approach based on shared values needs persistence and patience from all concerned: government agencies, community leaders and organizers and participants. These qualities always seem to be in short supply.

Reflections on governance in practice

All five of us have experienced good and terrible examples of governance approaches to community engagement with sustainability. Wendy, however, has over 40 years of experience observing what works and what doesn't. She's witnessed the consequences of ignoring good governance principles, when the laundry is left undone. In this section, we reflect on two community engagement processes. They are two very different tales of how governance was taken into account and the subsequent consequences.

Good governance principles ignored: The tale of BlueWater Cove

It's sad to report that a project that had so much going for it ended up as a failure. And we believe it's largely because nobody was willing to do the *laundry*. When Steph, Wendy and Yollana think back on the sad tale of BlueWater Cove, we're reminded of a provocative book by Jack Kornfield, *After the Ecstasy, the Laundry: How the Heart Grows Wise on the Spiritual Path*.[10] Kornfield, a wise spiritual teacher, explains that even the most enlightened beings have to take time out to 'do the laundry'. Life is not one continual ecstatic spiritual experience, even for a guru. We believe that the same applies to community engagement with sustainability and especially to the 'governance' component, which is so often ignored. We have to make time for the time-consuming, boring and repetitive work of community engagement. And that's often the governance components, which is one reason we have featured 'governance' in this book.

> Kornfield, a wise spiritual teacher, explains that even the most enlightened beings have to take time out to 'do the laundry

In the case of BlueWater Cove, a waterfront site near a large northern Australian city, we designed and implemented a sophisticated programme of community engagement and capacity-building process with the full support of the developer, DevelopersRUs. That was necessary because the project was a 'rescue mission' for a project that had previously fallen apart under suspicious circumstances, leaving some local people financially burnt and others who had bought neighbouring properties very disappointed. They had been promised a marina, various resort and recreation facilities, and all manner of delightful beachside amenities on their doorsteps. None had eventuated. And, sadly, several years after our involvement in the enthusiastic relaunch, described by one local as 'clowns and elephants dancing down the street,' it appeared that nothing was happening. Again.

Initially, we were so proud of our sophisticated engagement processes that we intended to make the BlueWater Cove story the cornerstone of this book, using its full identity. However, when we returned to BlueWater Cove to see how things were proceeding, we discovered that the project had stalled and that local people felt dispirited and betrayed by inaction. The delays were not the developer's fault. Quite the contrary. But nobody was telling the community what was going on. More than that, the community members didn't know what to do. They had no formal processes, protocols, or further ways to be empowered. The developer was holding only occasional meetings and the locals were slipping into passivity and despair. They had never taken charge – as a community – of the governance components of the engagement process after the 'clowns and elephants' departed. They had not built their capacity and they felt completely disempowered by the inexplicable delays.

The community came to believe that they had been let down again

As we explored matters further, it became clear that the developer and their consultants (and community members) had found participatory design exercises, bus trips, site visits and long lunches with residents more fun than developing and refining consensus-based decision-making processes and protocols for the community group that was to guide the project. Thus, the whole governance process had fallen apart. Further, the charismatic and courageous project manager had resigned, leaving instead an inexperienced, nervous and risk-adverse deputy, terrified of even speaking with the community when he had 'nothing to report'. In a fertile ground of silence that continued for months and years, suspicion again took root. The community came to believe that they had been let down again (when, actually, there were some hopeful signs behind the scenes). Inside the developer's office, however, it was 'business as usual' and the openness and community capacity-building approaches that characterized our earlier work and that of the courageous project manager were nowhere to be seen. In fact, she was now vilified. She had said that the culture change and internal governance changes had been the most difficult of all to achieve in the relaunch of this complex project. Now, no longer part of 'the family', she had to admit to the failure of her attempts at cultural change within the organization.

Some very simple – but possibly boring – processes could have contributed to an ongoing relationship between the developer and the community and much higher levels of trust

Some very simple – but possibly boring – processes could have contributed to an ongoing relationship between the developer and the community and much higher levels of trust. An empowered community might have been able to help the developer put pressure on others who were delaying progress. We discuss these processes in this chapter. We also show how, in a very different community some years earlier, careful attention to boring matters of governance resulted in strong and enduring community strengthening and empowerment processes. Those processes helped to transform a depressed and disenchanted community into one that was full of energy and ready to embrace change. That community was the low-income community of Eagleby, described in the next story. In Eagleby, with the help of a committed and thoughtful project manager, community members did the laundry. Lots of it.

Good governance principles in action: The tale of the Eagleby Residents Action Group (ERAG)

Wendy was leafing through some old photos when she came upon the one showing members of the Eagleby community making the award of the first Order of Eagleby to Mike Allen in 2000. As the second recipient of that honour the following year, she holds these matters very dear to her heart. What is a nondescript low-income community on the edge of Brisbane doing giving an award to a consultant? And what for? And what did it matter? And what does this mean for governance in a community engagement context?

What is a nondescript low-income community on the edge of Brisbane doing giving an award to a consultant?

A lot, truly. But first, a bit of background:

When Wendy began working in Eagleby in 1999, it was regarded as one of the most disadvantaged communities in Queensland. Bureaucrats ticked off a long list of things that were supposedly wrong there. The usual: high levels of welfare dependence, little community infrastructure, too much drug use and pregnancy among teens. Two state government departments, Queensland Housing and Queensland Health, had massive projects operating and Wendy was managing the community engagement processes for both of them. Like it or not, Eagleby was being 'renewed'.

Sad feelings about governance

The residents were very sceptical about the process. Sadly, some of their scepticism was well founded. Their comments below (in the public record) are typical of community members who have experienced poorly organized community engagement processes with inadequate attention to governance:

> When CRP [Community Renewal Program] first commenced the community was stumbling, but when we asked for information about how other CR [community renewal] areas had done their community reference group we were not provided with anything. There was very little guidance offered by the Department of Housing about how we should go about it.

The ERAG [Eagleby Residents Action Group] was functioning prior to CRP as the Eagleby Action Team which evolved into the ERAG. Our name was RAGE (Renewal Action Group for Eagleby) but senior staff of the Department of Housing came to one of our meetings and advised that this was an 'unfortunate' name for the group and that we would have to change it to ERAG.

> ...it [the demand for the name change] immediately set the Department up in conflict with us. It caused a lot of negative feeling towards Housing and a loss of trust. We felt that once staff of CRP decided the group should go down this path, that was it and we were just forced to go down that path.

> Another example was the terms of reference for the ERAG were given to us (without discussion/consultation) and we were expected to simply accept them. We felt no credibility was accorded the group as a representative body, or that Eagleby residents would have skills – 'it was a Big Brother statement' ... they were doing things to us rather than working with us.[11]

The farmer from Toowoomba

These experiences simply added to residents' earlier experiences of being ignored by successive local and state governments for several decades. Naturally, they were suspicious of new programmes and especially suspicious of consultants. But Mike Allen, first recipient of the coveted Order of Eagleby award, was something else. He was a farmer in his day job – in Toowoomba, a rural community some 150 kilometres away. He came to work in jeans and spoke with people in plain English. He knew how to listen and he never put people down. Furthermore, he understood bureaucracies. What a blessing!

In a wide-ranging series of workshops over about six weeks, Mike helped the Eagleby residents and members of the newly formed ERAG tackle the issues of how the Eagleby community would relate to the bureaucrats, funding programmes, administrative requirements and the management of several millions of dollars for social and physical infrastructure that was eventually poured into the community. As one resident commented, 'We were on a steep learning curve and made it up as we went along.' The first meeting of the community organization (a requirement of the funding) was poignant. Nobody felt confident enough to take minutes or had much experience with meeting procedures. It was embarrassing and frightening. The woman who tried to take the meeting notes ran sobbing from the room. It felt like it was going to be a long haul.

Mike's tireless and patient tutoring helped the Eagleby residents to develop their confidence, to remember what they already knew from other organizations and processes, to build solidarity and get a sense of their mission and their identity as a group. All agreed that they had to be protected from unwelcome intrusion until they were ready: until the group had properly 'formed'. One memorable day when ERAG was meeting, early in its formation, the Minister's minder arrived at the door, demanding to attend the meeting.

Mike's tireless and patient tutoring helped the Eagleby residents to develop their confidence, to remember what they already knew from other organizations and processes, to build solidarity and get a sense of their mission and their identity as a group

Wendy and the local community development worker stood with their backs to the door, protesting that ERAG was not ready to meet with anyone and when they were, his boss (who was also the local member) would be the first to know. This local member was not the housing or health minister – but had another Cabinet portfolio. He was a powerful man, an old-style Queensland politician.

With Mike's gentle tutoring, ERAG flourished: no subject was too embarrassing; no shy question seen as too foolish to ask. It took about six weeks of group-development workshops, learning meeting procedures, unpacking the intricacies of *Robert's Rules of Order*, developing decision-making models, electing and training officers, learning how to take meeting notes, chair meetings, propose motions, read and prepare budgets...

At the same time that Mike Allen was working with ERAG on governance issues, Wendy's husband Karl Langheinrich, a qualified social worker, was helping the new community organization grapple with meeting procedures and protocols so that they would be effective in working with the various government departments that had programmes operating there. Karl was adamant that this form of 'laundry' needed attention, partly because of problems he and Wendy had recently experienced in projects in Sydney, where community groups refused to tackle the boring tasks of governance and decision making. Karl prepared a paper called, 'Suggestions for Procedural Rules for Use with a Consensus Interaction Method Decision-Making Framework'. He began by explaining the weaknesses of formal meeting procedures, the role of a facilitator as opposed to a Chair, the role of the recorder, common rules for managing meetings, process guides and examples of how to work through various roles. His work supported Mike Allen's coaching and mentoring.

When all of this was absorbed – with lots of practice runs and role playing – ERAG was ready.

Then they invited the bureaucrats to lunch.

In some ways, Eagleby has been a poster child for community renewal in Queensland and Australia. Other projects have been successful, too, but if you look at Eagleby's website (www.eagleby. org.au), you can see what we mean. All those weeks doing the laundry and learning how to do boring and repetitive (but neces- sary) administrative tasks helped the community strengthen their capacity to deal with all the issues they faced in subsequent years. They've taken initiatives in many realms, including community safety, park regeneration, development of a wetlands recreation area and community employment programmes. ERAG was recently disbanded, as the formal renewal funding has finished and life is more or less 'normal' there now. But ERAG 'graduates' work for pay now – in community renewal programmes throughout Queensland – helping other communities. We believe that this is as it should be.

All those weeks doing the laundry and learning how to do boring and repetitive (but necessary) administrative tasks helped the community strengthen their capacity to deal with all the issues they faced in subsequent years

Early forays into partnership and collaboration

There is more to the Eagleby governance story than the personal qualities of Mike Allen, however. In 2000, ERAG negotiated a milestone agreement with Queensland Health that represented the type of governance structures we have been discussing in this chapter. The words, 'whole-of-government approach' are easy to roll off the tongue but fraught in practice, as different government agencies have different agendas, different manage- ment cultures and different attitudes and approaches to commu- nity engagement. In Eagleby, the South Coast Public Health Unit consciously pioneered a leading-practice approach to community engagement and made great commitment to it. After many months of negotiation with the local community, an exemplary protocol or Memorandum of Understanding (a Partnership Agreement) was signed with ERAG. This approach guided the Eagleby *Stories in a Park* project that Wendy, Karl and their colleague community artist and activist Graeme Dunstan worked on for many months.

This commitment won the confidence of Eagleby residents. But there was much to be learned on all sides. Much of consultants' time was spent consolidating and affirming ERAG as a working committee and a confident community voice, and, as described above, tutoring committee members in meeting skills, acronyms and the ways of bureaucrats. The success of this governance work was evident in the prevailing good feeling within ERAG meetings and the goodwill towards, and support for, the Stories project. It was also evident in the number of government representatives who were drawn to attend ERAG's weekly meetings. For a bureaucrat obliged to consult a community, finding a stable, intelligent and receptive community committee to work with is a very important matter.

The partnership agreement was a formal document signed by Queensland Health and the President of ERAG in December 2000. It commits each party to work collaboratively with the other. The effectiveness of this document is testament to the work of another remarkable professional who was willing to 'do the laundry', Project Manager, Rebecca Cotton. This is Rebecca's recollection of the process of negotiating the governance agreement:

Rebecca's story

I'll always remember how it felt.

We decided to have a session that would help us to build trust with these folk we were only just getting to know before we commenced with the 'supportive environments for physical activity' work as government representatives. I sensed that many of them had been damaged by their experiences of dealing with government authorities – and I had heard that some of them had quite tragic stories (Jane having her kids removed – how heart-breaking).

To be honest, I felt a bit embarrassed coming in from a state government body. I felt like an intruder who was

Continued

preceded by a history of intruders who left damage in their wake. I wanted to prove somehow that I wasn't like the others. Wanted to prove that the South Coast Public Health Unit (Kate and I) weren't like the others – that we were fair dinkum. I know that Kate felt the same way. So we planned a session that would begin by allowing the (later to be called) ERAG folk a chance to *tell us their horror stories'* (and that is exactly how I said it) about dealing with government people and representatives.

After each horror story, we paused in the group for a moment to think about how that must have felt for the person telling the story. Together we looked for the lesson that the government could learn from the story. We then made a reciprocal agreement about the story. That became the Partnership Agreement. Basically we said, 'OK, we promise to XYZ. And what can you promise us in return?'

And we did this for each story told:

1   Horror story told.
2   Reflect as a group on how it must have felt.
3   What can we learn from that story?
4   What do we promise you as a result of hearing this story?
5   And what do you promise us in return?

Each of these reciprocal promises became a *reciprocal agreement*. And all the agreements together made our partnership agreement. Each session was very moving and intense – very intimate. And we were always held to the agreement. ERAG and the Eagleby people quickly reminded us if we weren't living up to what we promised. I heard a few years later (after I had left) that ERAG continued to be happy to deal with Queensland Health 'because we have a partnership agreement with them'. I was so pleased that the Partnership Agreement had a lasting effect.

I heard a few years later (after I had left) that ERAG continued to be happy to deal with Queensland Health 'because we have a partnership agreement with them'. I was so pleased that the Partnership Agreement had a lasting effect

The Queensland Health Partnership Agreement

What makes the process described above so potent is that the Partnership Agreement was written in the form of guidelines between Queensland Health and ERAG members. It's a precise, signed and dated statement about what each group promises the other with respect to the SEPA-Q (Supportive Environments for Physical Activity) project.

In our experience, careful attention to the mundane tasks in the 'laundry' of community governance is never wasted

This Agreement is still spoken about as a benchmark in engagement processes. It took many weeks of painful and sometimes boring 'laundry' work to come up with such a straightforward and helpful document. But, as Rebecca Cotton explained above, it worked. In our experience, careful attention to the mundane tasks in the 'laundry' of community governance is never wasted.

Partnership Guidelines, 2000

1. Input and guidance

- Queensland Health staff will ensure that ERAG is given the opportunity to provide input and guidance for all stages of project development and implementation.
- ERAG members will actively follow the progress of the SEPA-Q project in Eagleby and provide input and guidance to the Queensland Health staff.

2. Best practice

- Queensland Health staff will strive to base all work on proven best practice at every stage of the process.
- ERAG will hold the Queensland Health project staff accountable for using proven best practice in all their work.

3. Keeping up to date

- Queensland Health staff will provide an update at an ERAG meeting on all SEPA-Q activities at least once per month. This update will include a written progress brief and a spoken update by one of the Queensland Health staff.
- ERAG will ensure that a Queensland Health staff member is given an opportunity to provide a progress update at least once per month at an ERAG meeting.

Continued

4. Raising and listening to issues

- Queensland Health staff will listen actively to all comments and concerns raised by ERAG members. We welcome discussion and negotiation on any issue pertaining to SEPA-Q.
- ERAG will raise all concerns about the SEPA-Q project with the Queensland Health staff according to the ERAG policy guidelines for communications.

5. Respect

- Queensland Health staff will treat all members of ERAG and the Eagleby community with the utmost respect, recognizing that every person has a valuable contribution to make to the project.
- ERAG will treat the Queensland Health staff with respect and value them as equals in this process.

6. Preferred processes

- Queensland Health staff will honour the preferred processes of ERAG, adapting work to align with these processes.
- ERAG will clearly explain their preferred processes to the Queensland Health staff so that the SEPA-Q project may come into alignment with these processes at every stage.

7. Asking and answering questions

- Queensland Health staff will answer questions honestly, with courtesy and respect and with appropriate language. If we cannot answer your questions straight away due to a lack of knowledge, we will research the issue and return an answer to you as soon as possible.
- ERAG members will ask and answer questions with honesty and integrity.

8. Courtesy

- Queensland Health staff will always be mindful that they are guests in the Eagleby community and will behave with courtesy and respect at all times.
- As hosts, ERAG will behave with courtesy and respect at all times.

Continued

9. Preparation and punctuality

- Queensland Health staff will arrive at all ERAG meetings and other SEPA-Q related events on time and well prepared.
- ERAG members will arrive at meetings with Queensland Health staff on time and prepared.

10a. Decision making

- Queensland Health staff will respect and honour the decisions made by ERAG.
- ERAG will clearly explain all decisions made concerning the SEPA-Q project and ensure that Queensland Health staff understand the reasoning behind the decisions.

10b. Decision making

- Queensland Health staff will engage ERAG in all decision-making processes concerning the project.
- ERAG members will honour decisions made in consultation and cooperation with Queensland Health staff.

11. Positive representation

- Queensland Health staff will always present Eagleby in a positive manner in all discussions, meetings and media-related activities.
- ERAG will strive to positively promote the SEPA-Q activities to the wider Eagleby community, and to prevent and resolve any rumours that may develop.

12. Acknowledgement and opportunity

- Queensland Health staff will acknowledge and reward the effort made by ERAG members and the community in the SEPA-Q process.
- ERAG will endeavour to link local people with specific skills and talents with appropriate SEPA-Q initiatives.

13. Overcoming 'red tape' frustration

- Queensland Health staff will assist ERAG members by identifying and clearly explaining any bureaucratic processes and procedures which may delay SEPA-Q

Continued

activities. Queensland Health staff will also strive to overcome any bureaucratic restrictions that do not support best practice community participation in the SEPA-Q project.

- ERAG members will express any dissatisfaction with delays in progress and will ask for clarification from Queensland Health staff in this event. ERAG members will also identify any blocks to the progress of the SEPA-Q project as soon as they become evident.

Rebecca Cotton's story and the Partnership Guidelines are testament to what is possible in community engagement. The willingness of government to engage with mistakes of the past is far too rare. In refusing to be open to negative feedback, government agencies often lose a valuable opportunity to build trust and improve relationships and community engagement processes. We hope that this story will inspire more people in 'positions of power' to admit and to learn from the mistakes of their organization, so that the real (the 'everyday' laundry) work of community engagement can begin and flourish.

The willingness of government to engage with mistakes of the past is far too rare. In refusing to be open to negative feedback, government agencies often lose a valuable opportunity to build trust and improve relationships and community engagement processes

Coming to public judgement

One of the important stages in participatory governance is called 'coming to public judgement'. This means moving from public *opinion* to public *judgement*. Coming to judgement requires three steps: (1) consciousness raising, (2) working through and (3) resolution. It also involves local people accepting that they no longer have to bow to expert views and what has been called 'a culture of technical control'. As Costanza explains, 'Coming to judgment is the process of confronting and resolving these inconsistencies by breaking down the barriers between the mutually exclusive compartments into which knowledge and information have been put'.[12]

Costanza argues that, 'This can be done most effectively by formulating the choices as complete visions of the alternative states of the world, and incorporating all the divergent elements.'[13] We strongly support this view, as we have found that community groups must work through divergent thinking and move into more convergent thinking modes. This is the difficult work: the 'groan zone'.[14] Demanding work for communities and for facilitators, it can be enormously assisted by strong governance structures that give community members confidence that their contributions will not be trumped by 'expert' views and that their contributions will reach decision makers and make a difference.

Recipes for good governance

As the tales above illustrate, when governance arrangements fail, people jump ship. Sometimes the ship goes down, with some people still on board. On the other hand, when good governance arrangements are addressed up front and centre, conditions for a possibly transformative journey are optimized. The ERAG story is a wonderful demonstration of this. We want to keep the ship afloat.

Below we provide four recipes for good governance that will ensure better community engagement with sustainability.

- Recipe 1: *Resourcing*
- Recipe 2: *Processes and procedures*
- Recipe 3: *Capacity strengthening*
- Recipe 4: *Learning opportunities*

Recipe 1: Resourcing

We advocate a participatory approach to governance which requires addressing how we can resource the community involved in any engagement process to enable full participation. Resourcing includes access to funding, meeting spaces in which to meet and organize and access to information and knowledge. Community Assistance Schemes (CAS) and similar programmes provide specific resource and infrastructure funding to community organizations working for broad community outcomes. Providing funding and access to shared community spaces, noticeboards, equipment and other resources strengthen opportunities for action to occur and trusting relationships between proponents and the wider community. Shared community spaces help the local community to participate more effectively, as they can be used for meeting, gathering, information dispersal, storage and other activities associated with community organizing.

A *coproduction* model allows for participant assistance in financial terms, adequate budgets for resourcing of community groups, to pay their expenses so that they can participate fully and easily (the argument being that the bureaucrats and consultants are paid but the community members are volunteers).

Access to information and knowledge is another aspect. Information made available to a community organization or group needs to be in a form that they can digest, taking issues of cultural and linguistic diversity into account. Reports and plans need to be in understandable formats and plain words. Community groups need sufficient notice and time to review reports and respond to plans and proposals so that the group can convene a meeting, gather advice, seek professional assistance, if required, workshop a plan or proposal, and prepare a thoughtful response. Regular and convenient meeting times of appropriate length are also important.

Information made available to a community organization or group needs to be in a form that they can digest, taking issues of cultural and linguistic diversity into account

Recipe 2: Processes and procedures

Many practical processes and procedures are necessary to keep wind in the sails of community engagement processes to support transformative change: decision-making processes, conflict-resolution procedures, accountability mechanisms and meeting protocols, to name but a few. As with any decision-making structure, there are always opportunities for groups of like-minded people to dominate, control and manipulate community governance processes and structures. However, when we incorporate good governance principles, we can help participants self-manage and regulate inappropriate behaviour. Appropriate conflict-resolution processes can maintain balance and reduce domination, offering participants confidence that there are systems for maintaining balance, equity and equal access.

When designing governance processes and procedures, six questions require our attention:

1 *High-Level Decision Makers*: How can we enable access to high-level decision makers so that the passions and concerns of the local community can be heard directly and not filtered though bureaucratic language?

2 *The Same Faces*: How can we provide assurance that the same people will be able to be contacted (so that the time spent in relationship-building with bureaucrats is not wasted), and that that person *has* authority to make decisions when meeting with a representative of a community group?

3 *Children and Young People*: How can children and young people be incorporated into the decision-making processes as full participants to ensure they are included and that their views are not exclusively communicated by adult gatekeepers?

4 *Status in Open Forums*: How can we establish open forums where community members have status to speak and be heard and can also hear the planners and proponents with respect to the plan or proposal?

How can we establish open forums where community members have status to speak and be heard and can also hear the planners and proponents with respect to the plan or proposal?

5   *Coaching and Mentoring*: What coaching and mentoring opportunities can we make available for community members to participate in submissions, panels and formal review processes?

6   *Accountability*: How can we design community engagement processes with directly accountable links between community members and the proponent and government representatives?

As the ERAG story above demonstrates, there is no simple formula. However, with a commitment to participatory processes and sufficient time, participants can agree on locally appropriate processes and procedures. Like the ERAG Partnership Guidelines.

Recipe 3: Capacity strengthening

Participatory governance practice demands a focus on strengthening community and individual capacity to participate effectively. This requires resources (as discussed above), as well as community education approaches that create localized and broader exchange of high-quality information, learning tools and experience to broaden people's understanding of governance practice, community needs and sustainability imperatives. We discussed this requirement at length in Chapter 5, Education. We need to develop capacity-strengthening opportunities in tandem with building community connectivity through intergenerational approaches such as mentoring programmes and through skill-sharing and support exchanges among individuals, groups, professionals and academics.

Participatory governance practice demands a focus on strengthening community and individual capacity to participate effectively

Capacity strengthening can include assistance to any of the following matters:

• knowledge and practice of small-group consensus decision-making processes

- iraining in how to manage a community advisory group: how it is formed, statutory and formal reporting requirements (especially if the group manages any money), how to work up an agenda, a report to a meeting, how to run meetings, take minutes, report on meetings, manage conflict and resolve it effectively within meetings, determine the representativeness of any group and seek to widen membership to be more representative
- education about reading balance sheets, understanding plans and drawings, reading plans in three dimensions, understanding technical matters like Crime Prevention through Environmental Design (CPTED)
- coaching and mentoring for community members to participate in panels and formal review processes that can be frightening contexts.

Often found at the core of resistance to participatory governance is an unwillingness to share or devolve power. Our educator colleague Noel Wilson reminds us that power structures exist within all organizations. And the lessons are the same: change the basic power structure or in the endgame, you change nothing. To change the power structure, we have to deepen our *Promise to the Public*, as discussed in Chapter 3. And communities with a stake in the matter must have authentic opportunities to strengthen their capacities.

Cathy visited the Castle Vale Housing Action Trust (CVHAT) in Birmingham in 2002 as part of a study tour focusing on learning from innovative urban renewal projects in Great Britain.[15] The CVHAT was a community-based housing association, established with significant funding in 1993 to improve housing and general living conditions in Castle Vale, following 30 years of physical, social and economic decline. It was to have a ten-year life span. From the outset, a priority was to strengthen community capacity so that when the CVHAT wound down there would be sufficient local capacity to carry on the work. The CVHAT dissolved in 2005, having achieved tangible health, education and living standard improvements across the community through multi-agency approaches. Most importantly, over ten years, people worked together to strengthen the community's capacities, and successor organizations were established to enable the local community to manage its own affairs into the future. These included a credit union and junior credit union, a community development trust (focused on employment and training linked to local job creation), the Castle Vale Community Care Partnership and the Castle Vale Community Environmental Trust.

Local people now see the potential to transform the cycle of poverty entrenched for generations at Castle Vale. The capacity to maintain and extend the hard work lies within the local community. What was so special about this project was the active community strengthening designed into the process *from the outset*. It was no afterthought. This is a critical component of governance that must be on the agenda of any community engagement with sustainability process from the very beginning.

What was so special about this project was the active community strengthening designed into the process *from the outset*

Recipe 4: Learning opportunities

There are no formulaic solutions to sustainability problems. We are all in this together and need to create deep learning cultures so we can learn from one another, from our mistakes and our successes, not at the end of the process but during it. Governance arrangements must provide the time and space for learning opportunities. We have spoken a great deal about learning in this book. In Chapter 5, Education, we introduced concepts of 'transformational learning' and a 'learning society'. 'Transformational learning' is a deep kind of learning that has the capacity to transform our values and approaches into the future. A learning society recognizes that for us to develop, evolve and live sustainability, we must be willing to evaluate our decisions, learn from our mistakes and gain knowledge from our successes. Governance for community engagement needs to be designed to support this type of learning.

In Chapter 6, Action, we recommend the formative evaluation approach as one way to build learning opportunities into community engagement processes. Here are some other practical suggestions:

- Opportunities (formally sanctioned and definitely used) to give feedback to proponent, planners and bureaucrats about how community people feel they are being treated by them. Carefully managed, this can foster good working relationships. However, this requires 'safe' contexts where there will not be punishment later on for speaking openly.
- Senior people regularly attending local workshops, meetings and other engagement processes so that they know exactly what is going on.
- Opportunities for community people to share successes and feel good – together with the planners and bureaucrats – about how they are working together and celebrating common successes.
- An action learning approach to conducting projects, where participants collectively review a project's outcomes and what they have learned from being involved.[16]

Kitchen table conversation starters

What changes would be required in your life for you to be able to participate in community governance? How would you prefer to participate?

- How do you feel about current systems of governance where you live?
- In a practical sense, how could greater access to decision making change they way your local community operates and looks?
- How effective have you found the governance components of community engagement processes?

- What changes would be required in your life for you to be able to participate in community governance? How would you prefer to participate?
- What skills would you like to strengthen to participate in governance processes?

For more opportunities to continue the conversation about community education for sustainability, please visit www.kitchentablesustainability.com.

Final thoughts

Our values directly inform the conversations and interactions we have at our kitchen tables. They inform our worldview – the lens through which we assess sustainability and how we relate it both to our communities and to our individual vision, hope and sense of possibility. Without governance, we cannot achieve successful sustainability strategies and programmes. However, if people in communities perceive governance structures as inaccessible, remote and unrelated to their personal perspectives and aspirations, how can they be expected to engage? We need a better fit between people in communities and governance structures. When governance structures and processes accurately reflect our values, sustainability actions will flourish – grounded in local culture. Then, and only then, will we see our dreams translated into practical outcomes.

Encouraging active engagement in governance for sustainability is strongly linked to kitchen tables. Good governance practice, based on authentic community involvement, relies on those involved understanding and engaging with the complex requirements for creating sustainable communities. We can make progress only if we can speak openly about sustainability issues at our kitchen tables. And at all the other tables we set up for this purpose. We need opportunities for deep conversations about sustainability at many, many tables.

Good governance practice, based on authentic community involvement, relies on those involved understanding and engaging with the complex requirements for creating sustainable communities

11 CONCLUSIONS, CHALLENGES AND A WAY FORWARD

Many kitchen tables await us and over time we may again sit at the kitchen tables of our past.

Rachel Naomi Remen, 2006, p331

Introduction: The heart of the matter

Kitchen Table Sustainability outlines our *EATING* approach to sustainability, incorporating *Education, Action, Trust, Inclusion, Nourishment* and *Governance.* Deep understanding of all of these components combined is essential to community engagement with sustainability, just as proper and non-toxic nutrients are necessary for a well balanced diet. Our concepts go to the heart of sustainability. Our hope is that they will also reach into the heart of individuals and communities, stimulating cross-cultural kitchen table conversations with people everywhere: community members, activists, educators, students, innovators, community engagement practitioners, planners, developers, decision makers, bureaucrats and many others. We are committed to empowering processes with influence far beyond the life of an individual policy, plan or development project.

We are committed to empowering processes with influence far beyond the life of an individual policy, plan or development project

Our vision of community engagement with sustainability

Creating a truly sustainable environment for all life on Earth is a long and complex journey. As a species, we have lost our way and must now find our direction. There is no time to lose. This is why we must begin now, knowing that every step is important, as it brings us closer to our goal. To move forward on this path, we must have a clear vision of where we are going. A vision for the future must influence every step. Our vision is that this approach will help communities *to make the critical transitions from intention to action*, through education, action, trust, inclusion, nourishment and good governance.

Our vision is that this approach will help communities *to make the critical transitions from intention to action*, through education, action, trust, inclusion, nourishment and good governance

Education offers an opportunity for communities to take charge of the knowledge and literacy components of community engagement with sustainability. Education has a critical role, based on leading-practice community education for sustainability, grounded in the best of environmental and adult education principles.

Action and activism are also critical. It is futile to tinker at the margins of a paradigm that is outdated and now seen as dangerous to life on Earth. As we seek to rework our 'master metaphorical templates', we cannot afford to exclude or alienate activists. Many of them have turned their backs on formal community engagement processes for good reasons. Community engagement models must prepare a welcoming place at the table for activists and their range of perspectives so that the resulting conversations and actions reflect their knowledge, wisdom, experience and passion.

By understanding the importance of *trust* and how to repair and maintain it, we can begin to heal the 'expectation of betrayal' so prevalent in community engagement processes. Then we can reconnect the diverse knowledges and skills of people from diverse backgrounds.

By *inclusion*, we mean that we are eager to see *everyone* sitting at the table, empowered to understand and contribute to discussions about sustainability. *Inclusion* means a place for children and young people and those from diverse cultural and linguistic backgrounds. It also means people who may be angry, emotional and not rational in their expressions of concern about sustainability issues. All are welcome. We respectfully prepare a seat at the table for our unfamiliar guest: nonhuman Nature.

By *nourishment*, we seek to ensure that individuals and communities are nourished as they engage with sustainability: physically, emotionally, mentally and spiritually. Well resourced and nourishing community engagement processes can be fun, as well as productive. We can encourage people to maintain their involvement over the long term.

Finally, we affirm that effective, transparent and open *governance* structures – the mundane but essential 'laundry' of community engagement and community building – must be built into our processes from the very start. We seek to empower communities to make decisions about local, bioregional *and* global futures. Participants need strong and repeated reassurances that formal processes will keep their interests and their contributions alive for the *long term*. Where formal processes and existing structures refuse to engage or are unable to engage precisely because of those processes or structures, we must be willing to persevere until the processes are changed or the structures are modified, or if necessary, dismantled.

Participants need strong and repeated reassurances that formal processes will keep their interests and their contributions alive for the long term

Challenges (opportunities) for everyone

As worldchanging.com reminds us, 'another world is not just possible, it's here. We only need to put the pieces together'.[1]

Our vision for community engagement with sustainability provides challenges and opportunities for many people to play a variety of roles. We don't need to wait for more information. What we know is more than enough to prompt us to engage in action toward sustainability.

The following actions by different responsible bodies would represent a good start on the journey toward sustainability.

For governments (local, state, provincial and federal): Community engagement with sustainability means a completely new way of relating with communities that is profoundly respectful of the contributions that community members bring to the table. Resourcing, educating and empowering community members with the skills for good governance within communities will ensure higher quality contributions and improved communication between communities and government. Processes may take longer than they have in the past and require greater levels of resourcing to be effective. More fundamentally, the power of values such as efficiency, control, conformity and blame that permeate such institutions must be diminished. The values of complexity, ambiguity, diversity and compassion must become paramount.

More fundamentally, the power of values such as efficiency, control, conformity and blame that permeate such institutions must be diminished

For developers and the private sector: Community engagement with sustainability evokes a whole new way of doing business. It calls for 'radical accountability', making the facts, the figures and the bottom lines clearly available so that community members can participate with full comprehension of the constraints that private organizations face. There will be ample opportunities for visionary organizations to demonstrate leadership when governments are held back by formal processes, resistance or intransigence. It is time now to move beyond *greenwashing* to generate real sustainable solutions. We know that there *are* principled developers eager to embrace these challenges in our communities and we commend them.

> **We know that there *are* principled developers eager to embrace these challenges in our communities and we commend them**

For consultants in the land professions: For years, academics examining community engagement and sustainability issues have been throwing down challenges to consultants to 'raise the bar' of ethical and sustainable practice. Professional organizations need to rise to these challenges. Consultants need to find the courage to challenge briefs that are not sustainable and turn their backs on *exclusionary* processes. A planetary emergency provides the opportunity for planners and the other land professions to take leadership roles – roles that communities have been begging them to take for decades.

> **Consultants need to find the courage to challenge briefs that are not sustainable and turn their backs on *exclusionary* processes**

For community engagement practitioners: *Every* engagement process can be an opportunity to take another step toward sustainability. Even processes that do not directly address environmental or social issues can be designed to include and build trust among diverse participants. They can empower and foster networks for social innovators, incorporate community education approaches and strengthen community capacities, including the capacity for governance. Community engagement practitioners must continue to design, advocate for and facilitate such processes.

For social, environmental and community activists: As sustainability has transformed from a 'fringe' to a 'mainstream' agenda, activists may need to reconceptualize their roles and relationships to achieve their goals most effectively. Community engagement processes should support, not hinder, these goals. Because of the creativity, vision and experience that many activists bring to the table, we must seek ways to reduce the 'demonization' of activism in community engagement. Activists need to participate in and have more influence over formal engagement processes. *Inclusionary* engagement processes can support activist agendas and build community literacy about a wide range of sustainability options.

For non-government organizations: Community engagement with sustainability means embracing and radicalizing participation. This involves practical organizing methods to support diverse participation in organizational processes and projects. Because nowadays many people trust NGOs more than they trust other 'experts' in government, we must include their voices and knowledge, as well as their expanded concepts of 'community'. New approaches will require resources for community education and the support of NGO activists.

For artists and community development practitioners: These marvelously creative people have much to offer community engagement with sustainability. We must raise the profile of Community Cultural Development (CCD) practitioners and artists, particularly in the eyes of decision makers and organizers of engagement processes. Graeme Dunstan, an activist-artist colleague, reminds us of the importance of the CCD model, informed by an activist perspective:

> ... just begin by being brave, choosing to be different. Choose to speak up and seek to be heard. Lighting just one candle dispels darkness. When people speak from their hearts, truly and insightfully, about their concerns and their confusions, it's always empowering and revealing for the speaker and the listener.[2]

Inclusionary engagement processes can support activist agendas and build community literacy about a wide range of sustainability options

... just begin by being brave, choosing to be different. Choose to speak up and seek to be heard

Engagement must support active roles for community cultural development.

For teachers and academics: Many educators (some of whom are practitioners and/or activists) support the views espoused in this book. We bow deeply to their commitment and wisdom. Continuing professional development programmes for planners and others that foreground the work of inspirational people like Timothy Beatley, Lyn Carson, Des Connor, John Forester, Ann Forsyth, Patsy Healey, Randy Hester, Peter Newman, Bill Rees, Mark Roseland, Leonie Sandercock, James Whelan and Iris Marion Young will help keep community engagement with sustainability on the agendas of theoreticians and practitioners. And keep us on our toes.

For children and young people and their parents: Children and young people must be accorded opportunities to participate fully in community engagement with sustainability as empowered members of the community. This requires us to acknowledge and openly support more active citizenship and leadership roles for them, as they come to see themselves as fully fledged citizens, not citizens-in-the-making. To support them in their expanded roles, parents will need to attend to their own ecoliteracy and advocate for children's engagement processes to be fully integrated into processes for adults. Such engagement will count for little, however, if children and young people are denied such participatory power in the organizations in which they are most engaged – their schools.

As citizens: There are opportunities for *all of us* to continue to rise to the challenge of embodying an 'engaged citizenry'. If we understand how to nourish ourselves, we can sustain ongoing engagement with sustainability and grow into more empowered roles within our communities. Further, as consumers concerned about sustainability, we must be willing to speak out and express our views on bioregional and global, as well as local, issues.

The mother of all challenges

The ultimate challenge – and opportunity – that community engagement with sustainability presents to all of us is to *create caring communities*. We must repeatedly and critically ask ourselves these two questions:

- Can I extend my care beyond my individual and family circles to a wider and more diverse community?
- Can I then extend my care beyond an anthropocentric model of community life to embrace all of Nature and all future generations?

> **The ultimate challenge – and opportunity – that community engagement with sustainability presents to all of us is to *create caring communities***

The answer, we hope, is Yes! We can learn how.

We trust that this book provides you with inspiration and practical support to do just that. Mindful of the Buddhist prayer, 'May all beings be happy and free from suffering,' we pray that our work can help, if only in a small way, to create a world where all beings, now and in the future, are free from suffering.

Conclusion: At the kitchen table, where it all begins

As we commit to creating more inclusive, caring communities, we can begin to express this commitment most simply at our kitchen tables. We invite you to invite more people to sit at your kitchen table – friends, neighbours, the mayor, older people, children and young people, people like you and people who are very different. We need to extend our trust and consideration to those who are not familiar and to feel responsible to those we do not know.

> **We invite you to invite more people to sit at your kitchen table – friends, neighbours, the mayor, older people, children and young people, people like you and people who are very different**

It can take courage and commitment in today's busy world to make time for talking with others about complex issues like sustainability. As representatives of three living generations, we affirm that we must do that; for the sake of future generations, as well as for current generations. Right now, we may be sustaining human life on Earth, but *precariously*. There's no need for further data or information. If we want to create a truly sustainable world, we must converse. How else can we conceive of sustainable solutions? Or agree to collaborate in pursuing them?

Until now, kitchen table conversations about sustainability issues may have been hampered by thoughts like these: 'What difference can I (or my family or community) make?' We have also asked these questions. Many times. And we now realize that while not everyone may believe that they can make a difference at a global scale, *everyone* can make a difference in their communities. At their kitchen tables.

Kitchen Table Sustainability is about considering the local implications of global issues and crafting creative and effective *local* solutions. By engaging others within our communities around our kitchen tables, we will discover a richness of knowledge, skills, resources and networks to inform this process. Our solutions will become opportunities to inspire and be inspired by other communities, to emulate others and nurture creative and culturally appropriate approaches. We may even find ourselves contributing to sustainability on a bioregional, national or global level. This may not be because we worked at that level initially but because we engaged locally and sustainably, and inspired others to do the same.

By engaging others within our communities around our kitchen tables, we will discover a richness of knowledge, skills, resources and networks to inform this process

So let's gather round, set the table and pull up the chairs. We have lots of talking – and listening – to do. And we'd better get started right away.

*Let our descendants look back
upon this time as the time of the Great
Turning, when humanity made a bold
choice to birth a new era devoted to
actualizing the higher potentials
of our human nature.*

David Korten,
2006, p21

Notes

Chapter 1

1   Remen (2006), pxxxvii
2   Worldchanging (2008)
3   Steffen (2006), p24
4   Crawford Stanley (Buzz) Holling has made significant contri-
     butions to systems ecology including resilience theory, adaptive
     management and panarchy. He gave the advice referred to at
     an informal session for young scholars at the 2008 Resilience
     Conference in Stockholm, Sweden, 14–17 April 2008
5   See, for example, the following books on the technical aspects of
     sustainability: *Green Urbanism Down Under: Learning from
     Sustainable Communities in Australia* (Beatley with Newman, 2008);
     *Navigating Social-Ecological Systems: Building Resilience for
     Complexity and Change* (Berkes et al, 2003); *How Green is the
     City?: Sustainability Assessment and the Management of
     Urban Environments* (Devuyst et al, 2001); *The Sustainability
     Revolution: Portrait of a Paradigm Shift* (Edwards, 2005); *The Last
     Hours of Ancient Sunlight: The Fate of the World and What We
     Can Do Before It's Too Late* (Hartmann, 2004); *Cities and
     Natural Process: A Basis for Sustainability* (Hough, 2004); *Sustainable
     Fossil Fuels: The Unusual Suspect in the Quest for Clean and
     Enduring Energy* (Jaccard, 2006); *Sustainability and Cities* (Newman
     and Kenworthy, 1999); *Resilient Cities: Responding to Climate
     Change and Peak Oil* (Newman et al, 2008); *Taking Sustainability
     Seriously: Economic Development, the Environment and Quality of
     Life in American Cities* (Portney, 2003); *Sustainable Urban
     Development: A Literature Review and Analysis* (Wheeler, 1995); and
     The Sustainable Urban Development Reader (Wheeler and Beatley,
     2004)
6   According to Paul Ray and Sherry Anderson, Cultural Creatives are
     a subculture comprising over 100 million people worldwide who
     among other things 'love Nature and are deeply concerned about
     its destruction', 'are strongly aware of the problems of the whole
     planet (global warming, destruction of rainforests, overpopulation,
     lack of ecological sustainability, exploitation of people in poorer
     countries) and want to see more action on them', 'put more emphasis
     on children's education and well-being, on rebuilding our neigh-
     borhoods and communities and on creating an ecologically sustain-
     able future', and 'want to be involved in creating a new and better
     way of life'. Cultural Creatives (undated) 'Are You a Cultural
     Creative?', www.culturalcreatives.org/questionnaire.html, accessed
     6 June 2008. See also Ray and Anderson (2000)

7 *Kitchen Table Wisdom* was originally published in 1996 and re-issued in 2006. See Remen (2006)
8 United Nations (2008)
9 Victoria, Department of Planning and Community Development (2007)
10 Remen (2006), pxxii
11 This book focuses on community engagement for the developed world, as that is where our experience lies. However, community engagement is a vital tool for helping people in developing countries to move beyond 'survival' and redirect their communities to become sustainable communities. We are inspired by organizations like Sarvodaya, in Sri Lanka, dedicated to 'the sustainable empowerment of people through self-help and collective support, to non-violence and peace'. While their social and technological village development programmes have reached over 15,000 villages in Sri Lanka, they point out: 'It is not as much what we do to alleviate rural poverty but the way in which we do it which makes us so effective and sustainable – through the active participation and engagement of the villagers themselves'. Sarvodaya Shramadana Movement (2007) 'Why, who, what, where... Sarvodaya?', www.sarvodaya.org, accessed 6 June 2008
12 Westley et al (2007)
13 Bolen (1994), p272
14 Alice Walker, in an interview about her work in *Common Boundary* magazine (1990) reported in Bolen (2004)
15 Kercher (2002)
16 See, for example Cotgrove (1982)
17 See Bowers (1993) and Sarkissian (1996), p298
18 Sandercock (1998)
19 Sontag (1992)

Chapter 2

1 Glendinning (1994)
2 For more on the power of stories, see Mandelbaum (1991); Mellon (1992); Reason and Hawkins (1988); Simpkinson and Simpkinson (1993); Throgmorton (1992); Witherell and Noddings (1991)
3 Berry (1988), pxi
4 Western Australia, Department of Premier and Cabinet (2003)
5 The report was presented to the UN General Assembly in 1987 and published in 1988 as: *World Commission on Environment and Development*, and Brundtland, G. H. (1988) *Our Common Future*, Oxford University Press, Oxford and New York
6 Newman and Rowe (2003)
7 Culture as a key element of sustainability was introduced by Australians Jon Hawkes and David Yencken: Hawkes (2001); Yencken

(1991); Yencken and Wilkinson (2000)

8   Orr (2006)

9   Orr (2006)

10   McKibben (2007)

11   Hawkes (2001), p25

12   According to respected Australian researchers and writers like Jon Hawkes, David Yencken and David Throsby, and American David Orr. See Yenken (1991); Yenken and Wilkinson (2000); Throsby (2005); and Orr (2006)

13   Hawkes (2001), p4

14   Hawkes (2001), p11

15   Hart (2006)

16   Ecological Footprint Analysis is a way of measuring and visualizing the resources required to sustain human impacts on the Earth by converting seemingly complex concepts of carrying capacity, sustainability, resource use and waste disposal into a simple graphic form. It is used to aid environmental policy and personal decision making. It was developed over many years by Mathis Wackernagel, Bill Rees and their students, through the Healthy and Sustainable Communities Task Force at the University of British Columbia, BC. See Wackernagel and Rees (1996), p9 and McKibben (2007)

17   Stiglitz (2002)

18   In August 2001, economics students from 17 countries gathered in Kansas City to release their International Open Letter to all economics departments calling on them to reform economics education and research by adopting the broadband approach, which includes: a broader conception of human behaviour – beyond the 'economic rationalist man'; a recognition of culture within which economic systems are embedded; consideration of economics as a dynamic process within history; a new theory of knowledge that acknowledges subjectivity of the investigator; empirical grounding of theoretical claims; expanded methods; and Interdisciplinary dialogue. See Post-Autistic Economics Network, 'A brief history of the post-autistic economics movement', www.paecon.net/historypae.html, accessed 9 June 2008.

19   See Campaign for Sustainable Economics (2008); CASSE (undated); Costanza (2001); Daly and Farley (2004); and ISEE (undated)

20   For more information on participatory economics, see Albert (2003); Albert and Hahnel (1991a, 1991b); and Hahnel (2005)

21   See Costanza and Daly (1992) and Hawken et al (1999)

22   According to *Worldchanging*: 'In the sustainability framework, human capital – reflected in healthy, skilled, talented, creative, and engaged people – is often valued over economic capital. This acknowledges the need for a human-centred approach to development and the contribution of human capital to broader wealth creation' (Steffen, 2006)

23   See Dale (2005), p176 and Onyx and Osburn (2005)

24 Throsby (2005), p4
25 Berkes and Folkes (1991)
26 See Bowers (1993), p166; Orr (1994, 2006)
27 According to a report in *The Guardian*, 'The destruction of Sumatra's natural forests is accelerating global climate change and pushing endangered species closer to extinction, a new report warned today. A study from WWF claims that converting the forests and peat swamps of just one Sumatran province into plantations for pulp wood and palm oil is generating more annual greenhouse gas emissions than the Netherlands, and is endangering local elephant and tiger populations' (Aldred, 2008)
28 An ancient example of this is the tragic case of the decimation of both ecosystems and ultimately the population of Easter Island. See Diamond (2002, 2005)
29 Sontag (1992)
30 Bennet et al (1998)
31 Senbel (2005)
32 Seeking deeper explanations for this separation, Wendy undertook a PhD in environmental ethics, starting in 1992. She learned that we can partly blame our sense of separation from Nature on what our friend Leonie Sandercock calls Cartesian anxiety: mind–body duality and a search for ontological certainty. The roots of this separation are in the Enlightenment and the views of Descartes, Newton and Bacon. We are inheritors of this rationalistic thinking, another story that inaccurately portrays our reality. See Bernstein (1983) and Sandercock (1998, 2004)
33 Watts (2000)
34 Glendinning (1994)
35 See Lewin (1993) and Waldrop (1992)
36 See Holling (1973, 1986)
37 Glendinning (1994), p107
38 Hajer (1995), p277
39 Berkes (1989)
40 Hardin (1968)
41 Ostrom (2008)
42 Ostrom (1990)
43 Ostrom (2008)

Chapter 3

1 Steffen (2006), p22
2 See Isaacs (1993, 1999)
3 Isaacs (1993)
4 Young (1986)
5 Capra (2005), p24
6 International Association for Public Participation (IAP2): www.iap2. org, accessed 7 June 2008

7   O'Neill and Colebatch (1989)
8   Susskind and Elliott (1983)
9   See Nowlan and Nowlan (1970), p84 and Sarkissian et al (2003a), p3
10   Sarkissian et al (1997)
11   International Association for Public Participation (IAP2): www.iap2.org, accessed 7 June 2008
12   Arnstein (1969)
13   See Davidson (1998) and Sarkissian et al (2003a)
14   Sarkissian (1994), p20
15   Susskind and Elliott (1983)
16   See Albrechts and Van den Broeck (2004); Thomas (1995); Sarkissian et al (2003a), pp5–6; Van den Broeck (2006)
17   See Rosen and Knaster (1986); Sarkissian and Walsh (1994a)
18   See Clarke (1994)
19   See Sarkissian et al (1994b)
20   The model was developed in detail by Desmond Connor, a Canadian practitioner who has completed over 350 projects since 1965, mostly in Canada, some in the US and a dozen overseas. For his basic approach, see Connor (1994). Connor emphasizes the need to use open houses as part of a comprehensive and systematic process, including a preceding responsive publication. See Connor (1997)
21   City of Vancouver (2007)
22   The workshop was staffed by the Metropolitan Design Center of the University of Minnesota for the Minneapolis Center for Neighborhoods
23   Minneapolis' Corridor Housing Strategy aims to increase affordable housing along transit corridors – Minneapolis' 'Main Streets' – by acquiring critical sites, awarding priority funding to development tied to jobs and transit and giving neighbourhood organizations an early and comprehensive role in planning. In collaboration with the City of Minneapolis, the Center for Neighborhoods coordinates the Corridor Housing Initiative with support from a team of technical experts, the Family Housing Fund of Minneapolis and Saint Paul and the Twin Cities Local Initiatives Support Corporation (LISC). For details of the award received by the initiative, see City of Minneapolis (2007). For more details on the Minnesota Block Project and the Corridor Housing Initiative, see Center for Neighborhoods (2008a, b, c); Enterprise Community Partners, Inc. (2008); and Greater Minnesota Housing Fund, the Family Housing Fund and Enterprise (2008)
24   *The Corridor Housing Initiative: A Strategy for Successful Planning*, produced and directed by Tom DeBiaso (n.d.). This 30-minute video puts the viewer inside the Corridor Housing Initiative from the perspective of the technical team running the initiative, explaining how to work with cities and neighborhoods (see www.housinginitia tive.org/video.html)
25   Metropolitan Design Center (2005)

26   Center for Neighborhoods (2008c)
27   See Enterprise Community Partners, Inc. (2008) and Greater Minnesota Housing Fund, the Family Housing Fund, and Enterprise (2008)
28   See, for example Center for Neighborhoods (2008b)
29   See Center for Neighborhoods (2008b)

Chapter 4

1   Maslow (1943). See also Maslow (1998)

Chapter 5

1   Moore (2002)
2   For more information about the Moore Reserve Wetlands in Kogarah Council, see Kogarah Council (2008) 'Moore Reserve Wetlands', www.kogarah.nsw.gov.au/www/html/336-moore-reserve-wetlands.asp, accessed 9 June 2008
3   Stapp et al (1996), p5
4   Hansen and Allen (2002), p148
5   Tàbara et al (2005). The HarmoniCOP project was coordinated by Professor Claudia Pahl-Wostl, Institute of Environmental Systems Research, University of Osnabrück, Germany. This HarmoniCOP Integration Report was prepared under contract from the European Commission, Thematic programme: Energy, Environment and Sustainable Development of the 5th framework programme 1998–2002. See HarmoniCOP Project (2003) 'HarmoniCOP: Harmonising collaborative planning', www.harmonicop.info, accessed 9 June 2008
6   Finger and Asún (2001), p142. The principles we borrow from this educational philosophy pertain to people of all ages
7   See Bowers (1993) and Orr (1994), pp2, 32
8   Material for this table was sourced from a review of environmental education literature. Source: Adapted from Hofer and Stephenson (2007)
9   Hofer and Stephenson (2007). See also Brundage and Mackeracher (1980) and Zemke and Zemke (1995)
10   Sarkissian with Walsh (1994)
11   Theobald and Nachtigal (1995)
12   Boothroyd (1991)
13   Capra (2005), p20
14   According to Lafferty and Meadowcroft (1996): 'Capacity building in environmental policy is an important aspect of environmental success on three levels:

1   Informational capacity: defined by existence of epistemic communities, openness of media, adequate cognitive structures and paradigms, professionalism of relevant actors.

2   Participatory capacity: defined by openness of input mechanisms in policy processes, inclusiveness of policy networks which make the de facto decisions before the de jure decisions, adequacy of legal and material infrastructure for raising interventions within civil society.

3   Integrative capacity: defined by future-oriented dialogues, consensus-oriented policy culture and cooperative policy style, strategic capacity.'

15   See Sarkissian and Hurford with Wenman (2009b)
16   Steffen (2006), p344
17   Steffen (2006), p481
18   Generally, laypeople seem to understand drawings best when they are sketches or axonometrics (bird's eye views)
19   Sarkissian et al (2009a)
20   Barthel et al (2008)
21   Steffen (2006), p22
22   Biophilia theory is supported by 'a decade of research that reveals how strongly and positively people respond to open, grassy landscapes, scattered stands of trees, meadows, water, winding trails, and elevated views'. See Louv (2006), p43
23   Gould (1991), cited in Orr (1994), p140
24   See Cohen (1989, 1995)
25   Cohen (1993)
26   Greenway (1994b), p26
27   See Greenway (1994a, 1995)
28   See Peavey (2000a, 2000b) and Peavey et al (1986)
29   Hester (2006)
30   Hester (2006), p28
31   Churchman (2005), cited in Louv (2006), p171
32   'Nature-deficit disorder describes the human costs of alienation from nature, among them: diminished use of the senses, attention difficulties, and higher rates of physical and emotional illness'. See Louv (2006), pp34, 171
33   Orr (2006), p93
34   Glor-Bell (2007)
35   Bullard (2001)
36   See Jacobson et al (2006), p31; Gurevitz (2000); Thomashow (1996)
37   Nepo cited in Remen (2006), p261
38   Stone (2005), p165
39   See Sarkissian (1996)
40   See: Learning for a Sustainable Future (LSF) (undated) 'Learning outcomes', www.lsf-lst.ca/en/teachers/learning_outcomes.php, accessed 13 June 2008
41   Adapted from: Learning for a Sustainable Future (undated), pp37–39, accessed 13 June 2008

42   Orr (1992)
43   Hester (2006)
44   Selman (2001)
45   Jacobson et al (2006)
46   Queensland Government (2008) 'Queensland: The Smart State', www.smartstate.qld.gov.au, accessed 28 May 2008
47   Orr (1994), pp17, 30
48   Orr (1994), pp48–49. See also Bolan (1983), p32: 'The true task of the professional is not to display cleverness and intellectual dexterity but, rather, to create a new sense of value'
49   See: Bowers (1995), pp125, 132; Capra (1993); see also, p9
50   Although it would seem anathema to most educators, Thomas Berry suggests that we engage in postcritical naivete, 'a type of presence to the earth and all its inhabitants that includes, and also transcends, the scientific understanding that now is available to us from those long years of observation and reflection'. In other words, science had its value; now we must change modes to make sense of its lessons. See Berry (1988), p4
51   Meadows (2005), p201
52   Goleman (1995), p27
53   See Gardner (1999) and Goleman (2006)
54   Noddings also addresses the question of intelligence. She argues that educators must operate on the 'assumption of multiple intelligences' and a great variety and variability of students. She argues against what she sees as 'the persistent undervaluing of skills, attitudes and capacities traditionally associated with women', and proposes the notion of 'interpersonal reasoning'. See Noddings (1992), ppxiii, 53
55   Gardner (1993, 1999)
56   See Infed (the informal education homepage) (2002) 'howard gardner, multiple intelligences and education', www.infed.org/thinkers/gardner.htm, accessed 13 June 2008; Gardner (1999), p52; Louv (2006), p71
57   See Lang (1993, 1995) and Sarkissian (1996)
58   'The meaning of my communication is the response I get' is one of the presuppositions of neurolinguistic programming (NLP), outlined in Revell and Norman (1997)
59   Forester (1989), p108
60   Learning for a Sustainable Future (LSF) (undated) 'Learning Outcomes, www.lsf-lst.ca/en/teachers/learning_outcomes.php, accessed 13 June 2008

Chapter 6

1   According to the Institute for Intercultural Studies, Mead 'believed that cultural patterns of racism, warfare and environmental exploitation were learned, and that the members of a society could work together to modify their traditions and to construct new institu-

tions. This conviction drew her into discussions of the process of change, expressed in the slogan, "Never doubt that a small group of thoughtful, committed citizens can change the world"'. Institute for Intercultural Studies (2003) 'Margaret Mead (1901–1978): An anthropology of human freedom', www.intercultural studies.org/Mead/biography.html, accessed 11 June 2008 See also Mead (2001)

2   This story was transcribed and in part summarized from a video presentation: Westley (2008) 'Getting to Maybe. Social innovation: An agency based approach to transformation', keynote address, Resilience 2008 Conference, Stockholm University, Stockholm, 14–17 April, webcast proceedings, http://resilience.qbrick.com/view. aspx?id=6, accessed 30 May 2008

3   van der Brugge and van Raak (2007)

4   Kaplan and Kaplan (1989). See also Kaplan et al (1998)

5   Bill Moyer (1933–2002) was a United States social change activist, author and founding member of the Movement for a New Society. He outlines these four roles of activism in the following publications: Moyer (1990), p7; Moyer et al (2001). In a paper published online, Sam La Rocca (2003) describes how activists in the Gully Campaign, described later in this chapter, illustrate the Rebel and Reformer approaches

6   Based in northern NSW, Australia, Interhelp aims to assist community change agents to strengthen and renew their work through a process of reflection on and clarification of their core personal values and purpose (contact info@icef.info)

7   Urban Ecology Australia (UEA) is a United Nations-accredited, non-profit, non-government, educational association, based in Adelaide, South Australia. Incorporated in 1991, UEA is committed to trans-forming human settlements into EcoCities: vibrant, equitable, ecologically sustaining and economically viable communities. In a conventional development process, buildings are designed to suit a 'target market' and a community adapts itself to the environment after the development process is considered complete. In contrast, UEA gather together people wanting to embrace ecologically sound principles and help them create a not-for-profit private housing cooperative, which then acts as the developer for any proposed project. Because future residents are involved in decision making as their housing development evolves, they learn, in a hands-on fashion, the nuances of ecologically sustaining development (Urban Ecology Australia, 2008)

8   We thank Chérie Hoyle, Urban Ecology Australia and our dear friend and colleague, Sophia van Ruth, for this summary

9   Lotte Scharfman died aged 42 in 1970. According to the League of Women Voters of Massachusetts, Scharfman was a refugee from Hitler's Germany who devoted her life to working for the democratic process and helping citizens gain access to government. She is widely

credited with coining the phrase, 'Democracy is not a spectator sport'. See The League of Women Voters Massachusetts (undated) 'The LWV Massachusetts Citizen Education Fund', www.lwvma.org/cef.shtml, accessed 29 May 2008

10   Now Redland City Council, see Redland City Council (2008) 'Redland City Council', www.redland.qld.gov.au, accessed 12 June 2008

11   We are hopeful that recent changes in representation in Redland City Council will mean better environmental outcomes and more inclusive processes

12   Steffen (2006), p461

13   Leach, M. (Highgate Hill resident) cited in SPIRAL (undated) 'Development Issues: The Gully', www.spiral.org.au/sos/index.php?page=7&show=1, accessed 12 June 2008

14   Spiral Community Hub (undated) 'Development Issues: The Gully', www.spiral.org.au/sos/index.php?page=7&show=1, accessed 12 June 2008

SPIRAL (Steps to Participation, Initiative, Resources Action & Learning) is a community hub located in West End, Brisbane, which assists community members to develop community based initiatives including cooperatives, campaigns and ethical business. SPIRAL works towards social/ecological justice and sustainability, through: local–global community development and action; ethical economic development and community empowerment through education. See SPIRAL (2002) 'spiral community hub', www.spiral.org.au, accessed 12 June 2008

15   Gene Sharp has produced a brilliant foundational text for non-violent direct action, which provides a theoretical framework for non-violent action case studies, and presents a practical guide for strategic planners which aims to bring non-violent direct action from an 'improvised response' to a reflexive and deliberate strategy for positive change. See Sharp (2005)

16   La Rocca (2003)

17   See Rosa and Raymond Parks Institute for Self Development (2008) 'About Us', www.rosaparks.org/about.html, accessed 12 June 2008

18   See Curthoys (2002); 'The Australian Freedom Rides' (undated), www.freedomride.net, accessed 12 June 2008

19   For more information on the Franklin River campaign, see Hutton and Connors (1999); The Wilderness Society (2006) 'Campaigns: History of the Franklin River Campaign 1976–83', www.wilderness.org.au/articles/franklin, accessed 19 June 2008

20   This view evolves from the work of Melucci, Habermas, Offe and others (see below). For a more general discussion of how social movements shape – and are shaped by – societies, see Dalton and Kuechler (1990); Habermas (1981, 1985); Melucci (1985); Offe (1987); and Wapner (1995)

21   See Whelan (2005, 2007)

22   See Driskell (2002); Hart (1997); Sarkissian and Cook (2002); White (2001)

23   Loorbach (2007), p20
24   Croggon (2008)
25   Karvelas (2008)
26   Allard (2008)
27   Loorbach (2007), p19
28   B. Fuller quoted in Steffen (2007)
29   Dirven et al (2002)
30   Rittel and Webber (1984)
31   Lane and Maxfield (1996)
32   Zimmerman and Hayday (1999)
33   Zimmerman and Hayday (1999), p299
34   See Green et al (1994)
35   Carroll (2001). Maleny has a population of approximately 4000 and
      boasts 28 cooperatives (at 2003). The cooperative structures are used
      to support many of the town's activities, including:

      • financing, consumer services, environment, eco-development,
        environmental and strategic planning and economic
        development; arts and crafts, film, performance and social
        venues
      • education, community information, community radio,
        publishing
      • social services, family support services, women's services and
        youth services
      • employment, alternative trading, intra- and inter-regional
        networking and buying and recycling

      Jordan (2001, 2003)
36   A poll conducted by an independent market research company
      found that '79% of its sample of Maleny residents oppose a
      "Woolies" on the Obi Obi site. The main reasons given were traffic
      chaos, adverse local business impact and environmental concerns.'
      See Sturtz (2005)
37   Maleny Voice (2008). The Maleny Voice is a community-driven
      website designed to assist with the collation and dissemination of
      information for and on behalf of the Maleny community. It aims
      to cover a wide range of social, environmental and economic issues
      of concern, to protect the town's character, and to foster support for
      local food producers and their retailers
38   Maleny Voice (2008)
39   Mt Evelyn RAW: Residents Against Woolworths, MEEPPA (2007)
40   Peavey (2000a)
41   Green et al (1994)
42   Carson (1995). See also Sarkissian et al (1994b)
43   Loorbach (2007)
44   Loorbach (2008). See also Multi-level Approach to Transition
      Management, illustrated in Kemp et al (2007), p81; The Transition
      Management Cycle, illustrated in Loorbach (2007), p115
45   Tamarck Institute for Community Engagement (2006). For a summary

of the PLAN Institute's social innovation achievements, see Westley et al (2007)

46   Tamarck Institute for Community Engagement (2006)
47   Tamarck Institute for Community Engagement (2006)
48   Sarkissian (1994b), pp44–47
49   Moyer (1987)
50   See Moyer (1987); Moyer et al (2001). Our colleague Sam La Rocca outlines how the Gully Campaign, discussed earlier in this chapter, sits within the MAP framework. See La Rocca (2003), p21
51   For a useful summary of simple, complicated and complex problems see Westley et al (2007), p9
52   Westley et al (2007), p9
53   Victoria, Department of Infrastructure (DOI) (2002)
54   Cameron and Johnson (2004)
55   Geoffrey Syme is a scientist with the Australian Research Centre for Water in Society CSIRO, Division of Water Resources and Brian Sadler works within the Water Resources Directorate of the Water Authority of Western Australia. See Syme and Sadler (1994), p539
56   Westley (2008). See also Westley et al (2007)
57   See 'Why activists bypass community engagement processes', earlier in this chapter, and Whelan (2007)
58   The Change Agency is a collective of activist educators and researchers who help communities achieve social and environmental justice outcomes by providing facilitation, workshops, resources, research and other learning opportunities. See The Change Agency Education and Training Institute (undated)
59   Training for Change was founded in 1992 to help groups stand up for justice, peace and the environment through strategic non-violence. They have a unique approach to direct action training which they call direct education: 'Education that directly confronts and challenges the current system of injustice'. See: TFC (undated)
60   Evolving from a Permaculture design certification course, Earth Activist Training (EAT) presents principles of Permaculture, earth-based spirituality and regenerative activism to a diverse range of participants through lectures, exercises and hands-on learning opportunities. See Earth Activist Training (EAT) (2008)
61   Hawken (2007), p41
62   Hawken (2007), p143
63   Shadow networks are of increasing interest in governance literature and within systems ecology; for example see Gunderson and Holling (2002) and Olsson et al (2006)
64   Institute of Science in Society (2008)
65   Barthel et al (2008)
66   Food Connect is a dynamic, farmer–direct, community food distribution enterprise, based on the Community Supported Agriculture (CSA) model, and operating in south-east Queensland. They aim to 'provide genuine food for families, a decent living for farmers,

support the nurturing of the land and the establishment of local community networks'. See Food Connect (2008)

67   Sandercock (1995)

68   This list includes actions from the complete summary of progress against the agreed solutions, documented at Greatbearwatch.ca (2008) 'Solutions', www.savethegreatbear.org/solutions, accessed 4 June 2008

Chapter 7

1   See Forester (2004); Goudzwaard (2007); Newman et al (1986); Newman and Rowe (2003); Sacks (1997); and Suzuki and Dressel (2002)

2   See Isaacs (1993, 1999)

3   Isaacs (1993, 1999)

4   The programme was originally aired on British television by Channel 4 in March 2007: C4 (undated) 'The Great Global Warming Swindle', www.channel4.com/science/microsites/G/great_global_warming_swindle, accessed 13 June 2008.
     In Australia, the Australian Broadcasting Commission (ABC), clearly concerned about the reliability of technical and scientific information presented in the film, featured it in a prime-time programme on 12 July 2007. The programme (simulcast on ABC 2 and ABC NewsRadio) included an in-depth interview with writer and director Martin Durkin, followed by an expert panel discussion with a studio audience. Jones' interview with Durkin canvassed contentious issues raised in Durkin's piece: its impact when it premiered in the UK in March 2007; the science on which the documentary is based; credibility of scientists interviewed; their satisfaction with how they were portrayed; and the filmmaker's assertion that capping CO_2 emissions would be devastating to developing nations

5   G. Dunstan, personal communication, 14 July 2007

6   Clarke (1994), p17

7   La Rocca (2004)

8   Senbel (2005)

9   Sarkissian (1996)

10   Nick Wates Associates (2006) 'Glossary', www.communityplanning.net/glossary/glossary.htm, accessed 12 June 2008

11   US Department of Health and Human Services, Centers for Disease Control and Prevention (undated), 'Social Capital', www.cdc.gov/healthyplaces/healthtopics/social.htm, accessed 12 June 2008

12   Dale (2005)

13   Wilson (2005), p15

14   Onyx and Bullen (2000)

15   In Bonnyrigg, Sydney, the Khmer community, whom we meet in Chapter 8, exhibited strong bonding social capital but had not been successful in bridging or linking to the wider community or neighbouring communities

16   See Memmott and Meltzer (2005) and Onyx and Bullen (2000)
17   Tompkins and Lawley (2008)
18   Richmond (1999), p22
19   Adams (1995)
20   Sarkissian, W. (2007) Interview with Trisch Muller, Peter Muller, Lynn McNeilly and Les Turner, 18 October
21   Sarkissian (2005)
22   Clarke (1994)
23   See Albrechts and Van den Broeck (2004) and Thomas (1995, pp156–160)
24   See Sarkissian et al (1994a) and Sarkissian et al (2003b)
25   On the value of humour, see also Forester (2005)
26   Westley (2008)

Chapter 8

1   This poem is translated by Coleman Barks with John Moyne, in Mitchell (1989), p59
2   Coombes, P. (2000), personal communication with Cathy Wilkinson, November.
      Penny Coombes is the founder and managing director of The People for Places and Spaces in Sydney, Australia. See The People for Places and Spaces (undated)
3   Senbel (2005)
4   Hester (2006), p371
5   Healey (1997), p249
6   Hester (2006), p77
7   See Young (1990, 2000)
8   See Sandercock (1998, 2003)
9   Sandercock (2003)
10   Attili and Sandercock (2006) *Where Strangers Become Neighbours: The Story of the Collingwood Neighbourhood House and the Integration of Immigrants*, film, National Film Board of Canada, www.nfb.ca. For information about the film, see: 'Where Strangers Become Neighbours: The Story of the Collingwood Neighbourhood House and the Integration of Immigrants' (undated), www.mongrel-stories.com, accessed 6 June 2008. See also Giovanni Attili (2008, p348). This film is accompanied by their book *Where Strangers Become Neighbours: Integrating Immigrants in Vancouver, Canada* (Sandercock and Attili, 2008)
11   Young (1997), p68
12   Young (1997), p63
13   This is a common problem. In this case, some bureaucrats and others treated some immigrants as ignorant villagers likely to keep chickens in their bathtubs, when they had, in fact, emigrated from cities and large towns

14   Hart (1997), pp49–50
15   See Sarkissian et al (1997, 2003b, 2009)
16   Arnstein (1969), p217. These and other models are discussed in detail in the books in the *Community Participation in Practice* suite (1994–2003)
17   Sarkissian et al (1997)
18   See Sidhu (1994); Walsh with Cook (1994); and Walsh et al (1990)
19   See Driskell (2002) and White (2001, 2007)
20   See Driskell (2002); Sarkissian et al (1997, 2003b)
21   See WWF (2008). Another experience Yollana's family enjoyed during Earth Hour is documented in Chapter 9, Nourishment
22   Meadows (2005)
23   Young (1997), p57
24   Source: extracted from Sarkissian et al (2003b), pp12–18
25   See Sarkissian (2005) and Sarkissian with Dunstan (2003)
26   Seed et al (1988)
27   See Sarkissian and Hurford with Wenman (2009b)
28   See Sarkissian with Dunstan (2003); Sarkissian and Hurford with Wenman (2009b); and Sarkissian (2005)
29   Healey (1997), p249
30   Healey (1997), p264
31   Forester (1993)
32   Healey (1997), p278
33   Healey (1997), pp271–274
34   Sarkissian (1996)
35   Healey (1997), pp267–268
36   Sarkissian et al (2009a)
37   Forester (1993)
38   See Sarkissian et al (2009a)
39   See Sarkissian et al (2003a); Sarkissian and Hurford with Wenman (2009b) and Sarkissian et al (2009a)
40   Mabee and Hoberg (2006)
41   Healey and Hillier (1995) cited in Healey (1997), p274
42   Healey (1997), p274
43   Healey (1997), pp272, 278
44   Kaner et al (1996)
45   Cameron and Johnson (2004)
46   Hajer (1995) cited in Healey (1997), p277
47   Sarkissian (2005). See also Sarkissian and Hurford with Wenman (2009b)
48   See: www.kitchentablesustainability.com

Chapter 9

1   Lerner (2008)
2   Dictionary.com Unabridged (v 1.1) (2008)

3   Dictionary.com Unabridged (v 1.1) (2008)
4   Westley (2008)
5   Gould (1991), p140
6   Ash et al (2008)
7   Miller (2005)
8   See Birkeland (1993, p3; 1996, p48) and Naess (1978), cited in Fox (1990), p244
9   Naess (1988), p20
10   See Kaplan (1995); Kellert (2005); Hartig et al (1991); Humphries (2007); Maller et al (2005); and Staats et al (2003)
11   For an introduction to citizen science, see Irwin (1995)
12   Coastal CRC (2006). The Coastal CRC completed seven years of coastal research in 2006. Their website remained active until June 2008. A major output of their research was The Citizen Science Toolbox, developed in partnership with Griffith University and the Department of Natural Resources, Mines and Water, Queensland. This resource has been renamed as the URP Toolbox. The URP Toolbox is a free resource of principles and strategies to enhance meaningful involvement, from communities, scientists and decision makers, in community decision making. See Griffith University (2008)
13   Wendy Sarkissian, personal communication, 2008
14   Louv (2006), p43
15   Wilson (1990)
16   Wallace (1990)
17   WWF (2008)
18   Remen (2006), p217
19   See Sidhu (1994); Walsh with Cook (1994); and Walsh et al (1990)
20   Stubbs (2005), p151
21   Stewart et al (1994)
22   Armstrong (2005), p16
23   Prechtel (1999), pp340–341
24   Prechtel (1999), p338
25   Steffen (2006), pp514–516
26   More information about the Personal Sustainability Action Plan – and a complimentary downloadable workbook – can be found on our website: www.kitchentablesustainability.com
27   As ecological economist Robert Costanza argues: 'Practical problem-solving in complex, human dominated ecosystems requires the integration of three elements: (1) active and ongoing envisioning of both how the world works and how we would like the world to be, (2) systematic analysis appropriate to and consistent with the vision and (3) implementation appropriate to the vision.' Costanza (2001), p459
28   Steffen (2006), p536
29   According to Shields, positive visions help us: 'unglue ourselves from the way things appear to be'; buffer and balance negativity about the

future that pervades modern media, literature, art and film; and provide a framework for evaluating the present. See Shields (2000), p25

30 Shields (2000), p25

31 From the passage:

In conventional economics, a commodity is valuable to the extent it contributes to the goal of individual welfare, as assessed by individuals' willingness to pay. The point is that one cannot state a value without stating the goal being served. Conventional economic value is based on the goal of individual utility maximization. But other goals, and thus other values, are possible. For example, if the goal is sustainability, one should assess value based on the contribution to achieving that goal, in addition to value based on the goals of individual utility maximization, social equity, or other goals that may be deemed important. This broadening is particularly important if the goals are potentially in conflict (Costanza, 2001, p462)

32 In Chapter 6, Action, we discuss some of the different approaches to personal and community engagement with sustainability, such as Moyer's citizen, reformer, change agent and rebel

33 Mead (1935)

34 For example, turning a 60W light bulb off for two hours more each day can save approximately 38 kilowatt hours per year. Not huge. But if you multiply this number by, for example, the number of households in Australia (7.1 million according to the 2006 Australian Bureau of Statistics Census of Population and Housing), the saving increases to 271.5 million kilowatt hours

35 Hawken (2007), p163

36 Lerner (2008)

37 Johnson (1993)

38 According to Shields, archetypal aspects of our personalities can interfere with our effectiveness in social change. For example, she has observed the internal Critic, the Rebel, the Victim and the Hero creating problems in personal and community engagement with sustainable action. See Shields (2000), p35

39 Bennet et al (1998)

40 Bennet et al (1998), p11

41 Bennet et al (1998), p11

42 Adams (1995)

43 Shields (2000), pp104–114

44 Mary Maher, personal communication, 30 April 2008

45 Crying is another one of nature's stress-relieving strategies. Psychiatric chemist William Frey, PhD, showed that not all tears are the same. Unlike tears caused by eye irritants, emotional tears contain abundant amounts of adrenaline and other stress-related chemicals. See Frey (1985)

46 Abel (2002)

47   Abel (2002)
48   Sarkissian (1996)
49   See Noddings (1984, 1992)
50   Prior (2007)
51   This quotation is attributed to Helen Keller, an American author, activist and lecturer, famous for being the first deaf-blind person to graduate from college
52   Abelman (2005), p183

Chapter 10

1   The Redland Youth Plaza is the largest skate and BMX facility in South-East Queensland. See Redland City Council (2008b)
2   Paitson (2008), p5. See also Nimbin Community Development Association (2008)
3   Healey (2006)
4   van der Brugge and van Raak (2007)
5   Loorbach (2007)
6   Flyvberg (1998)
7   Kohler-Koch (2008), p3
8   See, for example, Fung (2004) and Fung and Wright (2003)
9   The Frankfurt School is not so much an institution as a school of thought. It refers to a group of German-American theorists, who developed powerful analyses of the changes in Western capitalist societies that occurred following the classical theory of Marx. Working at the *Institut für Sozialforschung* in Frankfurt, members of the Frankfurt School accepted Marx's analysis of social forces, while recognizing that communism, as advocated at the time, was not a long-term solution. Their ideas came to be known as 'critical theory'
10   Kornfield (2000)
11   Extracts from Eagleby Residents Action Group meeting minutes, 5 December 2000
12   See Costanza (2001), p460; Yankelovich (1991)
13   Costanza (2001), p460
14   Kaner et al (1996)
15   Castle Vale Housing Action Trust (2005)
16   For more information on Action Learning, see Dick (1997)

Chapter 11

1   Worldchanging (undated)
2   Sarkissian, W. (2007) Interview with Graeme Dunstan, 14 July

References

Abel, M. H. (2002) 'Humor, stress, and coping strategies', *Humor*, vol 15, no 4, pp365–381

Abelman, M. (2005) 'Raising whole children is like raising good food: Beyond factory farming and factory schooling', in M. K. Stone and Z. Barlow (eds) (2005) *Ecological Literacy: Educating our Children for a Sustainable World*, Sierra Club Books, San Francisco

Adams, D. (1995) 'Affiliation', in *Psychology for Peace Activists*, Second edition, Advocate Press, New Haven, CT

Adams, D. (1995) 'Anger vs fear and pessimism', in *Psychology for Peace Activists*, second edition, Advocate Press, New Haven, CT

Adams, D. (1995) *Psychology for Peace Activists*, second edition, Advocate Press, New Haven, CT

Albert, M. (2003) *Parecon: Life After Capitalism*, Verso, London and New York

Albert, M. and Hahnel, R. (1991a) *Looking Forward: Participatory Economics for the Twenty-first Century*, South End Press, Boston, MA

Albert, M. and Hahnel, R. (1991b) *The Political Economy of Participatory Economics*, Princeton University Press, Princeton

Albert, M. and Hahnel, R. (2002) 'In defense of participatory economics', *Science & Society*, vol 66, no 1, pp7–21

Albrechts, L. and Van den Broeck, J. (2004) 'From discourse to acts: The case of the ROM-project in Ghent, Belgium', *Town Planning Review*, vol 75, no 2, pp127–150

Armstrong, J. C. (2005) 'En'owkin: Decision-making as if sustainability mattered', in M. K. Stone and Z. Barlow (eds) (2005) *Ecological Literacy: Educating our Children for a Sustainable World*, Sierra Club Books, San Francisco

Arnstein, S. (1969) 'A ladder of citizen participation', *Journal of the American Institute of Planners*, vol 35, no 4, pp216–224

Ash, C., Jasny, B. R., Roberts, L., Stone, R. and Sugde, A. M. (2008) 'Reimagining cities', *Science*, vol 319, p739

Attili, G. (Director) and Sandercock, L. (Producer) (2006) *Where Strangers Become Neighbours: The Story of the Collingwood Neighbourhood House and the Integration of Immigrants*, film, National Film Board of Canada, www.nfb.ca

Barthel, S., Folke, C. and Colding, J. (2008) 'Socio-ecological memory for management of ecosystem services', in Barthel, S. (2008) *Recalling Urban Nature: Linking City People to Ecosystem Services*, Doctoral Thesis, Stockholm University

Beatley, T. with Newman, P. (2008) *Green Urbanism Down Under: Learning from Sustainable Communities in Australia*, Island Press, Washington DC

Bennet, M., Edwards, S., Houghton, N. and Wilkinson, C. (1998) 'Navigating nihilism: Towards a sustainable world', Masters of Environmental Science group thesis, Monash University, Melbourne

Berkes, F. (1989) *Common Property Resources: Ecology and Community-based Sustainable Development*, Belhaven, London

Berkes, F. and Folkes, C. (1991) 'A systems perspective on the interrelations between natural, human-made and cultural capital', *Ecological Economics*, vol 5, no 1, pp1–8

Berkes, F., Colding, J. and Folkes, C. (eds) (2003) *Navigating Social-Ecological Systems: Building Resilience for Complexity and Change*, Cambridge University Press, Cambridge and New York

Bernstein, R. J. (1983) *Beyond Objectivism and Relativism*, Basil Blackwell, Oxford

Berry, T. (1988) *The Dream of the Earth,* Sierra Club Books, San Francisco

Birkeland, J. (1993) 'The environ-mental illness', conference paper, 'Health and Ecology: A Nursing Perspective', Nursing and the Environment National Conference, 26 March, Sydney

Birkeland, J. (1996) 'Ethics-based planning: The case for a new public forum', *Australian Planner*, vol 33, no 1, pp47–49

Bolan, R. S. (1983) 'The structure of ethical choice in planning practice', *Journal of Planning Education and Research*, vol 3, no 1, pp23–34

Bolen, J. S. (1994) *Crossing to Avalon: A Woman's Midlife Pilgrimage*, HarperSanFrancisco, San Francisco

Boothroyd, P. (1991) 'Developing community planning skills: Applications of a seven-step model', *CHS Research Bulletin*, bulletin 91, no 10, pp1–9

Bowers, C. A. (1993) *Education, Cultural Myths, and the Ecological Crisis: Towards Deep Changes*, State University of New York Press, New York

Bowers, C. A. (1995) *Educating for an Ecologically Sustainable Culture: Rethinking Moral Education, Creativity, Intelligence, and Other Modern Orthodoxies*, State University of New York Press, Albany

Brundage, D. H. and Mackeracher, D. (1980) *Adult Learning Principles and their Application to Planning*, Ministry of Education of Ontario, Toronto

Bullard, R. (2001) 'Environmental justice', in N. J. Smelser and P. B. Baltes (eds) *International Encyclopedia of the Social & Behavioral Sciences*, Pergamon, Oxford

Cameron, J. and Johnson, A. (2004) 'Evaluating for development: Planning for public involvement in SEQ2021', *Australian Planner*, vol 41, no 1, pp49–55

Capra, F. (1993) 'What is ecological literacy?' in *Guide to Ecological Literacy*, The Elmwood Institute, Berkeley, CA, pp4–8

Capra, F. (2005) 'Speaking nature's language: Principles of sustainability', in M. K. Stone and Z. Barlow (eds) (2005) *Ecological Literacy: Educating our Children for a Sustainable World*, Sierra Club Books, San Francisco

Carson, L. (1995) 'Perspectives on community consultation: Strategic questioning in action', *Australian Planner*, vol 32, no 4, pp217–221

Churchman, D. (2005) 'Reinstilling the love of nature among children', *American Forests*, vol 98, no 10, cited in Louv, R. *Last Child in the Woods: Saving Our Children from Nature-Deficit Disorder*, Algonquin Books of Chapel Hill, North Carolina

Clarke, H. (1994) 'Public participation in Alexandria', in W. Sarkissian and D. Perlgut (eds) (1994) *Community Participation in Practice: Handbook*, second edition, Murdoch University, Institute for Sustainability and Technology Policy, Perth

Cohen, M. J. (1989) *Connecting with Nature: Creating Moments that Let the Earth Teach*, World Peace University, Eugene, OR

Cohen, M. J. (1993) 'Integrated ecology: The process of counselling with nature', *The Humanistic Psychologist*, vol 21, no 3, pp43–55

Cohen, M. J. (1995) 'Counselling and nature: A greening of psychotherapy', *The Interpsych Newsletter*, vol 2, no 4

Connor, D. M. (1997) 'The open house', in *Public Participation: A Manual*, Development Press, Victoria, BC

Coombes, P. (2000) personal communication with Cathy Wilkinson, November

Costanza, R. (2001) 'Visions, values, valuation, and the need for an ecological economics', *BioScience*, vol 51, no 6, pp459–468

Costanza, R. and Daly, H. (1992) 'Natural capital and sustainable development', *Conservation Biology*, vol 6, no 1, pp37–46

Cotgrove, S. F. (1982) *Catastrophe or Cornucopia: The Environment, Politics and the Future*, John Wiley & Sons, New York

Curthoys, A. (2002) *Freedom Ride: A Freedom Rider Remembers*, Allen & Unwin, Sydney

Dale, A. (2005) 'Social capital and sustainable community development: Is there a relationship?', in A. Dale and J. Onyx (eds) *A Dynamic Balance: Social and Sustainable Community Development*, UBC Press, Vancouver

Dalton, R. and Kuechler, M. (eds) (1990) *Challenging the Political Order: New Social and Political Movements in Western Democracies*, Oxford University Press, New York

Daly, H. E. and Farley, J. (2004) *Ecological Economics: Principles and Applications*, Island Press, Washington DC

Davidson, S. (1998) 'Spinning the wheel of empowerment', *Planning*, April, pp14–19

Devuyst, D. (ed) with Hens, L. and De Lannoy, W. (2001) *How Green is the City?: Sustainability Assessment and the Management of Urban Environments*, Columbia University Press, New York

Diamond, J. (2002) 'Easter Island's end', in D. E. Lorey (ed) *Global Environmental Challenges of the Twenty-First Century: Resources, Consumption and Sustainable Solutions*, Rowman and Littlefield, Lanham, MD

Diamond, J. (2005) *Collapse: How Societies Choose to Fail or Succeed*, Viking, New York

Dirven, J., Rotmans, J. and Verkaik, A. P. (2002) 'Society in transition: An innovative viewpoint', transition essay, LNV, ICIS and Green Space and Agrocluster Innovation Network, The Hague, The Netherlands

Driskell, D. with the Growing up in Cities Project (2002) *Creating Better Cities with Children and Youth: A Manual for Participation*, Earthscan, UNESCO Publishing and MOST, London

Edwards, A. R. (2005) *The Sustainability Revolution: Portrait of a Paradigm Shift*, New Society Publishers, Gabriola Island, BC

Finger, M. and Asún, J. M. (2001) *Adult Education at the Crossroads: Learning our Way Out*, NIACE, Leicester

Flyvberg, B. (1998) *Rationality and Power*, University of Chicago Press, Chicago

Forester, J. (1989) *Planning in the Face of Power*, University of California Press, Berkeley

Forester, J. (1993) *Critical Theory, Public Policy and Planning Process: Toward a Critical Pragmatism*, State University of New York Press, Albany

Forester, J. (2004) 'The politics of planning communities: The art of collaborative consensus building', paper presented at NSW Safe Communities Symposium, Sydney, 28–29 July

Forester, J. (2005) 'Irony and critical moments in negotiations: On humor and irony, recognition and hope', in U. Johansson and J. Woodilla (eds) *Organizations: Epistemological Claims and Supporting Field Stories*, Copenhagen Business School Press, Copenhagen

Fox, W. (1990) *Toward a Transpersonal Ecology: Developing New Foundations for Environmentalism*, Shambhala, Boston and London

Frey, W. H. (1985) *Crying: The Mystery of Tears*, Winston Press, Minneapolis

Fung, A. (2004) *Empowered Participation: Reinventing Urban Democracy*, Princeton University Press, Princeton

Fung, A. and Wright, E. O. (eds) (2003) *Deepening Democracy: Institutional Innovations in Empowered Participatory Governance*, The Real Utopia Project: Volume 4, Verso, London

Gardner, H. (1993) *Multiple Intelligences: The Theory in Practice*, Basic Books, New York

Gardner, H. (1999) *Intelligence Reframed*, Basic Books, New York

Gerard, L. and Teurfs, L. (1995) 'Dialogue and organizational transformation', in K. Gozdz (ed) *Community Spirit: Renewing Spirit and Learning in Business*, New Leaders Press, San Francisco, pp143–153

Glendinning, C. (1994) *My Name is Chellis & I'm in Recovery from Western Civilization*, Shambhala, Boston

Glendinning, C. (2007) *My Name is Chellis & I'm in Recovery from Western Civilization*, New Society/New Catalyst, Gabriola Island, BC

Glor-Bell, J. (2007) *Bibliography of Climate Justice Literature*, Canadian Centre for Policy Alternatives, BC, Vancouver, December

Goleman, D. (1995) *Emotional Intelligence: Why It Can Matter More Than IQ for Character, Health and Lifelong Achievement*, Bantam Books, New York

Goleman, D. (2006) *Social Intelligence: The New Science of Human Relationships*, Bantam Books, New York

Goudzwaard, B. (2007) *Hope in Troubled Times: A New Vision for Confronting Global Crises*, Institute for Christian Studies, Citizens for Public Justice, Baker Academic, Ada, MI

Gould, S. J. (1991) 'Enchanted evening', cited in Orr, D. W. (1994) *Earth in Mind: On Education, Environment, and the Human Prospect*, Island Press, Washington DC, p140

Green, T. and Woodrow, P. with Peavey, F. (1994) 'Strategic questioning: An approach to creating personal and social change', in *Insight and Action: How to Discover and Support a Life of Integrity and Commitment to Change*, New Society, Philadelphia

Green, T. and Woodrow, P. with Peavey, F. (1994) *Insight and Action: How to Discover and Support a Life of Integrity and Commitment to Change*, New Society, Philadelphia

Greenway, R. (1994a) 'Boundary crossings: Wilderness and culture', paper to International Transpersonal Association, 13th International Conference, Killarney, Ireland, 25 May, Conference Recording Service, Berkeley, CA, Tape 042

Greenway, R. (1994b) 'The wilderness experience: A doorway Into ecopsychology?', unpublished paper, Corona Farm and Northstar Wilderness Institute, Port Townsend, WA

Greenway, R. (1995) 'The wilderness effect and eco-psychology', in T. Roszak, M. E. Gomes and A. D. Kanner (eds) *Ecopsychology: Restoring the Earth, Healing the Mind*, Sierra Club, San Francisco

Gunderson, L. H. and Holling, C. S. (eds) (2002) *Panarchy: Understanding Transformations in Human and Natural Systems*, Island Press, Washington DC

Gurevitz, R. (2000) 'Affective approaches to environmental education: Going beyond the imagined worlds of childhood?', *Ethics, Place and Environment*, vol 3, no 3, pp253–268

Habermas, J. (1981) 'Social movements', *Telos*, vol 49, pp33–37

Habermas, J. (1985) 'Introduction', in J. Habermas (ed) *Observations of 'The Spiritual Situation of the Age'*, MIT Press, Cambridge, MA

Hahnel, R. (2005) *Economic Justice and Democracy: From Competition to Cooperation*, Routledge, New York and London

Hajer, M. (1995) *The Politics of Environmental Discourse: A Study of the Acid Rain Controversy in Great Britain and the Netherlands*, Oxford University Press, Oxford

Hames, R. (2007) *The Five Literacies of Global Leadership*, Jossey-Bass, San Francisco

Hansen, M. V. and Allen, R. G. (2002) *The One Minute Millionaire*, Harmony Books, New York

Hardin, G. (1968) 'The tragedy of the commons', *Science*, vol 162, pp1243–1248

Hart, R. A. (1997) *Children's Participation: The Theory and Practice of Involving Young Citizens in Community Development and Environmental Care*, Earthscan, London

Hartig, T., Mang, M. and Evans, G. W. (1991) 'Restorative effects of natural environment experiences', *Environment and Behavior*, vol 23, no 3, pp3–26

Hartmann, T. (2004) *The Last Hours of Ancient Sunlight: The Fate of the World and What We Can Do Before it's Too Late*, Three Rivers Press, New York

Hawken, P. (2007) *Blessed Unrest: How the Largest Movement in the World Came into Being and Why No One Saw it Coming*, Viking, New York

Hawken, P., Lovins, A. B. and Lovins, L. H. (1999) *Natural Capitalism: The Next Industrial Revolution*, Earthscan, London

Hawkes, J. (2001) *The Fourth Pillar of Sustainability: Culture's Essential Role in Public Planning*, Common Ground Publishing Pty Ltd in association with the Cultural Development Network (Victoria), Melbourne

Healey, P. (1997) *Collaborative Planning: Shaping Places in Fragmented Societies*, Macmillan Press, London

Healey, P. (2006) 'Transforming governance: Challenges of institutional adaptation and a new politics of space', *European Planning Studies*, vol 14, no 3, pp299–319

Hester, R. T. (2006) *Design for Ecological Democracy*, MIT Press, Cambridge, MA

Hofer, N. and Stephenson, C. (2007) 'Educating for sustainability', unpublished paper, University of British Columbia, Vancouver

Holling, C. S. (1973) 'Resilience and stability of ecological systems', *Annual Review of Ecology and Systematics*, vol 4, pp1–23

Holling, C. S. (1986) 'Resilience of ecosystems: Local surprise and global change', in W. C. Clark and R. E. Munn (eds) *Sustainable Development of the Biosphere*, Cambridge University Press, Cambridge

Hough, M. (2004) *Cities and Natural Process: A Basis for Sustainability*, Routledge, London

Humphries, C. (2007) 'The path to nature: Contact with nature as a planning opportunity', unpublished student paper, School of Community and Regional Planning, University of British Columbia, 9 July

Hutton, D. and Connors, L. (1999) 'Taking to the bush', in *A History of the Australian Environment Movement*, Cambridge University Press, Cambridge

Irwin, A. (1995) *Citizen Science: A Study of People, Expertise and Sustainable Development*, Routledge, London

Isaacs, W. N. (1993) 'Dialogue: The power of collective thinking', *The Systems Thinker*, vol 4, no 3, pp1–4

Isaacs, W. N. (1999) 'Dialogic leadership', *The Systems Thinker*, vol 10, no 1, pp1–5

Jaccard, M. (2006) *Sustainable Fossil Fuels: The Unusual Suspect in the Quest for Clean and Enduring Energy*, Cambridge University Press, Cambridge

Jacobs, J. (1961) *Death and Life of Great American Cities*, Random House, London

Jacobson, S. K., McDuff, M. D. and Monroe, M. C. (2006) *Conservation Education and Outreach Techniques*, Oxford University Press, New York

Johnson, R. (1993) *Owning Your Own Shadow: Understanding the Dark Side of the Psyche*, HarperCollins, New York

Kaner, S. with Lenny, L., Toldi, C., Fisk, S. and Berger, D. (1996) *Facilitator's Guide to Participatory Decision-Making*, New Society Publishers, Gabriola Island, BC

Kaplan, R. and Kaplan, S. (1989) *The Experience of Nature: A Psychological Perspective*, Cambridge University Press, Cambridge

Kaplan, R., Ryan, R. L. and Kaplan, S. (1998) *With People in Mind: Design and Management of Everyday Nature*, Island Press, Washington DC

Kaplan, S. (1995) 'The restorative benefits of nature: Toward an integrative framework', *Journal of Environmental Psychology*, vol 15, pp169–182

Kellert, S. R. (2005) *Building for Life: Designing and Understanding the Human-Nature Connection*, first edition, Island Press, Washington DC

Kemp, R., Loorbach, D. and Rotmans, J. (2007) 'Transition management as a model for managing processes of co-evolution towards sustainable development', *International Journal of Sustainable Development and World Ecology*, vol 14, no 1, pp78–91

Kercher, B. (2002) 'Native Title in the shadows: The origins of the myth of Terra Nullius in early New South Wales courts', in G. Blue, M. Bunton and R. Crozier (eds) *Colonialism and the Modern World Order: Selected Studies*, M. E. Sharpe, New York

Kohler-Koch, B. (2008) 'Does participatory governance hold its promises?', conference presentation, CONNEX Final Conference: Efficient and Democratic Governance in a Multi-Level Europe, Mannheim, 6–8 March

Kornfield, J. (2000) *After the Ecstasy, the Laundry: How The Heart Grows Wise on the Spiritual Path*, Bantam Books, Westminster, MD

Korten, D. (2006) *The Great Turning: from Empire to Earth Community*, Kumarian Press, Bloomfield, CT and Berrett-Koehler Publishers, San Francisco, p20

Lafferty, W. M. and Meadowcroft, J. (eds) (1996) *Democracy and the Environment: Problems and Prospects*, Edward Elgar, Cheltenham

Lane, D. and Maxfield, R. (1996) 'Strategy under complexity: Fostering generative relationships', *Long Range Planning*, vol 29, no 2, pp215–231

Lang, R. (1993) 'Learning style', handout material for a workshop, ENVS. 5101, York University Faculty of Environmental Studies, September

Lang, R. (1995) 'Strategic planning and personality type: Toward constructive and contingent use of difference: Summary of findings and conclusions', Ed.D. Thesis, University of Toronto

Lewin, R. (1993) *Complexity: Life at the Edge of Chaos*, Collier Books, New York

ICLEI (1996) *Local Agenda 21 Planning Guide: An Introduction to Sustainable Development Planning*, ICLEI, Toronto

Loorbach, D. (2007) *Transition Management: New Mode of Governance for Sustainable Development*, International Books, Utrecht, The Netherlands

Loorbach, D. (2008) 'Transition management: "Organised panarchy" in social systems?', conference paper, Resilience 2008: Resilience, Adaptation and Transformation in Turbulent Times: International Science and Policy Conference, Stockholm, 14–17 April

Louv, R. (2006) *Last Child in the Woods: Saving our Children from Nature-Deficit Disorder*, Algonquin Books of Chapel Hill, Chapel Hill, North Carolina, p320

Lowe, I (1994) 'Performance Measurement', *Proceedings of the Fenner Conference on the Environment*, ANU, Australia

Mabee, H. S. and Hoberg, G. (2006) 'Equal partners? Assessing comanagement of forest resources in Clayoquot Sound', *Society and Natural Resources*, vol 19, no 10, pp875–888

Maller, C., Townsend, M., Pryor, A., Brown, P. and St Leger, L. (2005) 'Healthy nature, healthy people: "Contact with nature" as an upstream health promotion intervention for populations', *Health Promotion International*, vol 21, no 1, pp45–54

Mandelbaum, S. J. (1991) 'Telling Stories', *Journal of Planning Education and Research*, vol 10, p209–214

Maslow, A. (1943) 'A theory of human motivation', *Psychological Review*, vol 50, pp370–396

Maslow, A. (1998) *Toward a Psychology of Being*, third edition, Wiley & Sons, New York

McKibben, B. (2007) *Deep Economy: The Wealth of Communities and the Durable Future*, Times Books, New York

Mead, M. (1935) *Sex and Temperament in Three Primitive Societies*, William Morrow, New York

Mead, M. (2001) *New Lives for Old: Cultural Transformation: Manus, 1928–1953*, 2001 edition, HarperCollins, New York

Meadows, D. (2005) 'Dancing with systems', in M. K. Stone and Z. Barlow (eds) (2005) *Ecological Literacy: Educating our Children for a Sustainable World*, Sierra Club Books, San Francisco

Mellon, N. (1992) *Storytelling and the Art of the Imagination*, Element, Shaftesbury, UK, Rockport, MA and Brisbane

Melucci, A. (1985) 'The symbolic challenge of contemporary movements', *Social Research*, vol 52, no 4, pp789–816

Memmott, P. and Meltzer, A. (2005) 'Modelling social capital in a remote Australian Indigenous community', in A. Dale and J. Onyx (eds) *A Dynamic Balance: Social Capital and Sustainable Community Development*, UBC Press, Vancouver

Miller, J. R. (2005) 'Biodiversity conservation and the extinction of experience', *Trends in Ecology & Evolution*, vol 20, pp430–434

Mitchell, S. (1989) *The Enlightened Heart: An Anthology of Sacred Poetry*, HarperPerennial, New York

Moore, J. (2002) 'Lessons from environmental education: Developing strategies for public consultation within the Georgia Basin Futures Project', *Canadian Journal of Environmental Education*, vol 7, no 2, pp179–192

Moyer, B. (1990) *The Practical Strategist: Movement Action Plan (MAP) Strategic Theories for Evaluating, Planning, and Conducting Social Movements*, Social Movement Empowerment Project, San Francisco

Moyer, B., with McAllister, J., Finley, M. L. and Soifer, S. (2001) *Doing Democracy: The MAP Model for Organizing Social Movements*, New Society Publishers, Gabriola Island, BC

Naess, A. (1988) 'Self realization: An ecological approach to being in the world', in J. Seed, J. Macy and P. Fleming, *Thinking like a Mountain: Towards a Council of All Beings*, New Society Publishers, Gabriola Island, BC

Newman, P. and Jennings, I. (2008) *Cities as Sustainable Ecosystems: Principles and Practices*, Island Press, Washington DC

Newman, P. and Kenworthy, J. R. (1999) *Sustainability and Cities*, Island Press, Washington DC

Newman, P. and Rowe, M. (2003) *Hope for the Future: The Western Australian State Sustainability Strategy*, Western Australian Government, Perth

Newman, P., Beatley, T. and Boyer, H. (forthcoming 2008) *Resilient Cities: Responding to Climate Change and Peak Oil*, Island Press, Washington DC

Newman, P., Duxbury, L. and Neville, S. (1986) *Case Studies in Environmental Hope*, Picton Press, Perth

Noddings, N. (1984) *Caring: A Feminine Approach to Ethics and Moral Education*, University of California Press, Berkeley

Noddings, N. (1992) *The Challenge to Care in Schools: An Alternative Approach to Education*, Teachers College Press, New York

Noddings, N. (2003) *Happiness and Education*, Cambridge University Press, Cambridge, p131

Nowlan, D. and Nowlan, N. (1970) *The Bad Trip: The Untold Story of the Spadina Expressway*, New Press, Toronto

Offe, C. (1987) 'Challenging the boundaries of institutional politics: Social movements since the 1960s', in C. Maier (ed) *Changing Boundaries of the Political*, Cambridge University Press, Cambridge

O'Neill, N. and Colebatch, H. K. (1989) *Public Participation in Local Government*, Hawkesbury City Council, Sydney

Onyx, J. and Bullen, P. (2000) 'Measuring social capital in five communities', *Journal of Applied Behavioural Science*, vol 36, no 1, pp23–42

Onyx, J. and Osburn, L. (2005) 'The case of Broken Hill', in A. Dale and J. Onyx (eds) *A Dynamic Balance: Social Capital and Sustainable Community Development*, UBC Press, Vancouver

Orr, D. W. (1992) *Ecological Literacy: Education and the Transition to a Postmodern World*, State University of New York Press, Albany

Orr, D. W. (1994) *Earth in Mind: On Education, Environment, and the Human Prospect*, Island Press, Washington DC

Orr, D. W. (2005) 'Place and pedagogy,' in M. K. Stone and Z. Barlow (eds) (2005) *Ecological Literacy: Educating our Children for a Sustainable World*, Sierra Club Books, San Francisco

Orr, D. W. (2006) 'Framing sustainability', *Conservation Biology*, vol 20, no 2, pp265–268

Ostrom, E. (1990) *Governing the Commons: The Evolution of Institutions for Collective Action*, Cambridge University Press, Cambridge

Ostrom, E. (2008) 'Updating the design principles for robust resource institutions', keynote address, Resilience 2008 Conference, Stockholm University, Stockholm, 14–17 April

Paddison, S. (1992) *The Hidden Power of the Heart: Discovering an Unlimited Source of Intelligence*, Planetary Publications, Boulder Creek, CA

Paitson, E. (2008) 'Friends of Nimbin Skatepark update', *Nimbin GoodTimes*, June

Peavey, F. (2000a) *By Life's Grace: Musings on the Essence of Social Change*, New Society, Philadelphia

Peavey, F. (2000b) *Heart Politics Revisited*, Pluto Press, Annandale, NSW

Peavey, F. with Levy, M. and Varon, C. (1986) *Heart Politics*, New Society, Philadelphia

Percy, M. 'The Common Living Dirt', extract from *Stone, Paper, Knife* (1983) cited in L. Anderson (ed) (1991) *Sisters of the Earth: Women's Prose and Poetry about Nature*, Vantage Books, New York, pp340–342

Perschel, R. (2002) 'Work, Workshop, and the Natural World: A Challenge for the Land Use Professions', in S. R. Kellerman and T. J. Farnham (eds) *The Good in Nature and Humanity: Connecting Science, Religion, and Spirituality within the Natural World*, Island Press, Washington DC, p160

Portney, K. E. (2003) *Taking Sustainability Seriously: Economic Development, the Environment and Quality of Life in American Cities*, MIT Press, Cambridge, MA

Prechtel, M. (1999) *Long Life Honey in the Heart: A Story of Initiation and Eloquence from the Shores of a Mayan Lake*, Tarcher-Putnam, New York

Ray, P. H. and Anderson, S. R. (2000) *The Cultural Creatives: How 50 Million People Are Changing the World*, Harmony Books, New York

Reason, P. and Hawkins, P. (1988) 'Storytelling as inquiry', in P. Reason (ed) *Human Inquiry in Action: Developments in New Paradigm Research*, Sage, London

Remen, R. N. (2006) *Kitchen Table Wisdom: Stories that Heal*, 10th anniversary edition, Riverhead Books, New York

Revell, J. and Norman, S. (1997) *In Your Hands: NLP in ELT*, Saffire Press, London

Richmond, L. (1999) *Work as a Spiritual Practice*, Broadway Books, New York

Rittel, H. and Webber, M. (1984) 'Dilemmas in a general theory of planning', in N. Cross (ed) *Developments in Design Methodology*, J. Wiley & Sons, Chichester, pp135–144

Rosen, B. and Knaster, A. (1986) 'Managing complex environmental decision-making processes', conference paper, University of California at Davis Conference, 21–22 October, Interaction Associates, San Francisco

Sacks, J. (1997) *The Politics of Hope*, Jonathan Cape, London

Sandercock, L. (1995) 'Voices from the borderlands: A meditation on a metaphor', *Journal of Planning Education and Research*, vol 14, no 2, pp77–88

Sandercock, L. (1998) *Towards Cosmopolis: Planning for Multicultural Cities*, John Wiley & Sons, Chichester and New York

Sandercock, L. (2003) *Cosmopolis II: Mongrel Cities in the 21st Century*, Continuum, London

Sandercock, L. (2004) 'Towards a planning imagination for the 21st Century', *Journal of the American Planning Association*, vol 70, pp133–141

Sandercock, L. and Attili, G. (2008) *Where Strangers Become Neighbours: Integrating Immigrants in Vancouver, Canada*, Springer, Heidelberg

Sarkissian, W. (1994) 'Introduction: Community participation in theory and practice', in W. Sarkissian and K. Walsh (eds) *Community Participation in Practice: Casebook*, Murdoch University, Institute for Sustainability and Technology Policy, Perth, pp1–32

Sarkissian, W. (1996) 'With a Whole Heart: Nurturing an Ethic of Caring for Nature in the Education of Australian Planners', PhD thesis, Murdoch University, Perth

Sarkissian, W. (2005) 'Stories in a park: Giving voice to the voiceless in Eagleby, Australia', *Planning Theory and Practice*, vol 6, no 1, pp103–117

Sarkissian, W. (2007) Interview with Graeme Dunstan, 14 July

Sarkissian, W. (2007) Interview with Trisch Muller, Peter Muller, Lynn McNeilly and Les Turner, 18 October

Sarkissian, W. and Cook, A. (2002) 'Savvy cities: Helping kids out of the bubble wrap', keynote address, International CPTED Association Annual Conference, Calgary, Alberta, October

Sarkissian, W. and Walsh, K. (eds) (1994a) 'The Williamstown Rifle Range: A design negotiation exercise with 500 participants', in *Community Participation in Practice: Casebook*, Murdoch University, Institute for Sustainability and Technology Policy, Perth

Sarkissian, W. with Walsh, K. (1994b) 'Teamwork and collaborative planning for a new suburban development in Melbourne: The case of Roxburgh Park', in W. Sarkissian and K. Walsh (eds) *Community Participation in Practice: Casebook*, Institute for Sustainability and Technology Policy, Murdoch University, Perth

Sarkissian, W., Cook, A. and Walsh, K. (1994a) *Community Participation in Practice: A Practical Guide*, Institute for Sustainability and Technology Policy, Murdoch University, Perth

Sarkissian, W., Cook, A. and Walsh, K. (1994b) 'Recent developments in participatory planning', in *Community Participation in Practice: A Practical Guide*, Institute for Sustainability and Technology Policy, Murdoch University, Perth

Sarkissian, W., Cook, A. and Walsh, K. (1997) 'Core practices of community participation in practice', in *Community Participation in Practice: A Practical Guide*, Murdoch University, Institute for Sustainability and Technology Policy, Perth

Sarkissian, W., Hirst, A. and Stenberg, B. (2003a) 'Reconceptualising community participation', in *Community Participation in Practice: New Directions*, Murdoch University, Institute for Sustainability and Technology Policy, Perth

Sarkissian, W., Hirst, A. and Stenberg, B. (2003b) *Community Participation in Practice: New Directions*, Institute for Sustainability and Technology Policy, Murdoch University, Perth

Sarkissian, W. and Bunjamin-Mau, W. with Cook, A. and Walsh, K. (2009a) *SpeakOut!: The Step-by-Step Guide to SpeakOuts and Community Workshops*, Earthscan, London

Sarkissian, W. and Hurford, D. with Wenman, C. (2009b) *Creative Approaches to Community Planning: Nurturing Inclusion with Insight and Method*, Forthcoming

Seed, J., Macy, J., Naess A. and Fleming, P. (1988) *Thinking Like a Mountain: Towards a Council of All Beings*, New Society Publishers, Gabriola Island, BC

Selman, P. (2001) 'Social capital, sustainability and environmental planning', *Planning Theory and Practice*, vol 2, no 1, pp13–30

Senbel, M. (2005) 'Empathic leadership in sustainability planning', PhD thesis, University of British Columbia, School of Community and Regional Planning

Sennett, R. (1971) *The Uses of Disorder: Personal Identity and City Life*, W.W. Norton and Co, New York

Sharp, G. (2005) *Waging Nonviolent Struggle: 20th Century Practice and 21st Century Potential*, Extending Horizons Books, Manchester, NH

Shields, K. (2000) *In the Tiger's Mouth: An Empowerment Guide for Social Action*, 2000 Edition, Katrina Shields, The Channon, NSW

Shields, K. (2000) 'Support and accountability groups', in *In the Tiger's Mouth: An Empowerment Guide for Social Action*, 2000 edition, Katrina Shields, The Channon, NSW

Sidhu, M. (1994) 'Timbarra: Five years on', in W. Sarkissian and K. Walsh (eds) *Community Participation in Practice: Casebook*, Institute for Sustainability and Technology Policy, Murdoch University, Perth

Simpkinson, C. and Simpkinson, A. (eds) (1993) *Sacred Stories: A Celebration of the Power of Story to Transform and Heal*, HarperSanFrancisco, San Francisco

Sontag, S. (1992) 'The view from the Ark', in R. Misrach (ed) *Violent Legacies: Three Cantos*, Aperture, New York

Staats, H., Kieviet, A. and Hartig, T. (2003) 'Where to recover from attentional fatigue: An expectancy-value analysis of environmental preference', *Journal of Environmental Psychology*, vol 23, no 2, pp147–157

Stapp, W. B., Wals, A. E. J. and Stankorb, S. L. (1996) *Environmental Education for Empowerment: Action Research and Community Problem Solving*, Kendall/Hunt Publishing Company, Dubuque, Iowa

Steffen, A. (ed) (2006) *Worldchanging: A User's Guide for the 21st Century*, Abrams, New York

Stewart, K. with Forsyth, A., Sarkissian, W. and Coates, B. (1994) 'The 1992 Northern Territory housing plan', in W. Sarkissian and K. Walsh (eds) *Community Participation in Practice: Casebook*, Institute for Sustainability and Technology Policy, Murdoch University, Perth

Stone, M. K. (2005) 'It changed everything we thought we could do: The STRAW project', in M. K. Stone and Z. Barlow (eds) (2005) *Ecological Literacy: Educating our Children for a Sustainable World*, Sierra Club Books, San Francisco

Stone, M. K. and Barlow, Z. (eds) (2005) *Ecological Literacy: Educating our Children for a Sustainable World*, Sierra Club Books, San Francisco

Stubbs, J. (2005) *Leaving Minto: A Study of the Social and Economic Impacts of Public Housing Estate Redevelopment*, Residents Action Group Minto, NSW, March

Susskind, L. and Elliott, M. (1983) *Paternalism, Conflict and Co-production: Learning from Citizen Action and Citizen Participation in Western Europe*, Plenum, New York

Suzuki, D. and Dressel, H. (2002) *Good News for a Change: Hope for a Troubled Planet*, Allen and Unwin, St Leonards, NSW

Syme, G. J. and Sadler, B. S. (1994) 'Evaluation of public involvement in water resources planning: A researcher–practitioner dialogue', *Evaluation Review*, vol 18, no 5, pp523–542

Theobald, P. and Nachtigal, P. (1995) 'Culture, community and the promise of rural education', *Phi Delta Kappan*, October, pp123–135, cited in Kemp, A. T. (2006) 'Engaging the environment', *Curriculum and Teaching Dialogue*, vol 8, nos 1/2, pp125–142

Thomas, J. C. (1995) *Public Participation in Public Decisions: New Skills and Strategies for Public Managers*, Jossey-Bass, San Francisco

Thomashow, M. (1996) *Ecological Identity: Becoming a Reflective Environmentalist*, MIT Press, Cambridge, MA

Throgmorton, J. A. (1992) 'Planning as persuasive storytelling about the future: Negotiating an electric power rate settlement in Illinois', *Journal of Planning Education and Research*, vol 2, no 1, pp17–31

Throsby, D. (2005) 'On the sustainability of cultural capital', research paper, Macquarie University, Department of Economics, Sydney

Tompkins, P. and Lawley, J. (2008) 'Rapport: The magic ingredient', www.cleanlanguage.co.uk/articles/articles/112/1/Rapport-The-Magic-Ingredient/Page1.html, accessed 30 May 2008, originally published in *Personal Success*, January 1994

Tulku, T. (1978) *Skillful Means: Patterns for Success*, Nyingma Psychology Series 5, Dharma Publishing, Berkeley

United Nations (2008) *Urban Population, Development and the Environment*, United Nations Population Division, New York

Van den Broeck, J. (2006) 'What kind of spatial planning do we need?: An approach based on visioning, action and co-production!', conference paper presented at Europe and China: Which Future? International Conference, Leuven University, Belgium, 29–30 September

Victoria, Department of Infrastructure (DOI) (2002) *Melbourne 2030: Planning for Sustainable Development*, Department of Infrastructure, Victorian Government, Melbourne

Victoria, Department of Planning and Community Development (2007) *Melbourne 2030 Audit: Analysis of Progress and Findings from the*

2006 Census, Department of Planning and Community Development, Melbourne

Wackernagel, M. and Rees, W. (1996) *Our Ecological Footprint: Reducing Human Impact on the Earth*, New Society, Gabriola Island, BC and Philadelphia

Waldrop, M. (1992) *Complexity: The Emerging Science at the Edge of Order and Chaos*, Penguin Books, London

Wallace, D. R. (1990) 'The Forever Forests', *Greenpeace*, vol 15, no 5, p10

Walsh, K. with Cook, A. (1994) 'The beginning of something: The Timbarra "Welcome Home" workshops', in W. Sarkissian and K. Walsh (eds) *Community Participation in Practice: Casebook*, Institute for Sustainability and Technology Policy, Murdoch University, Perth

Walsh, K. with Sarkissian, W., Dunstan G. and Cook, A. (1990) 'A report on the Timbarra "Welcome Home" workshop, Sunday 24 June 1990', prepared for the Urban Land Authority by Sarkissian Associates Planners, Pty Ltd, Melbourne

Wapner, P. (1995) 'Politics beyond the State: Environmental activism and world civic politics', *World Politics*, vol 47, no 3, pp311–340

Wates, N. (2008) *The Community Planning Event Manual: How to use Collaborative Planning and Urban Design Events to Improve your Environment*, Earthscan, London

Wates, N. (2009) *The Community Planning Handbook: How People can Shape their Cities, Towns and Villages in any Part of the World*, second edition, Earthscan, London

Watts, A., cited in Walsh, R. (2000) 'Conventional and authentic lives', *Transpersonal Psychology Review*, vol 4, no 3, pp4–12

Western Australia, Department of Premier and Cabinet (2003) *Hope for the Future: The Western Australia State Sustainability Strategy*, Government of Western Australia, Perth

Westley, F., Zimmerman, B. and Patton, M. Q. (2007) *Getting to Maybe: How the World has Changed*, Vintage Canada, Toronto

Westley, F. (2008) 'Getting to Maybe. Social innovation: An agency based approach to transformation', keynote address, Resilience 2008 Conference, Stockholm University, Stockholm, 14–17 April, webcast proceedings, http://resilience.qbrick.com/view.aspx?id=6, accessed 30 May 2008

Wheeler, S. M. (1995) *Sustainable Urban Development: A Literature Review and Analysis*, Urban Ecology Inc., Oakland, CA

Wheeler, S. M. and Beatley, T. (eds) (2004) *The Sustainable Urban Development Reader*, Routledge, London

Whelan, J. M. (2005) 'Six reasons not to engage: Compromise, confrontation and the commons', conference paper, International Conference on Engaging Communities, Queensland Department of Main Roads, Brisbane

White, R. (2001) 'Youth participation in designing public space', *Youth Studies Australia*, vol 20, no 1, pp19–26

White, R. (2007) 'Public spaces, consumption, and the social regulation of young people', in S. A. Venkatesh and R. Kassimir (eds) *Youth, Globalization, and the Law*, Stanford University Press, Palo Alto

Wilson, V. (2005) 'Ecological and social systems: Essential system conditions', in A. Dale and J. Onyx (eds) *A Dynamic Balance: Social Capital and Community Development*, University of British Columbia Press, Vancouver

Witherell, C. and Noddings, N. (eds) (1991) *Stories Lives Tell: Narrative and Dialogue in Education*, Teachers College Press, New York

World Commission on Environment and Development and Brundtland, G. H. (1988) *Our Common Future*, Oxford University Press, Oxford and New York

Yankelovich, D. (1991) *Coming to Public Judgment: Making Democracy Work in a Complex World*, Syracuse University Press, Syracuse

Yencken, D (1991) *Mapping our Culture: A Policy for Victoria*, Victorian Government, Melbourne

Yencken, D. and Wilkinson, D. (2000) *Resetting the Compass: Australia's Journey Towards Sustainability*, CSIRO Publishing, Melbourne

Young, I. M. (1986) 'The ideal of community and the politics of difference', *Social Theory and Practice*, vol 12, no 1, pp1–26

Young, I. M. (1990) *Justice and the Politics of Difference*, Princeton University Press, Princeton

Young, I. M. (1997) *Intersecting Voices: Dilemmas of Gender, Political Philosophy, and Policy*, Princeton University Press, Princeton

Young, I. M. (2000) *Inclusion and Democracy*, Oxford University Press, Oxford

Zemke, R. and Zemke, S. (1995) 'Adult learning: What do we know for sure?' *Training*, vol 32, no 5, pp31–40

Zimmerman, B. J. and Hayday, B. C. (1999) 'A board's journey into complexity science', *Group Decision Making and Negotiation*, vol 8, pp281–303

Internet References

Aldred, J. (2008) 'Sumatran deforestation driving climate change and species extinction, report warns', *The Guardian, UK*, 27 February, www. guardian.co.uk/environment/2008/feb/27/climatechange.forests, accessed 11 June 2008

Allard, T. (2008) 'Diverse input, but little output', *Sydney Morning Herald*, 21 April, p14, www.smh.com.au/news/national/diverse-input-but-little-output/2008/04/20/1208629731352.html, accessed 13 June 2008

Attili, G. (Director) and Sandercock, L. (2006) 'Where Strangers Become Neighbours: The Story of the Collingwood Neighbourhood House and the Integration of Immigrants' (undated), www.mongrel-stories.com, accessed 6 June 2008

The Australian Freedom Rides' (undated), www.freedomride.net, accessed 12 June 2008

C4 (undated) 'The Great Global Warming Swindle', www.channel4. com/science/microsites/G/great_global_warming_swindle, accessed 13 June 2008

Campaign for Sustainable Economics (2008) 'Sustainable Economics', www.sustainableeconomics.org, accessed 10 June 2008

CASSE (undated) 'Center for the Advancement of the Steady State Economy', www.steadystate.org, accessed 10 June 2008

Carroll, A. (Presenter) (2001) 'The legend of Frogs' Hollow and the Men's Movement', episode, S. Butler (Producer) and K. Taylor (Researcher) *The Australian Story*, ABC TV, 6 September, transcript published online, www. abc.net.au/austory/transcripts/s355648.htm, accessed 12 June 2008

Castle Vale Housing Action Trust (2005) 'Castle Vale Housing Action Trust', www.cvhat.org.uk, accessed 30 May 2008

Center for Neighborhoods (2008a) 'Corridor Housing Initiative: Green Space and Yards', www.housinginitiative.org/greenspace.html, accessed 7 June 2008

Center for Neighborhoods (2008b) 'Corridor Housing Initiative: Nicollet Avenue in Kingfield', www.housinginitiative.org/kingfield.html, accessed 7 June 2008

Center for Neighborhoods (2008c) 'Minnesota Block Exercise', www. housinginitiative.org/blockexercise.html, accessed 19 June 2008

Center for Neighborhoods (2008d) 'Corridor Housing Initiative', www. housinginitiative.org, accessed 12 June 2008

'The Change Agency Education and Training Institute (undated) 'The Change Agency: Supporting effective community action', www. thechangeagency.org, accessed 11 June 2008

City of Minneapolis (2007) 'Corridor Housing Strategy wins national "grassroots initiative" award', www.ci.minneapolis.mn.us/cped/corridor_apa_award_2007.asp, accessed 7 June 2008

City of Vancouver (2007) 'Neighbourhood Energy Utility: Leading the way with low emissions, renewable energy and innovation', www.vancouver.ca/sustainability/building_neu.htm, accessed 2 June 2008

Coastal CRC (2006) 'Citizen Science: Community learning through citizen science', www.coastalzone.org.au/citizen%5Fscience, accessed 12 June 2008

Connor, D. M. (1994) 'Preventing and resolving public controversy', conference paper, 'Public Affairs and Forest Management', Canadian Pulp & Paper Association, Toronto, 25–27 March 1985 (revised 1994), www.connor.bc.ca/preventing.html, accessed 2 June 2008

Croggon, A. (2008) 'Sparkle stifled by a pre-set agenda', *The Australian*, 22 April, published online, www.theaustralian.news.com.au/story/0,,23577235-16947,00.html?from=public_rss, accessed 12 June 2008

Cultural Creatives (undated) 'Are You a Cultural Creative?', www.culturalcreatives.org/questionnaire.html, accessed 6 June 2008

DeBiaso, T. (Producer and Director) (undated) *The Corridor Housing Initiative: A Strategy for Successful Planning*, film, Center for Neighborhoods, www.housinginitiative.org/video.html, accessed 12 June 2008

Dick, B. (1997) 'Action learning and action research', published online, www.scu.edu.au/schools/gcm/ar/arp/actlearn.html, accessed 27 May 2008

Dictionary.com Unabridged (v 1.1) (2008) 'nourish', http://dictionary.reference.com/browse/nourish, accessed 25 May 2008, based on *Random House Unabridged Dictionary* (2006), Random House, New York

Earth Activist Training (EAT) (2008) 'Earth Activist training: Planting Seeds of Change', www.earthactivisttraining.org, accessed 12 June 2008

Enterprise Community Partners, Inc. (2008) 'Green communities', www.enterprisecommunity.org/programs/green%5Fcommunities, accessed 7 June 2008

Food Connect (2008) 'Food Connect Project', www.foodconnect.com.au, accessed 12 June 2008

GiovanniAttili (2008) 'Where Strangers Become Neighbours: Trailer', YouTube, www.youtube.com/watch?v=YWzcGXUWsl8, added 30 March 2007, accessed 6 June 2008

Greatbearwatch.ca (2008) 'Solutions', www.savethegreatbear.org/solutions, accessed 4 June 2008

Greater Minnesota Housing Fund, the Family Housing Fund, and Enterprise (2008) 'Minnesota Green Communities', www.mngreencommunities.org, accessed 7 June 2008

Griffith University (2008) 'URP Toolbox', www3.secure.griffith.edu.au/03/toolbox, accessed 12 June 2008

HarmoniCOP Project (2003) 'HarmoniCOP: Harmonising collaborative planning', www.harmonicop.info, accessed 9 June 2008

Hart, M. (2006) 'An Introduction to Sustainability', www.sustainablemeasures.com/Sustainability/index.html, accessed 11 June 2008

Infed (the informal education homepage) (2002) 'howard gardner, multiple intelligences and education', www.infed.org/thinkers/gardner.htm, accessed 13 June 2008

Institute for Intercultural Studies (2003) 'Margaret Mead (1901–1978): An anthropology of human freedom', www.interculturalstudies.org/Mead/biography.html, accessed 11 June 2008

Institute of Science in Society (2008) 'Organic Cuba without Fossil Fuels', www.cityfarmer.info/organic-cuba-without-fossil-fuels-the-urban-agricultural-miracle/#more-87, accessed 23 January 2008

International Association for Public Participation (IAP2) (undated) www.iap2.org, accessed 7 June 2008

ISEE (undated) 'International Society for Ecological Economics', www.ecoeco.org, accessed 10 June 2008

Jordan, J. (2001) 'Community & economic development: Towns shaping their destiny', ACCORD Paper No 4, Australian Centre for Co-operative Research and Development, University of Technology, Sydney, June, www.accord.org.au/publications/ACCORD_MalenyPaper_4.pdf, accessed 12 June 2008

Jordan, J. (2003) 'Cooperatives and the "Triple Bottom Line"', conference presentation, Annual Conference of the Cooperative Federation of Western Australia, September, www.australia.coop/cs_maleny.htm, accessed 12 June 2008

Karvelas, P. (2008) 'Invitees depart feeling hijacked', *The Australian*, 21 April, p9, www.theaustralian.news.com.au/story/0,25197,23571477-5013871,00.html, accessed 13 June 2008

Kitchen Table Sustainability: Practical recipes for community engagement with sustainability (2008) 'The Book', www.kitchentablesustainability.com, accessed 19 June 2008

Kogarah Council (2008) 'Moore Reserve Wetlands', www.kogarah.nsw.gov.au/www/html/336-moore-reserve-wetlands.asp, accessed 9 June 2008

La Rocca, S. (2003) 'Gully Insights: Lessons for local planning and NIMBY campaigning, presentation, a case study', published online, www. thechangeagency.org/_dbase_upl/CaseStudy_Gully.pdf, accessed 12 June 2008

La Rocca, S. (2004) 'Making a difference: Factors that Influence participation in grassroots environmental activism in Australia', Honours thesis, Faculty of Environmental Sciences, Griffith University, Australia, November

The League of Women Voters Massachusetts (undated) 'The LWV Massachusetts Citizen Education Fund', www.lwvma.org/cef.shtml, accessed 29 May 2008

Learning for a Sustainable Future (LSF) (undated) 'Learning outcomes', www.lsf-lst.ca/en/teachers/learning_outcomes.php, accessed 13 June 2008

Lerner, Rabbi M. (2008) 'Obama's Error – and what it would really take to rectify it', email newsletter, *TikkunMail* (www.tikkun.org),17 April

Maleny Voice (2008) 'Fourth Anniversary of the Woolworths Site Clearance', www.malenyvoice.com, 14 April, accessed 30 May 2008

Metropolitan Design Center (2005) 'The Corridor Housing Initiative in brief,' Metropolitan Design Center, University of Minnesota, Minneapolis, 21 July, www.housinginitiative.org/pdfs/CHIinBrief_072605.pdf, accessed 19 June 2008

Moyer, B. (1987) *The Movement Action Plan: A Strategic Framework Describing the Eight Stages of Successful Social Movements*, Movement for A New Society, Cambridge, published online, www.thechangeagency. org/_dbase_upl/movement_action_plan.pdf, accessed 30 May 2008

Mt Evelyn RAW: Residents Against Woolworths, MEEPPA (2007) 'Victory to Mount Evelyn: I am so proud of your fight', www.mtevelynraw.com, accessed 30 May 2008

Nick Wates Associates (2006) 'Glossary', www.communityplanning.net/ glossary/glossary.htm, accessed 12 June 2008

Nimbin Community Development Association (2008) 'Nimbin Skatepark', www.sk8park.nimbincommunity.org.au, accessed 12 June 2008

Olsson, P., Gunderson, L. H., Carpenter, S. R., Ryan, P., Lebel, L., Folke, C. and Holling, C. S. (2006) 'Shooting the rapids: Navigating transitions to adaptive governance of social-ecological systems', *Ecology and Society*, vol 11, no 1, article 18, published online, www.ecologyandsociety.org/ vol11/iss1/art18, accessed 12 June 2008

Post-Autistic Economics Network, 'A brief history of the post-autistic economics movement', www.paecon.net/historypae.html, accessed 9 June 2008

Prior, S. (2007) 'From anger to inspiration, *The Age*, 10 March, published online, www.theage.com.au/news/opinion/from-anger-to-inspiration/2007/03/09/1173166985832.html, accessed 12 June 2008

Queensland Government (2008) 'Queensland: The Smart State', www.smartstate.qld.gov.au, accessed 28 May 2008

Redland City Council (2008a) 'Redland City Council', www.redland.qld.gov.au, accessed 12 June 2008

Redland City Council (2008b) 'Redland Youth Plaza', www.redland.qld.gov.au/Residents/Parks/RedlandYouthPlaza/Pages/default.aspx, accessed 6 June 2008

Rosa and Raymond Parks Institute for Self Development (2008) 'About Us', www.rosaparks.org/about.html, accessed 12 June 2008

Sarkissian, W. with Dunstan, G. (2003) 'Stories in a park: Reducing crime and stigma through community storytelling', *Urban Design Forum Quarterly*, vol 64, published online, www.udf.org.au/archives/2004/02/stories_in_a_pa.php, accessed 7 June 2008

Sarvodaya Shramadana Movement (2007) 'Why, who, what, where... Sarvodaya?', www.sarvodaya.org, accessed 6 June 2008

SPIRAL (2002) 'spiral community hub', www.spiral.org.au, accessed 12 June 2008

SPIRAL (undated) 'Development Issues: The Gully', www.spiral.org.au/sos/index.php?page=7&show=1, accessed 12 June 2008

Steffen, A. (2007) 'Transforming Philanthropy', www.worldchanging.com/archives/005755.html, 18 January, accessed 11 June 2008

Stiglitz, J. (2002) 'There is no invisible hand: People don't behave rationally. So why do orthodox economists still cling to their discredited rational expectations theory?', *The Guardian*, 20 December, published online, http://education.guardian.co.uk/higher/comment/story/0,,863559,00.html#article_continue, accessed 9 June 2008

Sturtz, L. (2005) 'Maleny's community spirit', *Maple Street Co-op News*, Aug/Sep, www.maplestreetco-op.com.au (click Maple Street Co-op News>Environment Features>Maleny's Community Spirit), accessed 30 May 2008

The People for Places and Spaces (undated) 'The People for Places and Spaces', www.p4ps.com.au, accessed 2 June 2008

Tàbara, D. with Cazorla, X., Maestu, J., Massarutto, A., Meerganz G., Pahl-Wostl, C., Patel, M. and Saurí D. (2005) 'Sustainability learning for river basin management and planning in Europe', HarmoniCOP Integration Report, Report of Work Package 6, August, published online, www.harmonicop.info/_files/_down/WP6%20Integration%20reportFINAL.pdf, accessed 12 June 2008

Tamarck Institute for Community Engagement (2006) 'Thinking Like a Movement', www.tamarackcommunity.ca/g3s10_M4C1.html, accessed 29 May 2008

TFC: Training for Change (undated) 'TFC's Direct Education Approach', www.trainingforchange.org, accessed 12 June 2008

Urban Ecology Australia (2008) 'Urban Ecology Australia', www.urbanecology.org.au, accessed 12 June 2008

US Department of Health and Human Services, Centers for Disease Control and Prevention (undated), 'Social Capital', www.cdc.gov/healthyplaces/healthtopics/social.htm, accessed 12 June 2008

van der Brugge, R. and van Raak, R. (2007) 'Facing the adaptive management challenge: Insights from transition management', *Ecology and Society*, vol 12, no 2, article 33, published online, www.ecologyandsociety.org/vol12/iss2/art33/, accessed 12 June 2008

Whelan, J. M. (2007) 'Six reasons not to engage: Compromise, confrontation and the commons', *COMM-ORG Papers*, vol 13, http://comm-org.wisc.edu/papers2007/whelan.htm, accessed 30 May 2008

The Wilderness Society (2006) 'Campaigns: History of the Franklin River Campaign 1976–83', www.wilderness.org.au/articles/franklin, accessed 19 June 2008

Wilson, E. O. (1990) 'Arousing biophilia: A conversation with E. O. Wilson', www.arts.envirolink.org/interviews_and_conversations/EOWilson.html, 8 June 2005, accessed 25 May 2008

Worldchanging (2008) 'Worldchanging: change your thinking', www.worldchanging.com, accessed 13 June 2008

Worldchanging (undated) 'Our Manifesto', www.worldchanging.com/about/, accessed 10 June 2008

WWF (2008) 'About Earth Hour', www.earthhour.org, accessed 3 June 2008

About the authors

Wendy Sarkissian

I grew up as a lonely child in one of Vancouver's boring suburbs that was originally clear-cut for an airport. All the houses were identical. Not a living tree remained when the construction for the houses began in the late 1940s. My refuge was the nearby Capilano Indian Reservation, a second-growth temperate forest, where I spent most of my days, sheltering in the dark and aromatic bosom of the raining forest. These first two influences brought me to this book: an abiding love of the natural world and a deep concern about the complicity of planning in our global crisis.

I live with my husband, Karl, a passionate contributor to this book, in a tiny rural village in northern New South Wales. Nimbin is famous for its anarchist history and modern-day manifestations of independence and self-sufficiency. We are building a subtropical ecological house on half an acre of land in a Permaculture community.

For the past 27 years I have managed a small independent social planning firm in Australia, focusing on community engagement. In 1991, puzzled by my planning colleagues' avoidance of sustainability challenges, I closed my consulting firm to undertake a full-time PhD in environmental ethics with Peter Newman and Patsy Hallen at Murdoch University. After a year living in solitude in rough conditions near Darwin in northern Australia, I emerged with a strengthened passion for environmental reform.

My community engagement experience has also contributed to the ideas I bring to this book. I am committed to finding creative ways to listen across difference in community engagement processes.

I have found great joy in this collaborative project which has given life to this book. My dear friend and colleague, Steph Vajda and I began dreaming about it in late 2006 after my insightful coach,

Vivienne Simon, suggested that a 'green' book about practice might be helpful in the current crisis. Meeting Nancy Hofer, a planning student at the University of British Columbia, Vancouver, in late 2006, was an unexpected blessing. She joined us as an author early in 2007. My long-time friend, soulmate and colleague Yollana Shore joined us in early 2008. A new Australian friend Cathy Wilkinson, now living in Sweden, brought her keen eye, sharp mind and wide sustainability experience within government to the project at the same time.

Through the electronic marvels of Skype and the Internet, we have worked together joyfully and creatively. I have been supported in numberless ways by my Beloved, Karl Langheinrich, the best cook in Australia. With no running water, no kitchen and no kitchen table, he blesses me daily with his culinary and other sweetness. A wide circle of friends has embraced me for this writing project. I bow deeply in acknowledgement of their generous support. I pray earnestly that this book will make a difference.

Nancy Hofer

I grew up in the expanse of continental prairies outside the perimeter of Winnipeg, Manitoba in an area called St. Germain. My family lived on five acres of land that we didn't do much with. Occasionally my dad would cut mazes through the long grass with his John Deer riding lawnmower for my brother and I to make our way through, but mostly the land was left to grow naturally. And in this place I experienced living things and I saw them change with the seasons. After reading much on the psychological effects of children experiencing Nature, I realize now how important those years were for me in forming lasting relationships with nonhuman life.

When I was 12 I moved to Kelowna, British Columbia, where I again lived by Nature, this time in the form of dry Ponderosa Pine

(*Pinus ponderosa*) forests. There was a plateau in the forest near my house that looked over the valley Kelowna is situated in, and I would use that place to just sit and think or cool off if I had had a fight with my parents. At that time I relied on Nature as a refuge. I really think that contact with Nature helped get me through some tough adolescent times.

Now I live on British Columbia's coast in Vancouver. I came here for my undergraduate degree in Natural Resources Conservation at the University of British Columbia nine years ago. I had been accepted into both the environmental engineering and the forestry programmes and I didn't know which one to pursue. I took a road trip to Vancouver to check them both out and after walking in the buildings of both faculties my mind was made up. The engineering building had a subterranean feel with concrete walls and fluorescent lights. On the walls were pictures of chemical factories and people in site remediation suites. The forestry building had a large atrium four stories high lit entirely by natural light. Everything in the building was made of wood and on the walls hung pictures of bears, birds, trees, fish, insects, rivers and people in safety vests and rubber boots. My affinity with living things made me realize that forestry was the faculty for me and I never looked back on that decision.

I am now completing my degree in community and regional planning and I have found myself at home in this material and thinking about planning related challenges. I made the switch (or what I would see as a progression) from ecology to planning because it became clear to me that managing natural ecosystems was a misguided way to go about managing human demand on resources. From a solid background in ecology and an ever-expanding appreciation for the problems humanity is facing, I have come to realize that managing *humans* and their impact is the only approach to sustainability. Nature is an entity and force that is incapable of being controlled, and we need to act in a way that acknowledges that.

Yollana Shore

Growing up in the 1980s, I was well aware of environmental issues throughout my childhood and teen years. Sting was singing 'Fragile' on MTV in 1987. In 1989, Aussie folk singer John Williamson's song 'Rip Rip Woodchip' ('... turn it into paper, throw it in the bin, no news today!') reached top of the charts. We were participating in Cleanup Australia days in primary school. Litter was bad. Recycling was good. Chopping down trees was bad. Planting trees was good. I knew the Earth was in crisis. I believed that my generation had to be part of the solution. When people talked about making the world a better place for their children, they were talking about me! I felt cared for by the very principles of the sustainability movement and naturally wanted to be part of it.

In 1999, I enrolled in an environmental science degree at Griffith University in Queensland, Australia. I was so excited to be pursuing a career that would help me to really make a difference in the world. Griffith was the first University in Australia to establish a school in Environmental Studies back in 1975. It attracted many people who were genuinely concerned about environmental issues and how they could help.

I threw myself into the environmental activism that I saw happening around me. I wrote letters, signed petitions, organized events, put up posters, marched on the street, sat in trees, rode my bike through the traffic, argued with my family and sat in endless meetings. Some campaigns were colourful and creative. Many were chaotic and ineffective. Many were angry, chaotic and poorly attended. In short, unsustainable. In the end, I felt disillusioned and alienated by the emotionally charged processes of protest-centred activism. I realized it wasn't my scene, although I cared deeply about the issues. I had to find another way.

Ten years later, my area of expertise has broadened significantly. While continuing to care deeply about the natural world, I became an experienced community engagement practitioner through Wendy's mentorship in social planning, community planning and community engagement. I became certified in a personal transformation programme called The Journey™. In The Journey™, I found the tools that I believed the environment movement was missing: self-awareness and self-nourishment. And I am an entrepreneur who has embraced business as a vehicle for positive social, cultural and environmental change, as we transition towards a more sustainable world.

Steph Vajda

The kitchen table was a lively place where I grew up. We had a formal dining room, which we used only for formal occasions. Besides, you could see the TV from our kitchen table. Like many kitchen tables, ours wasn't even in the kitchen, but it was right next to it. Occasionally it found its way in there as my Nana spread out the torn foil squares she used to make up her rice packets to hand out to her children, my uncles and aunties, when they came over on Sundays.

Maybe it was to do with moving around a lot during my first eight years, but I didn't really think much about the household culture in my grandparents' house until I actually moved out in 1992. More now than then, I find myself thinking about the smells of fresh curries filling every pore, how our family ate at such odd times, and how much the whole household revolved around food. There were often lively conversations at our kitchen table, particularly when aunties and uncles were over. It was rare that everyone ate together; my family was more of an 'eat when you're hungry' type. But mostly everyone would sit at the table anyway; it was such a focal point.

One thing that I do remember is not talking about sustainability. That all came much later in life and more with friends. But we did talk, in a round-about way, about how different our family was to most of those around us. Never openly, and never negatively, but it was there. I remember feeling as if I was the only brown boy in the neighbourhood, never really sure what it took to fit in. The concept of community was quite alien to me growing up in the suburbs of Brisbane.

In her last months, my Nana and I would talk, her unable to do much more and I, keen to learn more about her, her life and beliefs. We would never talk directly about sustainability as a concept, but she would often end one of our conversations about some conflict or trouble or issue with the words 'why can't they all just get along?' It's a good question. I'm a firm believer that in some cases we just don't know how to talk to each other well enough to realize that there's much more benefit in cooperating than competing. In other cases, there are more fundamental differences; but this is the reason we have written this book. Our idea of community isn't a group of identical people with the same vision. We see community as a group of people who have access to an active role in decision making, strong social networks, some sense of broad shared values and diverse cultural approaches to growth and development.

My background is in community activism, then community planning work predominantly for local councils and, more recently, in facilitating community cultural development in Indigenous communities. I am mostly interested in the power dynamics of how our communities function and how we resolve our sustainability priorities given this and the often disparate 'needs' of government, industry and community members. And while I have often felt so discouraged by the dominant approach to community engagement and sustainability, through writing this book I am filled with hope that there are options for a better future that are within our grasp. We hope that you enjoy this book, which we've intended not to be a solution in itself, but a starting point for conversations about a future where we can learn to listen; to ourselves, to each other and to Nature and all its creations.

Cathy Wilkinson

Many, many years ago now, my late Grandmother single-handedly transformed a condemned house on the north shore of Sydney into her home – a sanctuary. Almost every school holidays my immediate family would make the trek up the Hume Highway from Melbourne, where I grew up, to her home. And there I began to learn the lived history and practice of deep but everyday sustainability. My Grandmother wasted nothing, respected everything and everyone (Nature included) and lived a simple life, full of music, reflection, healing and hard work. I have precious memories of lying awake on my fold-out bed, listening from my little alcove to my Grandmother, dad, uncle and sometimes visiting friends talking vigorously late into the night about how the world could be changed, could become more sustainable. That same calling drives me.

In my professional life as a planner and environmental scientist I have straddled boundaries between worlds – interested always in facilitating communication and understanding between academia and practice, between the local, regional and global, between the regime and the radical. I am fascinated by the complexity of socio-ecological systems – in particular cities – and believe that until we let go of our desire to 'control' and 'manage' these, we cannot re-imagine our relationship with Nature, or one another.

In 2006, after seven years working for the Victorian State Government and leading the development and implementation of Melbourne's most recent metropolitan strategy, I relocated to Sweden with my husband and two small children. We live now in Luleå, just south of the Arctic Circle in Lappland. The extremes of climate, peace of a small town and proximity to the hum of Europe are invigorating. I am currently undertaking my doctoral studies in Sweden and providing strategic advice on sustainable planning to governments across Europe.

Index

I

iceberg model 142–3
inaccurate reporting 165–6
'inaction' frustrations 129–38
inclusion 12, 75, 78, 185, 187–226
    activism and 134
    Easy-to-Hard Continuum 215–16
    governance and 272–3, 276–7, 294, 307
    visionary approaches 304
inclusionary argumentation model 213
information
    access 293
    management 111
    sharing 178–9
    transparency 222
    withholding 167
informational learning 85, 95
innovation 8, 151–2
    see also experimentation
institutional structures 155
instrumental rationality 194
integration 56, 79, 218
intelligences 57, 112–14, 168–9
interactions in communities 45
interconnectedness 32–5
interdependence 32–5, 248
intergenerational learning 97–8
interlocking circles model 22–3
International Association of Public Participation (IAP2) 49, 178
Isaacs, Bill 163

J

Jacobs, Jane 194
joyful service 258–9
judgement, coming to 291–2
justice 103–4, 251

K

Kaner, Sam 221
kanji symbols 115
Keller, Helen 259
Kenworthy, Jeff 23
Khmer communities 181, 202–3
kitchen table conversations 7–9
    building on 37
    definition 31
    future directions 309–10
    limitations 41–2
    'starters' 118–19, 156–7, 184–5, 225–6, 260–1, 298–9
knowledge
    blending 102–3
    eco-literacy 108
    evaluation for 223
    grounded 99–100, 110–11
    local 57, 103, 310
    management 111, 156
    soft skills 112–18
    see also education; expert knowledge
Kornfield, Jack 279

L

Ladder of Children's Participation (Hart) 204–5
land professionals 7, 306
Langheinrich, Karl 17, 46, 91, 200, 284
languages 46, 202–3, 220–1'latte set' 182, 198–9
'laundry' work 267, 278–9, 281, 283–8, 291, 304–5
learning
    environments 95–8
    models 77, 86–106, 112–14
    opportunities 297–8
    see also education
learning society concept 85–6, 102
Learning for a Sustainable Future (LSF) 108

publishing for a sustainable future

Other books in the *Tools for Community Planning* series

The Community Planning Handbook
How People Can Shape Their Cities, Towns and Villages in Any Part of the World
Nick Wates

'An excellent book that will have a host of valuable applications ... It is an important and timely contribution.' *Jules Pretty, University of Essex*

Community planning is a rapidly developing, increasingly important field. Growing numbers of professionals and local residents are getting involved and there is a powerful menu of tools available, from design workshops to electronic maps. This handbook provides a practical guide to community planning with tips, checklists and sample documents to help the reader get started quickly.

Paperback £18.99 • 236 pages • 978-1-85383-654-1 • 1999

The Community Planning Event Manual
How to use Collaborative Planning and Urban Design Events to Improve your Environment
Nick Wates with Foreword by HRH The Prince of Wales and Introduction by John Thompson

'Some books help you to learn - this one helps you to deliver! An invaluable tool.'
Professor Brian Evans, deputy chair, Architecture+Design Scotland and Partner, Gillespies LLP

Nick Wates' latest book is the first to explain why and how to organize community planning events. It includes a step-by-step guide, detailed checklists and other tools for event organisers. The method is user-friendly, flexible and easy to employ in any context from small neighbourhood improvements to major infrastructure and construction projects anywhere in the world.

Paperback £16.99 • 128 pages • 978-1-84407-492-1 • 2008

SpeakOut
The Step-by-Step Guide to SpeakOuts and Community Workshops
Wendy Sarkissian and Wiwik Bunjamin-Mau with Andrea Cook, Kelvin Walsh and Steph Vajda with Foreword by Karen Umemoto

This new manual is the product of nearly two decades of successful practice by internationally acclaimed community planning specialists. This book aims to enable both planning veterans and people with little or no experience in the field to conduct a wide variety of community engagement events with absolute confidence.

It introduces the SpeakOut, an innovative, interactive drop-in process with some of the qualities of an Open House and a participatory workshop. It provides hands-on, step-by-step guidance, detailed checklists and practical advice on how to manage community engagement processes, as well as advice on facilitation and recording and training of helpers.

Paperback £19.99 • 256 pages • 978-1-84407-704-5 • April 2009

www.earthscan.co.uk